Self Consciousness

An alternative anthropology of identity

Anthony P. Cohen

London and New York

First published 1994
by Routledge
11 New Fetter Lane, London EC4P 4EE

Simultaneously published in the USA and Canada
by Routledge
29 West 35th Street, New York, NY 10001

Reprinted 1995, 1998, 2000

Routledge is an imprint of the Taylor & Francis Group

© 1994 Anthony P. Cohen

Typeset in Times by
LaserScript, Mitcham, Surrey
Printed and bound in Great Britain by
TJ International Ltd, Padstow, Cornwall

British Library Cataloguing in Publication Data
A catalogue record for this book is available from the British Library

Library of Congress Cataloging in Publication Data
A catalog record for this book is available from the Library of Congress

ISBN 0–415–08323–0 (hbk)
ISBN 0–415–08324–9 (pbk)

Self Consciousness

What is the relationship of the individual to society? What *is* the individual besides being a participant in social relations? Like other social sciences, anthropology has tended to neglect these questions, treating individuals simply as micro-versions of larger social entities, and imputing to them consciousnesses modelled on those of the groups to which they belong.

In this book, Anthony Cohen establishes the importance of the individual, arguing that, in order to appreciate the complexity of *social* formations, we must take account of self consciousness – individuals' awareness of themselves and their authorship of their social contexts and conditions. Drawing comparatively on a wide range of ethnographic studies and anthropological topics from around the world, he proposes that anthropological concepts such as 'culture', 'society' and 'social relations' should be approached from the self upwards. He shows how social and cultural forms and processes such as ritual, symbolism, organisation, rhetoric, socialisation, marriage, naming, ethnicity and cultural nationalism are shaped and interpreted by the creative self. In the course of the argument, Professor Cohen dismisses the contention that selfhood is a predominantly Western idea, and shows that attention to the particular, the individual and to self consciousness both informs and disciplines the larger picture.

Self Consciousness reflects the author's deep concern with social identity and the dialectical relationship of individual and society. It will be of great interest not only to anthropologists but to students and teachers of the other social sciences, including sociology, social psychology and cultural studies.

Anthony P. Cohen is Professor of Social Anthropology at the University of Edinburgh.

This book is dedicated with love to

    L.N.C.
    I.P.C.
and M.A.C.

from whom I have learned the importance of trying to understand self consciousness – theirs, mine and other people's.

Contents

Preface and acknowledgements

I do not know, cannot remember, for how long I have been conscious of the matters taken up in this book, but I realise that some must have been with me throughout my self conscious experience. Therefore, I cannot date the origins of the book, and could not begin to acknowledge the influences, academic and other, which have contributed to it. I take instead an arbitrary moment in the early 1980s when, thinking about the ways in which individuals interpret symbols, I was led to hold deep reservations about how anthropologists tended to generalise the meanings of symbols to whole societies or to substantial groups within them. I realised then that, as an anthropologist who pursued an explicit interest in culture and culture theory, I was nevertheless dealing ethnographically with individuals, whose engagement with each other was problematic and fraught with misunderstanding, and who were reserved about their own generalisation into 'societies' or 'communities' or 'cultures' in ways to which anthropologists seemed insensitive.

As I write this, I remind myself that my first anthropological monograph, on local-level politics in Newfoundland, was essentially about seven individuals, and I squirm with some discomfort about how I made them stand for very large-scale social and cultural tendencies (Cohen 1985). It was in working through my long-term fieldwork in Whalsay, Shetland, that I became more aware of the inadequacy with which anthropology conventionally dealt with the complexities of individuals, and generalised them into collectivities. Just as one would expect, the better I came to know my friends and informants there, the more complex they seemed, and the more difficult appeared the task of committing them to paper. How well could any of us describe *ourselves* on paper within the disciplines of publishing and academic conventions? The problems delayed by some years my book on Whalsay (Cohen 1987) which, as I was even then uneasily aware, hardly avoided the ethnographic practices about which I was expressing grave doubt, in common with many of my academic generation.

It was finally my preoccupation with the diverse personal stances which the anthropologist adopts in the conduct and writing of ethnographic research which persuaded me of the need for anthropology to explore other people's self consciousness.[1] I was hardly early into the field. A catalogue of books published in the social and literary sciences over the last ten years and containing the word 'self' in their titles would be a very weighty tome indeed. Perhaps both for that reason, and because the problems I raise have long seemed so intractable to anthropologists, I sensed not a little despair among my friends and colleagues with my preoccupation, perhaps a sense of its futility. I have persisted in order to stress an aspect of this matter which I think has been inadequately recognised. Examining and reflecting on the self is not an alternative to addressing 'society' or social relations: they are mutually implicated. But I insist that we cannot properly do the latter, which I accept as the proper focus of anthropological enquiry, without the former. Anthropology will not fulfil its potential to offer sensitive accounts of social processes and formations unless it becomes self conscious – and, when it does so, will lead the way among the humane sciences.

Rather than just indulging me, my friendly interlocutors have helped me by their benevolent and expert criticism, both with their comments on earlier papers, or by taking the trouble to comment in detail on parts of the present book. I am especially indebted to Jim Fernandez, Ladislav Holy, Robert Paine, Nigel Rapport and Marilyn Strathern. Warmest thanks also to Malcolm Anderson, Frank Bechhofer, Jean Briggs, Roy Dilley, Katsuyoshi Fukui, Kirsten Hastrup, Paul Heelas, Wendy James, Carmelo Lisón-Tolosana, Martine Segalen, Cris Shore, Sandra Wallman and Barrie Wilson. The arguments contained in this book have been rehearsed on successive cohorts of Senior Honours students at Edinburgh University, for whose forbearance I am indebted. I have also had the good fortune and privilege of working at Edinburgh with a group of postgraduate students who have helped me far more than they probably realise: Sandra Brown, Rupert Cox, John Harries, Jon Mitchell, Gillian Munro, Amy Porter and Sarah Skerratt.

There is only so much that critics can accomplish in improving a colleague's work. In the end, I have to accept responsibility for everything that follows.

Returning to my opening remarks, I have drawn here on a series of working papers written since 1986, most of which have been published in journals or edited symposia. These are cited at the appropriate points in the text, but I would like to thank the editors and publishers concerned for allowing me to restate previously published work, specifically: Martine Segalen and Presses du CNRS; Judith Okely and Helen Callaway, and Paul Heelas and Paul Morris, and their publishers Routledge; my own co-editor Katsuyoshi Fukui, Murdo MacDonald and Edinburgh University Press; Ralph Cohen and Johns Hopkins University Press; Paul Bock and *Journal of Anthropological Research*.

I further express my gratitude to the following for permission to quote their work: Paul Bailey and Jonathan Cape, *Gabriel's Lament*; V.S. Naipaul and Penguin Group, *The Enigma of Arrival*; Tom Wolfe and Jonathan Cape, *The Bonfire of the Vanities*; M. Richler and Chatto & Windus, *Solomon Gursky was Here*.

APC, Edinburgh, November 1993

Chapter 1

The neglected self
Anthropological traditions

Most Indians do not reveal themselves because it does not occur to
them that they have unique selves to reveal.

(Gearing 1970: 146)

The self has no private space . . . but no need for privacy.

(Greenhouse 1986: 98)

POSITIONS

Fred Gearing's sympathetic study depicts the Fox Indians of Iowa as
defined by the statuses they occupy in their classificatory kinship
system. They regard their behaviour as inhering in the structural niches
in which they are placed, so that any other Fox who happened to be
similarly located would behave in the same way. Carol Greenhouse
imputes a comparable self consciousness – or lack of it – to the devout
Southern Baptists she studied in Hopewell, Atlanta, believers who
define themselves by their family roles, and who oppose individualism
to Christianity (see Chapter 6).

This selflessness seems so at odds with the ways in which most of us
might be assumed to think of ourselves that we have to work hard to
understand what Gearing and Greenhouse may mean and to envisage the
people they thereby describe. Anthropologists have laboured to elicit
notions equivalent to our 'self' and 'selfhood' which are held by the
people among whom they have lived and who they have studied. The
difficulties of imagining and interpreting these notions are compounded
by those of translation, which makes discourse about the self tricky
among the speakers of different European languages, let alone those of
more esoteric tongues. All sorts of metaphors and circumlocutions have
been called in aid, such as 'indigenous psychologies' and 'inner' (as

opposed to 'outer') consciousness, all of which attempt to evoke a distinction between the private and public aspects of a person.

The public–private dimension is a clumsy construction. Writers such as Lienhardt (1985) and Hsu (1985) have shown (for, respectively, Dinka and Chinese) that selfhood is a composite, the constituents of which vary in public and private modes. Thus, the self is not 'replaced' by something else as its bearer moves from privacy into public social space; rather, it adopts or discards elements which are not pertinent in more private contexts (for example, in intimate interaction or in solitary contemplation). The self is not a monolith; it is plastic, variable and complex. But that is to say that its description should acknowledge its complexity, a requirement in which anthropologists have not distinguished themselves. We shall consider some reasons for their failings.

Historically, another feature of this concern in anthropology has been the attempt to distinguish among such categories as 'individual', 'person' and 'self'. These distinctions are arbitrary, and are often difficult to sustain. They will be discussed at length. The motivation to make them clearly stemmed from theoretical influences at the turn of the century which demarcated the social and the psychological; and which elaborated the lineaments of social structure both to provide an analytic scheme and to demonstrate the primacy of society in the formation and determination of behaviour. For example, Durkheim was interested only in those aspects of the individual which could be socialised; he consigned the rest to psychology or physiology. And if these potentially social elements were not adequately socialised, this spoke, in his view, of the pathology of either the individual or society. In a normally functioning society, a person could not reasonably decide to behave in a way which defied social convention. In this theoretical perspective, selfhood was socially determined. The dominance of this perspective in British social anthropology is evident in that until quite recently 'the self' and 'selfhood' were simply not recognised as anthropological problems, other than in a methodological sense, despite the publication in 1938 of Mauss's classic essay on the self, a work only given appropriate recognition nearly fifty years later (see Carrithers et al. 1985).

There was a tradition in American anthropology of concern with the self, due in large part to the influence of the social psychologist G.H. Mead, a scholar whose work has remained almost entirely absent from the undergraduate syllabuses of British social anthropology. But in North American anthropology, concern with the self settled on a rather obscure subfield of the discipline as a whole, 'psychological anthropology' – again, a specialism which has never been recognised in

Britain – associated with writers such as A.I. Hallowell and Dorothy Lee. It did not attract mainstream attention until very much later, when, with the 'interpretive turn' (Rabinow and Sullivan 1979), anthropologists everywhere began to be interested in processes of symbolisation, rather than just in the decoding of cultural symbols.

Selfhood finally moved to centre stage in the late 1970s and 1980s with the linked developments in 'reflexivity' and the critical scrutiny of anthropological and ethnographic writing, a movement which is often trivialised by its description as 'post-modernism'. It was a trend of thought pertinent to selfhood because it interjected explicitly into the ethnographic scenario the figure hitherto proscribed by the canons of disciplinary practice, the anthropologist's self, appropriately caricatured by Crapanzano (1992) as a 'trickster' and by Hastrup (1992a) as a 'magician'; and, in so doing, triggered a critical examination of the distinction made by ethnographic style and convention between the self (the anthropologist) and the other (the anthropologised).

The convergence of these themes, selfhood and the posture of the anthropologist, was not adventitious. As scholars began to focus on self-awareness and cognate phenomena such as thought, emotion and cognition, the characteristic anthropological problem inevitably arose to pose unanswerable questions: How do you *know* what the other person is thinking? How do you know *that* the other person is thinking? How can you discriminate between the other person's consciousness and your construction of his or her consciousness? The answer to the first and second questions, 'I cannot know for certain', leads inexorably to the answer to the third: 'I cannot'. What we *can* do, what anthropologists customarily have done, as recent work has shown us, is to use literary devices of one kind or another to convey in our authored texts the impression of such a discrimination. But it is one which we as authors have engineered.

The enormity of this admission should not be underestimated, for it calls into question the methodological pretensions of modern anthropology. It amounts to the admission that the inevitable starting point for my interpretation of another's selfhood is my own self. For at least the three decades since the philosopher Peter Winch pointed to this inevitability in his *The Idea of a Social Science* (1958), anthropologists have sought ever more sophisticated means of minimising, if not escaping, its limitations, and they have become very sophisticated indeed. The rigour of anthropological scholarship in validating its rendering of other cultures' systems of knowledge, belief, thought and communication has arguably been unmatched by the other humane sciences. But it was all predicated on the prescription to maintain the axiomatic difference between the anthropological self and the anthropologised other.

The argument of this book denies the authority of that axiom. It is plainly unacceptable to assume that anthropologist and anthropologised are alike; indeed, it could be perverse, for it might risk rendering anthropology redundant. But, equally, the assumption that they are *not* alike is unacceptable for it seems to lead inexorably to the construction of their difference. It is also perverse, for it denies the pertinence of the most potent investigative and interpretive weapons in the anthropologist's armoury: his or her own experience and consciousness.

OBJECTIVES

This argument cannot be made simply or briefly, but depends on extended demonstration. That is one of the purposes of this book. It is implicated in, but subsidiary to, its principal objective which is to show why we *must* address the question of the self since not to do so is to risk misunderstanding, and therefore misrepresenting, the people who we claim to know and who we represent to others.

It is always difficult to know quite when a book originated. I began to write the final version of this volume during the summer of 1992, but had been consciously and deliberately working on it during at least the previous six years. During this period as working papers and articles appeared, some of my friends and colleagues grew increasingly exasperated with the apparent futility of my argument which called for anthropologists to do what we all know cannot be done: to elicit and describe the thoughts and sentiments of individuals which we otherwise gloss over in the generalisations we derive from collective social categories. Some were more than sceptical about my suggestion that we should use in a rigorous and controlled fashion the only means which is available to us: our experience of our own selves. Still others insisted that this objective was simply not the proper business of anthropology. I hope to show in this book that, notwithstanding these entirely respectable objections, anthropologists inevitably engage with the self, their own and other people's, and that it is in the nature of their enquiry that they must do so. Because they are unaware of doing it, or are squeamish about it, it is often fudged. But, by drawing extensively on the work of anthropologists and on a wide spectrum of cultural experience and ethnographic expertise, I will try to demonstrate that social anthropology has incorporated self consciousness implicitly into its discourse, and should now come out of the closet in order to deal more faithfully and fully with the self.

There is nothing new in the argument that methodologically anthropologists cannot avoid the intrusion of their own selves. It has been rehearsed openly and repeatedly throughout the history of modern social anthropology, sociology and the philosophy of science. Further, the engagement with critical literary theory and with various 'post-modern' currents has extended this self-scrutiny from the investigative to the writing processes in ethnographic work. More recently, the argument has been further developed by systematic attempts to explore how what had previously been regarded as a methodological burden and inhibition might be transformed instead into a resource, even a virtue (see e.g. Okely and Callaway 1992).

This aspiration is the premise for the present study. The proposition is that anthropologists' self-consciousness may stimulate their sensitivity to the self consciousness of those they study. I am not advocating an egocentric anthropology, or anything so facile as the notion that 'we are all the same under the skin', and that we might therefore be justified in treating ourselves as models for others. But I do insist that if there is no justification for treating people axiomatically as being alike, then equally the assumption of their difference is also questionable. Modern social anthropology was built on the putative cultural distance between anthropologist and anthropolog*ised*, on the largely unexamined assumption of the differences between the self (observer) and the other (observed). Throughout the 1980s, anthropologists showed how this presumption had been made self-validating in anthropological analysis and writing. I shall argue later that one of its unfortunate consequences has been to deny to cultural 'others' the self consciousness which we so value in ourselves.

If my contention is correct, then our neglect of others' selves must be objectionable for all kinds of reasons and certainly raises serious ethical questions. But the implication on which I wish to focus is that it has probably rendered our accounts of other societies inaccurate in important respects, since they must be revealed as generalisations from the only partially perceived, at worst misperceived, elements of those societies – individuals to whom we have denied self consciousness.

Addressing self consciousness and selfhood thus brings us up critically and inevitably against two bulwarks of ethnographic practice: generalisation and cultural relativism. Indeed, acknowledging that other people have selves also means recognising that generalising them into such analytic collectivities as tribes, castes and ethnic groups may be a very crude means of categorisation, the inadequacies of which we have all experienced in similar categorisations of ourselves. Sensitive ethnography demands nothing less than attention to other people's selves, an inquiry which inevitably entails to some extent the use of our own consciousness as a paradigm.

However, I repeat that my concern is not with the self for its own sake, but is to consider critically and constructively the assumptions we conventionally make about the relationship of individual to society. Western social science proceeds from the top downwards, from society to the individual, deriving individuals from the social structures to which they belong: class, nationality, state, ethnic group, tribe, kinship group, gender, religion, caste, generation, and so on. We have concentrated on these collective structures and categories and by and large have taken the individual for granted. We have thereby created fictions. My argument is that we should now set out to qualify these, if not from the bottom upwards, then by recognising that the relationship of individual and society is far more complex and infinitely more variable than can be encompassed by a simple, uni-dimensional deductive model.

This book is written with reference to, and from the perspective of, social anthropology, partly because it is my own discipline and because I am therefore criticising my own practice. However, readers may note that at various points in the text I identify the subject more generally with social science. This is not careless writing or absent-mindedness. While anthropological experience reveals the practices which I identify in the argument, they are also present in other social science disciplines which may have been even less sensitive to them. I have also long taken the view that, both because of its theoretical focus on culture, and, notwithstanding my critical stance, its general methodological rigour, social anthropology should be regarded as fundamental to social scholarship. My argument is therefore addressed in a non-sectarian spirit to all those academic disciplines whose practitioners regard themselves as engaged in the humane sciences in the hope that it may contribute to the discourse among them.[1]

WHY SHOULD ANTHROPOLOGISTS BE CONCERNED WITH THE SELF?

Concern with the self has not been universally welcomed among anthropologists; indeed, it has provoked some trenchant comment and invective. There are those who dismiss it as mere 'self-indulgence' (*inter alia* Friedman 1987; Sangren 1988), a deliberate pun; those who argue that it is a Western-, Euro- or Anglocentric preoccupation; and those who maintain more substantially, if atavistically, that it detracts from our proper attention to social relations, or that it poses such intractable methodological difficulties that it is really a blind alley. The first comment is too trivial to require an answer, the second a contention which is at odds with the ethnographic record, as the case studies which follow will show. The present book attempts to address the three latter points.

There is no essential opposition between the consideration of the self and the description and analysis of social relations, indeed, quite the contrary. In the past, our concern with groups and categories, that is, with the social bases of social relations, has largely ignored the dimensions of the self and self consciousness, and may therefore be regarded as having dealt with bogus entities. In treating individuals either explicitly or by default as merely socially or culturally driven, ignoring the authorial or 'self-driven' aspects of behaviour, is to render them at best partially, and, perhaps more often, as fictitious ciphers of the anthropologist's theoretical invention. It was an approach with a pedigree at least as long as the sociological concept of role, a term which focuses wholly on what a person *does* socially to the exclusion of who the person *is*. To treat social relationships as encounters among roles seems odd, and ethnographers rarely present their descriptions in this modest way. They are much more inclined to pretend that they are dealing with *people*; but, as I have suggested, this seems an unjustifiable pretence.

Let us take a step backwards. If we regard social groups as a collection of complex selves (complex, because any individual must be regarded as a cluster of selves or as a multi-dimensional self) we are clearly acknowledging that they are more complicated and require more subtle and sensitive description and explanation than if we treat them simply as a combination of roles. Indeed, the aggregation of these complex entities into groups may itself be seen as more problematic than would otherwise be the case. Collective behaviour is then revealed as something of a triumph, rather than as being merely mechanical. I suspect that this is a description which gibes more closely with our personal experience as members of families, committees, clubs, platoons or whatever.

If these problematic aggregations are then magnified to the level of society, we can put into a quite different focus the question of how society is possible. Far from being sociologically gratuitous, the question is a real one. The conventional answers of European social theory, most of which point to determinism of some kind or other, are inadequate. They do not take account of the individual's capacity to reflect on his or her own behaviour – that is, to be self-conscious – and to come to any conclusion other than that there is no real choice about how to behave – the bleak, but unconvincing, views which Gearing and Greenhouse attribute to, respectively, the Fox and the Hopewell Baptists. Nor do they address the meaning which the decision has for the individual, which may be significantly different from its perception by others. For example, if I make a full and accurate statement of my annual income to the Inland Revenue, my behaviour would be interpretable at the macro-level as evidence of the power of the state to compel its subjects to make such disclosures and to penalise them if they are shown to be delinquent. The most this interpretation will allow to my discretion is the decision to be law-abiding. But a moment's reflection will suggest numerous other possibilities. The fact that these all eventuate in the same behaviour may not be irrelevant so far as the state and its revenues are concerned, but this simplistic view fails utterly to explain my be-haviour. It neglects my reasons for my complicity with laws with which I may disagree. This kind of account therefore leaves the cohesion of people into societies unexplained, or, at best, only partially explained.

So if we return to the question, 'how is society possible?' or the less grandiose enquiry, 'how are social groups possible?' I suggest that, far from taking selfhood for granted, the question cannot be sensibly addressed without putting the self at its very centre. The problem lies in the putative contradiction between selfhood, individuality and social-ness. It is perhaps an irony that we have to approach the fundamental problem of social cohesion through its apparent opposite, selfhood and personal identity.

COMPLEX SELVES

Perhaps the issue may be put into focus if we contemplate ourselves as anthropologists contemplate the societies which they struggle to under-stand: that is, if we try to do some fieldwork on ourselves. We have curious mixtures of allegiances. The issue is not that we belong to many different kinds of group and association, although of course we do. Rather, the curiosity lies in their incompatibility. Many are positively antagonistic to each other. For example, I remember as an adolescent finding the presence of my friends embarrassing if I was with my parents. But why? I felt reasonably at ease with my parents when we were just among family, comfortable with my friends when exclusively in their company; but when both sets of associates were together, I felt acute awkwardness. You may experience similar discomfort if you try to mix together different sets of friends. It is not an uncommon experience that people who get on well both with their consanguines and their affines nevertheless find it very difficult to resolve the apparently competing claims made on them by each set of relatives. We have routinely to juggle the incompatible claims of family and work, of family and friends, of friends and neighbours, of neighbours and co-religionists; of locality and ethnic peers, of ethnic peers and nationality, of nationality and locality, and so on. All of these associations pull us in different directions. It seems to me remarkable that, as individuals, we generally manage to cope with these many incompatible claims on our allegiance without cracking under the strain. It is little short of a triumph that we do so while also preserving a reasonable sense of loyalty to our own sense of self, that is, to our individuality. For it is a very odd characteristic of our kind of society (I write as a bourgeois British intellectual) that we are expected to be able to accommodate these plural claims which are made on us, while also having a strongly developed sense of self. Indeed, when a man or woman fails, or worries that they might fail, we say of them that 'they are not quite themselves'!

This demand which we are inclined to make of ourselves and others for a strong and stable sense of self makes all the more curious the penchant which British anthropologists have showed during the last thirty years for theories which depict social and personal identity as being highly contingent. These theories owe much to the American sociological tradition of symbolic interactionism, in the development of which Mead's influence was seminal. Mead was concerned with the ways in which individuals symbolise themselves in social interaction, a concern from which sprang the sociological tradition of symbolic inter-actionism. He distinguished between the 'me' – the unthinking being, the enduring product of experience – and the 'I', the *consciousness* of being which, through its ability to symbolise, is capable of behavioural control, precisely because it conceptualises the self. The 'I', the active agency of being, has to be continuously creative to keep viable the person (including the 'me'), a view of the self which has been echoed in recent anthropological work (e.g. Heelas 1981a: 13–14; also Lock 1981: 32). Much of Mead's work elaborated this creative aspect of the individual. For example, he dealt with the human's unique capacity to 'manipulate', to intercede, through 'mind', between means and ends, to intervene, through language, between perception and 'consummation'. This mediation takes the form of reflective thought, and is where indivi-duality reposes.

For Mead, the self is nurtured, rather than determined, by interaction with the other, since interaction stimulates reflexivity (e.g. Mead 1934).

Indeed, like Cooley before him, he saw social interaction as being the very foundation of self-conception: both are accomplished by 'taking the role of the other', viewing oneself and one's behaviour from what is imagined to be the perspective of an other, anticipating the other's reaction. The 'I' component of the self is the analyst of this self-observation who modifies or plans behaviour on the basis of this analysis. The conceptual material for the analysis, in the Meadian view, is derived partly from culture, which explains the similarities to be observed among the members of a society. It is also mediated through the individual's consciousness in ways which reflect cultural theories of the relationship of individual to society.

The symbolic interactionist tradition ran in a continuous line from Mead to Goffman. Goffman's early writing on personal identity was echoed in turn in Fredrik Barth's seminal statement on ethnicity which set the style for anthropological studies of ethnic identity for nearly twenty years. Goffman saw personal identity as an intentional construction designed to secure for its bearer the greatest advantage, or the least disadvantage, in his or her dealings with 'significant others'. Indeed he analyses all behaviour as if it was composed of tactical moves in a strategic game. The titles of his early books and articles make the point: 'On facework'; *The Presentation of Self in Everyday Life*; *Strategic Interaction,* and *Stigma: Notes on the Management of Spoiled Identity.*

Barth, trained both in Britain and the United States, based his transactional model of social behaviour on a similar calculus of advantage (1966). More specifically, in his seminal essay introducing the volume *Ethnic Groups and Boundaries* (1969), he argued that ethnic identity is malleable. It is articulated at 'the boundary' since that is where ethnic groups encounter each other, and the identity of any group is modulated to and moderated by that of the other. That is to say that ethnicity is impermanent, adjusting itself to the specific circumstances of any ethnic interaction.

This kind of argument was made with respect to personal identity by Leach, another important influence on Barth (see Paine 1974). In his famous series of Reith Lectures, *A Runaway World?*, Leach said: '*I* identify myself with a collective *we* which is then contrasted with some *other*. . . . What *we* are, or what the *other* is will depend upon context' (Leach 1967a: 34). It is not at all clear whether Leach really intended to depict the self as being so ephemeral, so contingent as this. Might he have confused self with persona? It seems unlikely. The wording seems deliberate: 'I identify myself . . .'. There is no suggestion in this formulation that I associate myself with a group for merely public purposes;

rather I see myself in the character of a group which is itself constituted by the requirement for contradefinition. This contingency theory of the self was later developed by Boon into a view of *all* identity – ethnic, cultural, linguistic, sectarian – as being contrastive. Boon characterises these boundary transactions as 'playing the vis-à-vis' (1982). How can this notion of shifting selfhood be squared with the demand for a stable, core self?

The answer, which we shall explore at some length later, again derives from American social psychology, in which it is especially associated with Ralph Turner. It sees the individual as essentially a basket of selves which come to the surface at different social moments as appropriate. The basket, the container of these selves, is the individual's identity. A.L. Epstein puts it as follows:

> Identity . . . is essentially a concept of synthesis. It represents the process by which the person seeks to integrate his various statuses and roles, as well as his diverse experiences, into a coherent image of self.
>
> (Epstein 1978: 101)

THE INDIVIDUAL AND SOCIETY

The compelling requirement for a strong sense of self extends beyond individuals to groups, large and small. A sense of collective self may be qualitatively different from that of individual self, but the imperative need for identity is not less. A self conscious perspective explains this imperative: groups have to struggle against their own contradictions, which lie precisely in the fact that they are composed of individuals, self conscious individuals, whose differences from each other have to be resolved and reconciled to a degree which allows the group to be viable and to cohere. Moreover, as a collective entity it has also to suffer and reconcile the competing claims made on it by its collective asso- ciates. The segmentary world view so familiar to Arabists is by no means limited to the Bedouin: I am an individual; I am a member of a sibling group. I compete with my siblings for the attention of our parents. I and my siblings together protect our interests with respect to groups of siblings who belong to other families in our village or our clan. We families, related to each other by descent or by locality or by some other means, identify our common interests against those of another group of allies, and so forth. But, at the same time, we are also having to satisfy, or to fend off, the claims of those with whom we have trading relations, ethnic peers, would-be political allies, etc., and to do so without impugning the integrity of the group's collective identity. It really is a bit of a puzzle how we manage to square these circles.

It may seem something of an intellectual mystification to characterise as a puzzle a social competence which we ordinarily take for granted. However, it is just an anthropological way of formulating the contradiction which we commonly experience between our sociality and our individuality, a contradiction which, far from being taken for granted, frequently causes us anguish, stress and perplexity. The state and other powerful social agencies compel us to compromise our individuality in our dealings with them by squeezing us into categories. The effect of this constraint is that we belong to society as members of collective entities (whether categories or groups) rather than as individuals. The application form compels me to render myself in ways which are not of my choosing. It would be a futile gesture to demand that whoever reviews my application for a passport or a driving licence or a job or a club membership should consider me – ME – the whole man. Instead, I have to contort my conscious self into: a husband; father of three sons; university professor; born in London; resident in Edinburgh; bearer of visible identifying features, etc., etc. My protest that these structural properties taken together do not add up to me are of no account: indeed, it is a mark of my eccentricity. Our social membership requires us repeatedly to belittle ourselves in this way. Individuality and socialness seem to be in contradiction to each other.

Of course, this is an entirely unoriginal thought in the tradition of Western social and political theory which bore on the development of social anthropology. It presages the need to distinguish individualism from individuality, a discussion which will be pursued in some detail in Chapter 7. The distinction has not always been clear. While Marx could entertain the idea of individuality as an aspiration for liberated humankind, individualism was clearly regarded as a symptom of the alienation of individual from class. In the condition of alienation, we are inclined to confuse the nature and cause of our travails: to see them as attaching peculiarly to us *qua* individuals; indeed, to see ourselves as specifically marked out as individuals by fate or by other people's malice. The rationale for the achievement of class consciousness is to bring about in such alienated individuals the recognition of their common condition since it can be rectified only by common action. There is thus an intriguing paradox in the Marxist scheme. The object of communism is to restore people to the condition of completeness ordained for them by nature but withheld from them by the development of capitalism. Although barely spelled out by Marx, this completeness is intelligible only as the total fulfilment of the individual as a hewer of wood, critic and drawer of water. Yet, this ideal can be accomplished only by the successive attenuation of individuality which marked the evolution of capitalism, and which has to be pursued to its logical conclusion through the revolutionary process which is to unwind the capitalist structure and to wither away its state mechanisms. The ultimate instrument of this revolution, the dictatorship of the proletariat, anathematises the individual, reduces him or her to the spiritual ashes of the cadre or the assembly line.

Although proceeding from a very different notion of human nature, Durkheim too saw an essential contradiction between individual and society. But whereas Marx's communism envisaged a reconciliation of the contradiction by eliminating the ways in which society compromises the individual, Durkheim's objective was just the opposite. In his view, individualism revealed the failure of social integration, and could therefore be regarded as pathological. It was a failure which eventuated in the condition of *anomie*. Anomic individuals, lacking the means to organise their behaviour, are literally normless. They behave in a kind of moral isolation. Without guidelines, they have no means of orientating themselves to others, no means of organising their behaviour through their expectations of how others might respond to them, simply because they cannot have any such expectations. Durkheim saw this awful normlessness as a consequence of a malfunctioning society, rather than of pathological individual psychology. Its extreme manifestation is suicide, and the examples of anomie which he gives in *Le Suicide* all point to the sudden loss of norm and normative constraint: the newly widowed man, unprepared for freedom from the regulations and restraints which inhere in the normal domestic routine; the speculator, unable to calculate the odds in an abnormally booming market. He generalised the condition from individuals and extended it to other individual components of society – groups of one kind or another – which were inadequately integrated into society as a whole and engaged in social analogues of anomic suicide: striking, fighting and pursuing unrealisable sectional interests.

Marx and Durkheim both saw a contradiction between society and the individual, but resolved it in opposite ways. Marx invoked the full panoply of state power over the individual to bring about a society in which social control of the individual would be minimised and replaced by something rather like a Rousseauian General Will to explain the compliance of individuals with each other. Durkheim argued for the maximisation of society's control over individuals (and over its individual parts). That was what motivated his advocacy of the division of labour which was, for Marx, the quintessential manifestation of alienation.

If we consider the ways in which modern social anthropology has treated the problematic relationship of individual to society, we find not surprisingly that the influence of Durkheim has predominated. Right through the traditions of structural-functionalism and British structuralism, the individual was consigned to membership of structural elements of a society: a lineage or segmentary lineage; a village, caste, or some other collectivity. In so far as they were considered at all, individuals were presented as refracting the conditions and characteristics of these collective entities. In fairness, this was less a reflection of ethnographers' lack of imagination than it was the consequence of prevailing theoretical fashion. For example, Radcliffe-Brown was consistent both with his positivist forebears and with subsequent Parsonian sociology in his view of society as a mechanism (in Durkheim's paradigm, an organism) the various parts of which could be objectively identified and specified by reference to their unique functions. Function was related to the logic by which the mechanism was configured: it was a matter of what any component contributed to the functioning of the whole. Its description and explanation were scientific matters which could be evaluated by the degree to which they conformed to the correct analytical procedures. There is little to choose in this respect between the positivism of Radcliffe-Brown's *A Natural Science of Society* (1957) and Durkheim's *Rules of Sociological Method* – nor even, come to that, of Weber's *Methodology of the Social Sciences*.

SOCIETY : INDIVIDUAL :: FORM : MEANING

Anthropologists did not attribute any importance to the problem of what these structures actually meant to those who populated them. In this kind of theoretical scheme, people, individuals, were important only as structures in themselves, or as related to structure in some identifiable way. The view has persisted into the present day, not least through the writings of Louis Dumont. Dumont is one of the scholars responsible for perpetuating the indefensible contention that the individual is a peculiarly Western concern, an error which is attributable to his failure to make the distinction between individuality and individualism to which I referred above (see, especially, Dumont 1986). Two mistakes follow from this neglect. The first is the denial to non-Western cultures of concepts and values of individuality, a contention which is clearly contradicted by the ethnographic record, even for India, the area of

Dumont's special ethnographic interest (see, for example, Mines 1988). The second is the axiomatic dichotomisation he makes between individualistic and holistic sociologies and ideologies, and which he reads into the very fabric of their respective societies. The opposition itself seems unsubtle in its attribution of monolithic character to so large-scale an entity as the aggregates we call 'societies'. But it is also a crude reduction of the variations among societies and their organising ideas into these polar types (see Morris 1992: 262–74).

Even in the rather different French structuralist tradition, known to us principally through the work of Lévi-Strauss, Barthes and de Heusch, individuality tends to be subordinated to the uniformities that are supposedly present in the ways in and through which human cognition is structured. With the important and intriguing exception of Mauss, the French holistic tradition sees individuality as a theoretical and practical problem. Theoretically, it is a deviation from the norm which requires explanation. Practically, it is an aberration which requires constraint. Hence, we encounter the implicit or explicit assumption that social structures, to which the analyst should be able objectively to assign functions, determine the meanings which their members find in the world, meanings which are consonant with the functions identified by socio-anthropological analysis. Both theoretically and normatively individuals are regarded as the determined products of their social environments.

The holistic tradition, so influential among American sociologists and the British structural anthropologists, stresses the need for society to impose itself over individuals and to imprint itself on their consciousnesses. It is out of this kind of programme that there emerged a concern with 'socialisation', the processes through which society retrieves its neophyte members from what would otherwise be a state of nature. The task is much more fundamental than one of explicit education, but inheres in such basic cultural concepts of cognition and classification as those of normality and deviancy, gender, sexuality and emotion (see Erchak 1992). In order to explain differences among members in their social behaviour, this kind of sociological determinism has to resort to such essentially psychological concepts as those of personality and intelligence, provided that society is functioning 'normally' (whatever that may mean). It is a theory which allows explanation to emerge from the more or less mechanical association of meaning with structure. Members are standardised by socialisation; even individuality may be socially ascribed, as when a community designates an individual as 'a character', and inscribes the character in a nickname (see e.g. Cohen

1978). And, when they depict social process in this bleak manner as a matter of conformity to social and cultural standards, it is hardly surprising that these anthropologists can indulge in generalisation with so few ethnographic and theoretical qualms.

Of course, this style of anthropology was not limited to accounts of individuals, but extended to the interpretation of social phenomena generally. It is the 'representational' style which regards symbols as 'standing for' particular referents which can be objectively identified (rather than just being means for conveying the raw material for individuals' interpretative work), which sees religions as comprehensible and explicable through the analysis of their dogmatic texts (rather than through their perception and interpretation by believers), and which in its later Lévi-Straussian incarnation sees myths as being explainable by their reduction into binary structures. It may not be too much to say that this was an anthropology in which people *qua* individuals were almost incidental, indeed, were ignorable if they could not be generalised into some category or other. It was only much later in the history of anthropology, when meaning was more generally recognised as problematic and when social differentiation in every respect was recognised as being normal, that problems of generalisation were pushed to the centre of the methodological stage and the approach to the individual changed appreciably.

This maturation out of the earlier generalising tendency was overdue. In saying this, I suggest neither that anthropology should be able to account for social behaviour and human nature in all their infinite varieties, nor that we should regard the individual as paramount. Both propositions seem manifestly absurd. My objection to the kind of generalisation in which we indulged is that it has little or no authenticity in our *own* experience. Therefore, I do not see how we can be content with it as an account of *other* people. Most of us will occasionally have felt ill-served, even outraged, by having had attitudes imputed to us because we are categorised in certain ways. We feel these impressions of ourselves to be inadequate or inaccurate expressions of the people we believe ourselves to be. Statements of these general kinds are made about 'students', 'Brits', 'Yids', 'Prods', 'Blacks', 'intellectuals', 'tourists' and so forth, labels which we may well regard as inappropriate descriptions of ourselves, even if we belong to these categories. Our disenchantment with them may even extend to a feeling of injustice: we take seriously the importance of representing ourselves precisely, and anything less is misleading, and may be demeaning.

There is nothing novel in saying that the stereotype is a crude device. The issues raised by its use in ethnography are not just those of its crudity, but also the question of whether we are aware that we are indulging in it. It is a mode of generalisation which ignores or neglects the rich diversity among people in a kind of deference to those features which they might be construed as having in common. As such, it confuses social *form* with substance, reiterating the fallacy of the 'representational' anthropology discussed above: the meaning conveyed to any individual by a symbol is neglected in favour of the symbol's formal character; the meaning of belief is obscured by its dogmatic statement; the character of an individual is displaced by the formal matrix into which our theories can squeeze the person.

I emphasise that it is not my intention to reinvent the wheel of methodological individualism, nor to allow individuality to obscure commonality. People *do* have things in common socially – culture has always been the premise of my own anthropology – and I do not dispute that they should be the focus of anthropological enquiry. All I plead for here is that we should pay more careful attention to their limits, and to the ways in which they impinge upon individuals, than we have done in the past.

SELF AGAINST ORTHODOXY

I have suggested above that we cannot take for granted the existence of common understandings and meanings among even closely knit groups of people: that is, that we should always be careful to distinguish between the appearance and the reality of an interpretation common to different individuals. I will argue and illustrate the point in greater detail in later chapters. But for the moment, let me hasten to acknowledge that within groups of people there will be a modicum of agreement; at the very least, there will be a feeling among the members that they do share a modicum of agreement. This sentiment may be regarded as a *sine qua non* of the group's very existence, suggesting that however little the members may actually share with each other, it must be more than they share with members of, what they recognise as, other groups.

The interpretations which people make of behaviour, of symbols, of the world, are not usually random. Although profoundly influenced by personal experience, they are made within terms which are characteristic of a given group, and are affected (I deliberately put it no more strongly than this) by its language, its ecology, its traditions of belief and ideology, and so on. The vehicles of interpretation are symbols, which are by their very nature malleable, manoeuvrable, manipulable by those who use them. It is this character of symbols which permits them to be shaped to the interpretative requirements or inclinations of their individual users, and which reveals as misguided the representational theory of symbols as 'standing for' other things. If symbols did indeed refer objectively to other things they would be redundant: why use a symbol if instead you can simply refer to the thing for which it supposedly stands? Their potency lies in their capacity to refer to these 'other things' in ways which allow their common form to be retained and shared among the members of a group, while not imposing on these individuals the constraints of uniform meaning. Symbols can be made to fit the circumstances of the individual (see Cohen 1985).

The argument may be illustrated by considering an ethnographic study of the relationship between religious believers and the dogmatic symbols of their organised religion. In his study of a Pietist congregation in Stockholm, Stromberg argues that the members use the Church's theology, the dogmas which they supposedly share by virtue of their common membership of the Church, and their common liturgy to make entirely personal commitments to their faith. This personal discretion, the individualisation of religious belief and practice, is an explicit and distinguishing feature of Pietism. It is a faith which denies the integrity of orthodoxy, and which makes personal experience the very foundation of its beliefs (Stromberg 1986: 16). The religion offers its members common forms, and the church offers them the opportunity for assembly; to this extent they are congregants. But so far as their meanings are concerned, these forms and structures are insubstantial. Members render them intelligible to themselves through their personal experience of their faith – experience which Stromberg renders as 'commitment'. By individualising these putatively common structures, members transform them to the extent that their common-ness may well become illusory. Therefore, Stromberg says,

> people may share commitments without sharing beliefs; it follows that they may constitute a community without that community being based in consensus.
>
> (Stromberg 1986: 13)

And further,

> the fundamental point which must be grasped . . . is not that the individual is more highly valued than the community but, rather, that the individual is in a logical and theological sense *prior to* community.
>
> (Stromberg 1986: 19)

And, finally,

common discourse is forged out of diverse meanings rather than shared ones.

(Stromberg 1986: 51)

I would suggest that although Pietism may be unusual within the Judaeo-Christian tradition in making explicit the creativity and agency of self, it is really making a virtue out of what is inevitably the case. However powerful their orthodoxies may be, however strictly enforced their dogmatic regimes, no Church or religion can legislate for a uniformity of experience and meaning. If I was a practising Jew, I would spend Yom Kippur, the Day of Atonement, in synagogue with my fellow Jews, fasting as they all fast, reciting the same liturgy as they do at more or less the same time, beating my breast to give emphasis to the confession of my misdeeds and to ask for forgiveness and a clean sheet in the divine ledger. I would bow with them in a gesture of reverence as the scroll of law, the *sefer torah*, is carried past us in procession. With my neighbours, I would almost certainly utter a comment of relief when the *shofar* was sounded in the evening to signal the end of the fast. I would nod in agreement or acceptance during the Rabbi's sermon as he pronounced authoritative interpretations of scripture. But nothing in all of this choreographed, uniform behaviour entails that my experience of prayer, or of faith, or of the religion generally is the same as anyone else's. We may weep together or exult together, but still the meanings which religious commitment have for us may be quite different. At the very least, we cannot know that they are the same. We deploy the same symbols to signal the commonality of our beliefs, but this says little about how we interpret and make meaningful to ourselves those symbols.[2]

Symbols enable individuals to experience and express their attachment to a society or group without compromising their individuality. Indeed, the members of a group may be unlikely to recognise the idiosyncratic uses to which each puts their shared symbols, so that they are unaware of these distortions of meaning. If a concert hall is acoustically deficient, the music played in it will not sound the same to members of the audience who are seated in different sections of it. Symbols mediate stimuli in a similar way, so that the stimuli are rendered sensible by members in ways which we cannot assume to be the same. We may all listen to the same Mahler symphony, but hear it differently. We may all participate in the same ritual, pray the same liturgy, speak the same language, but we cannot assume that these social forms convey to us the same meanings. That is why societies go to extraordinary lengths in the attempt to coerce their members into similar meanings, as we shall see in Chapter 3 when we examine some rites of initiation.

In representational accounts of ritual, the events tend to be described as if their participants are so choreographed that the prescribed orthodoxy of their behaviour displaces their freedom or necessity to think for themselves – as if they become automata. It is description which, perhaps unwittingly, makes audacious claims about the generality of states of mind: 'the Bemba think that . . .'; 'the Bedouin believe . . .'. Quite apart from generalisation, it also makes gross assumptions about the relationship of action to belief, as if the thoughts or mental states of ritual participants could be read off from their ritual behaviour. Why *do* we make these outrageous assumptions? We know from our own experience that while we *may* become absorbed by some activity, we frequently do not, and go through an apparently absorbing activity while thinking about something else altogether. Which academic has not listened to, even delivered, a lecture while thinking of something quite different? And even if genuinely absorbed, who is to say that the absorption produces a state of mind so hypnotic that it is identical to other people's who are also engaged in the same activity? This mode of description can be seen as based on a tacit premise that cultural others are different from ourselves. Intentionally or not, this essentially methodological prescription became a substantive statement as well: *we* are self-aware and therefore capable of detachment; *they* are not.

It may be because of this unconscious ethnocentrism that we find ethnographers treating as bizarre aberrations occasional instances of the failure of ritual to compel its participants, such as that of the Sebei girl who 'cried the knife', escaping at the last moment from the clutches of her initiators who were about to perform clitoridectomy on her. A week after the event, she claimed to have run in order to escape the malign attentions of a suspected sorcerer who she had spotted in the crowd. She was then made to feel such shame that she threatened suicide (Goldschmidt 1986: 102–4). This kind of ethnographic reporting implies that it is not only exceptional for people to resist the discipline of ritual (which it may well be), but unusual for them to think for themselves – a questionable position for anyone to take. It reveals an essentially deterministic anthropology which attributes to social structures the power to mould formulaic thinking among the members of society.

Common forms do not generate common meanings. Recent research which focuses on the personal experience of rituals of initiation, rather than on their sociological significance, shows that even the most coercive forms induce different kinds of reaction and are interpreted differently by different people, even though they are all coerced by them (Poole 1982; and see Chapter 3 below). This being so, the description and explanation of individuals in terms of their groups or categories must be misleading. Individual and society are too complex and too subtle to be reconciled satisfactorily in so mechanical a fashion. We have to see the relationship between group and individual as questionable. We cannot take belonging or social membership for granted: it is a problem which requires explanation.

One of the most sustained attempts to provide such an explanation for 'post-traditional' societies has been made by Giddens. In his *Modernity and Self-identity* (1991), he treats the self as a 'reflexive project', having to sustain itself by a continuous process of reflection and revision. The problem is to maintain the 'ontological security' of the self in a 'risk culture'. He concedes that 'The self is not a passive entity' but 'has to be reflexively made' (2–3), and considers factors such as trust which might attack this ontological security to see how the self fights back. Its reflexive project is continually to adjust itself as it is implicated in changes in the institutional order, having lost the protection which the individual enjoys in 'the small community' and 'tradition' (32–3), a strangely atavistic evocation of long-discredited distinctions made in anthropology between 'folk' and 'urban' cultures, and between Great and Little traditions.

For Giddens, self-identity (the object of self consciousness)

> has to be routinely created and sustained in the reflective activities of the individual.
>
> (Giddens 1991: 52)

It is

> the self as reflexively understood by the person in terms of her or his biography.
>
> (Giddens 1991: 53)

The trouble with this argument is its essentially Durkheimian posture. Giddens' 'structuration theory' treats society (rather than self) as an ontology which somehow becomes independent of its own members, and assumes that the self is required continuously to adjust to it. It fails to see society adequately as informed by, created by selves, and by implication, therefore, fails to accord creativity to selves. The 'agency' which he allows to individuals gives them the power of reflexivity, but not of motivation: they seem doomed to be perpetrators rather than architects of action:

> Agency refers not to the intentions people have in doing things but to their capability of doing those things in the first place. . . .
>
> (Giddens 1984: 9)

It seems a sadly attenuated self to which we attribute the capacity for action but whose intentionality we neglect either because it can be regarded as incidental (even adventitious) (ibid.), or because the agenda for action is set by superior powers (Giddens 1991). It is as if he answers the question of the possibility of society by defining out of existence the problems of selfhood and individuality.

By contrast, attention to selfhood, to the individual's consciousness, resurrects the fundamental question of how society can be possible. How is it that groups can cohere when their members perceive significant differences in them? How can the group 'speak' as a whole to the rest of the world when the internal discourse among its members is so diverse? How does it come to pass that individuals who have such disparate understandings of the group's symbols, and of the world in general, nevertheless come to have such a committed attachment to the group? Under what circumstances are groups mobilised into activity *qua* groups, and when do they languish? How do they mediate between their individual members and the wider society?

These are all recognisably authentic questions for anthropology, indeed for the social sciences generally. The argument I make in this book is that answers to them which somehow assume, explicitly or implicitly, that individuals are made in the image of their societies – to the extent that their consciousness of themselves can be ignored – are too simple to be plausible. We should focus on self consciousness not in order to fetishise the self but, rather, to illuminate society.

Chapter 2

The creative self

SELF-DIRECTION VS. SOCIAL DETERMINISM

In his book *Ethos and Identity*, Epstein quotes the Hasidic Rabbi Mendel of Kotzk as follows:

> If I am I, simply because I am I, and thou art thou simply because thou art thou, then I am I and thou art thou. But if I am I because thou art thou, and thou art thou because I am I, then I am not I and thou art not thou.

> (Epstein 1978: 1)

Rabbi Mendel seems here to reject contingency as an adequate explanation of selfhood and identity, and we should applaud his memory for it. His position stands in stark opposition to Leach's, which we encountered in the last chapter. It does not necessarily entail that we should think of the self as sovereign or wholly autonomous, but we should recognise that it has a unique essence formed by the individual's personal experience, genetic history, intellectual development and inclinations, and so on. This is the position of eminent common sense which the anthropological tradition has tended to deny, insisting, first, that the self is merely a reflex of superordinate determining forces; and second, that it is inconstant, a chameleon, adapting to the specific persons with whom it interacts and to the specific circumstances of each social interaction. I do not question the obvious: that society, through the media of its institutions and of culture, continuously intrudes upon the individual's capacity for self-direction. But we should not assume that individuals are complicit to the extent of abandoning their will to self-direction, nor that they have lost their consciousness of their selves.

The encounter between individual and society need not be seen just in micro/macro terms as a David-and-Goliath contest. It can become apparent at the microsocial level when the individual engages in a relationship which requires the transformation of 'I' into 'we' – say, by marriage, or by membership of a group. This transformation does not necessarily entail the contradiction of self, but, rather, the placing of certain limits on it. When I enter into such a relationship, I say, in effect, 'there are some aspects of "I" which are not relevant to "we", and which I will put into the background for the time being'. I take a particular version of myself into a 'we' relationship. Far from this entailing the loss of any aspect of my self, I regard my self as being augmented by my experience of and participation in this new relationship. I return to this matter in detail in Chapter 4. For the moment, I wish just to make the point that engaging in social relationships does not necessarily deprive the individual of self- (or authorial) direction. I begin with the following illustration.

In a series of monographs and essays, Kirsten Hastrup has brilliantly compiled an anthropological history of Iceland from the time of its initial settlement by Norse sailors in the ninth century, until the present day. She gives a comprehensive account of cultural history, encompassing law, language, kinship, cosmological beliefs, economics and so on. The achievement of her work lies not just in its meticulous research, but in the way in which she is able to demonstrate the emergence of these forms and beliefs and their articulation with historical circumstances. In the early period of settlement, the island was sparsely populated, with farmsteads and townships widely scattered. Such contact as the islanders had with each other was restricted to specific locations and times, such as the embryonic markets or other assemblies. In this condition of isolation, says Hastrup, their concepts of space and time were ego-centred (see Hastrup 1985).

This is simply explained. The measurement of time was material only in relation to the routines observed in the conduct of a person's own subsistence activities. Moreover, because its reckoning was based on observations of the sun and moon, it would vary with vantage point. Concepts of space were likewise related to the unique coordinates of ego's location.[1] Space was demarcated by reference to ego who was conceptualised as occupying its centre.

As Iceland's population increased and its settlements became more densely populated, social relations became more numerous and more complex; that is to say, society occupied an increasingly important place in the individual's life. The mechanisms of the state began to proliferate and to regulate social relations, and, indeed, to presage the need to regulate relations between ego and the state. Among the ways in which the state impinged directly on the lives of the settlers was the introduction of absolute (rather than egocentric) standard measures of time and space. But the new measures did not simply dislodge the previous ones. The two systems of reckoning coexisted, each prevailing in the area of the individual's life to which it was most appropriate. In the individual's immediate environment of the farmstead, there was retained a model of space, 'as a circular, multi-dimensional area with ego in the centre' (Hastrup 1985: 56).

However, when the space in question was beyond the personal static domain, for example, when the individual moved between two points, at least one of which was beyond the farmstead and immediate environs, then it was divided according to a scheme which was based on fixed, objective coordinates which reflected the socio-political division of the country into quarters. Rather than being ego-centred, this model of space was society-centred (ibid.: 66). As the individual moved between selfhood and society, as it were, so the measures of space and time which it was appropriate for him or her to use varied accordingly between the egocentric and the sociocentric. The imposition of a social system for the reckoning of space did not compromise the egocentric mode, at least not while the two systems coexisted.

A stuctural-functionalist reading of this history would see the state displacing the self to a degree at which the individual became merely a basket of social roles or a repository of social facts. For example, the Chicago School of urban sociology, from Robert Park onwards, saw urban life as being incompatible with the maintenance of a coherent self. Selfhood was fractured by the city into functional performances and contingent personae. This pessimistic view was expressed by Robert Park in a seminal statement:

> The processes of segregation establish moral distances which make the city a mosaic of little worlds which touch but do not inter-penetrate. This makes it possible for individuals to pass quickly and easily from one moral milieu to another, and encourages the fascinating but dangerous experiment of living at the same time in several different contiguous, but otherwise widely separated worlds.
>
> (Park 1925: 40–1)

The mosaic image in Park's statement is a clear echo of Durkheim's concept of organic solidarity. The model for Durkheim's notion was the interdependency implicit in a system of functionally divided labour. In order to make this model plausible as a matrix for social organisation generally, Durkheim tried to show how a 'moral' bond of solidarity could be overlaid on to a mechanism of structural integration. He was not optmistic about the prospects for creating this solidarity, for he found little evidence to suggest that people would rise easily above factionalism and sectional interest to promote it. But he argued passionately that the very absence of such a bond made its generation imperative. Park follows Durkheim in noting its absence, and warns that political leaders will exploit it to keep the populace divided and dependent on them.

But the mosaic image of society is replicated at the micro-level of the individual: a structure of little selves 'which touch but do not interpenetrate'. Park's view of the individual was not idiosyncratic, and has by no means passed from the conventional discourse of social science. There is a remarkable absence from it of any acknowledgement of the self's reflexivity: there is no self consciousness here, no sense that the self is an active and creative agent in managing and reconciling the plethora of obligations which tug its bearer in different directions. Rather, it is the determinate creature of its ecology.

Writing at the end of the 1930s, Louis Wirth took a similarly bleak view, but hinted at a greater sensitivity to the antithesis of urban life and creative selfhood. He recognised self beneath the role, but suggested that we have grown habitually blind to it:

> The urban world puts a premium on visual recognition. We see the uniform which denotes the role of the functionaries and are oblivious to the personal eccentricities that are hidden beneath the uniform.
>
> (Wirth 1938: 55)

His pessimism led him to suggest that, because of the power and influence of the city, this superficial orientation to persons would spread throughout society generally. No matter where we lived, our lives would become 'urban' in this respect. It is clear that these early Chicago sociologists had a Durkheimian view of the urban person: a person pressed into an organic matrix in which functional interdependency prevailed over individuality, partly by fracturing the self into discrete tasks and relationships. Individuality and difference were licensed only if they were functional and constructive for the society as a whole; if they did not meet these criteria, they were pathological. The simple, ghastly term which did all this work was 'role'. Role replaced the self. In the sociological eye, cities were populated not by individuals but by persons playing roles (in strictly defined situations [à la W.I. Thomas]), or as grouped into categories. The humanising influence which G.H. Mead was to throw on the concept, following earlier work by Cooley and Thomas, was yet to become apparent.

Mead certainly had more influence over American anthropologists than over their British counterparts, and was an important precursor of the Interpretative genre. His influence is clearly evident in the writings of later interactionists and phenomenologists, surfacing again among theorists of strategy, game and transaction. It seems to have missed most British scholars (Fortes [1973] being an honourable exception), at least until after the 'discovery of mind' and the demise of the deterministic and other modernist paradigms. Where Mead saw self-conception as founded on social interaction, they tended to a view of individuals as defined by their structural positions in society. It was not that a particular theory of structural determinism edged out all other explanatory possibilities, but that structure offered a compellingly tangible gloss to the insubstantial data with which anthropologists had to work, making 'consciousness' seem at best speculative, at worst downright mystical by contrast. Social relations were regarded as providing the proper stuff of anthropological analysis.

The analysis of social relations calls up status and role, but not self. Individuals were manipulated ethnographically into structural postures which obviated the need to consider their self-determination and self consciousness. Indeed, a theoretical virtue was made out of this ethnographic myopia, as ever more elaborate theories about the structural determination of the person followed. Ironically, the infection spread back into the academic tradition which derived from Mead himself, and reached its apotheosis in Goffman. The self, whose explication occupied so much of Goffman's concern, was a rather reactive entity, operating more or less mechanically a tactical calculus intended to optimise gain and minimise loss. Variations between such selves were provided by differences of intelligence and ingenuity, but not by a free-ranging and authorial intellect defining its own objectives. Presentations of self were dictated by strategic considerations emanating from structural context, rather than from individual creativity and imagination. It was, at best, a performing self[2] whose consciousness responded only to winning and losing rounds in the game of social life in which individuals were presumed to have to engage by virtue of their membership rather than of their conscious decisions to participate. It conjures up a peculiarly selfless society.

Even when the person's various roles were acknowledged to interact, even to cohere, it was as a consequence of structural imperatives rather than of a consciousness of self. Consider, for example, this concession by Gluckman to his critic, colleague and interlocutor, E.L. Peters:

while for analytic purposes it is essential to isolate a man's various roles, as if he plays each role separately at one time, in real life a man does not wear and act in a particular role as if it were a suit. . . . A man is known and acts as the occupant of several roles, and he carries all his roles even when one happens contextually to be dominant. Thus, most strongly, a man is not at one time a friend and at another an enemy, but always both a friend and an enemy. The roles are not as segregated as we have to make them appear in analysis.

(Gluckman 1962: 41)

Note that Gluckman and Peters do not question the integrity of the concept of role, nor its displacement of the self; nor, for that matter, are they disquieted by the distortion of reality which they see as required by the niceties of 'analysis'.

A historical curiosity of this monolithic concentration on the structural determinants of an individual's behaviour is that Mauss had hinted at some of its clumsiness in his essay published in 1938, the same year as Wirth's 'Urbanism as a way of life' (and republished in Carrithers *et al.* 1985). Mauss' concern with the person or self took the form of a cross-cultural review of the degrees of licence afforded by cultures (and their legal and religious institutions) to individuals and individualism. He attempted to distinguish the *moi*, the conscious self (Mead's 'I'), from the *personne* and the *personnage*, the socially and culturally constituted personalities. However, he still focused, not surprisingly, on structure rather than experience; and his *moi* was a poor, attenuated creature, governed and determined by cultural rules. While the discrimination of terms he proposed was promising, he simply did not take it very far. His motivation may well have been linguistic rather than theoretical – that is, as an attempt to sort out the variety of terms available in French to refer to the first-person subject (none of which is a precise analogue of the English 'self'), rather than to render structuralism more sensitive to human experience.

The kind of semantic puzzle which preoccupied Mauss in his essay remains evident in psychologists' attempts to distinguish among self, person and personality, and does not seem to have taken them far beyond a contingent view of the self as 'other-directed' (e.g. Gergen 1977). Indeed, they have barely progressed past the point reached by much earlier psychological anthropologists such as Hallowell, Florence Kluckhohn and Dorothy Lee. Lee added a Buber-esque ideological dimension to her view of the socialness of the self, arguing that its autonomy can be realised only in a person's 'relatedness' to others, the degree to which such relatedness is achieved being an expression of 'cultural value' (Lee 1976). This is a direction travelled by Hsu, among others, distinguishing among gross cultural types – Chinese, Japanese and Western – on the basis of the extent to which the individual's 'psychosocial homeostasis' is rooted in relationships of his or her own making. The Chinese are at the minimal pole, the Western at the maximal (e.g. Hsu 1985).

The approach here comes full circle with Mead's: a cultural predisposition to view oneself in social relationships in culturally typical ways. Hsu's gross types, Chinese, Western, Japanese, and so on, inevitably suggest a deterministic view of the relationship of individual to society. They are too indiscriminate to suggest anything more subtle. It may be fruitful, though, to proceed from Mead's promising opening in a different way: instead of moving deductively from society or culture to the individual, why not inductively, or, at least, experientially, from the individual to society? For example, instead of conceptualising the self as a replicate in miniature of society, we could begin by paying attention to the ways in which people reflect on themselves, and then see in what ways these reflections are indicative of social and cultural context, or require such contextualisation to be intelligible to us.

REFLECTING ON THE MBUTI REFLECTING ON THEMSELVES

The American social psychologist Ralph Turner insists that 'People are not just miniature reproductions of their societies'. Rather, a person's experience of his or her engagement with the social structure gives rise to a 'self-conception', a symbolisation of self which runs consistently through all of the person's activities (Turner 1976: 989–90). This essential self is informed by social engagement, but is not dependent on it. The self is not defined by its engagement with the other: to this extent, it is appropriate to think of it as autonomous rather than as contingent. Consider this disquisition on selfhood administered to Colin Turnbull by his Mbuti guide, who had just waded into the River Lelo, had addressed it, and had spoken also to *ema* and *eba*, mother and father (the Ituri rain forest):

> Stand at the edge of the water, I was told, and look at your reflection. Who is it? It looks like you, but its head is down there, looking up at the other you. Is it thinking the same thing, wondering who you are? Then put out your foot, over the water and gently lower it. The other

foot will come up to meet yours, and if you are very careful (not to break the surface of the water), you will feel that other foot touch yours. You are getting to know your other self. Then as you lower your foot further into the water the other foot comes up, passes through your foot, and disappears into your leg. The deeper you go into the water the more of your other self enters into you. Just before you go right down into that other world, look down, and see yourself down there, all but your head. Only your other self's head is there. And then look upward as you go right under the surface, and you see nothing. Your other self has passed into the world you left behind, taking your place. Now walk across the bottom of the river, and slowly come out on the far side. If you look up from under the water you will see nobody, just the forest. But as you emerge into that world something will leave you, passing through your body down into the water. Now who is the real self, and which is the real world?

(Turnbull 1983: 122)

It is possible to read into this reflection a theme which is prominent in Mbuti culture, the dialectic of self and society. The Mbuti pygmies lived nomadically within the Ituri forest (in what was then the Belgian Congo), speaking a wide variety of languages and revealing a plethora of extraneous cultural influences on them. They lived in and on the forest, and had a very fluid kin structure which enabled them to move from band to band and from place to place as they judged expedient. Around them on the forest's edge lived Mbira villagers who contrasted with them in most respects: they were tribal, sedentary, non-pygmy cultivators who were incompetent in the forest environment, depended on the Mbuti to supply them with its produce, but who nevertheless presumed to play patron to the Mbuti's client. The villagers were *alter* to the Mbuti *ego*.

So, here we have the Mbuti, contemplating his reflection in the river and talking about his two selves. Who or what might they be? They could be a metaphorical statement of this opposition between the forest nomad and the sedentary villager. This seems improbable: ethnic encounters do not often seem to be conceptualised in terms of mirror images, unless we think in terms of distorting mirrors. Rather more plausible is the idea that the reflection of two images may be a paradigm for the reconciliation of contradictory themes which are perceived as inherent in the human social condition, foremost among which is the opposition between self and society. So far as the Mbuti are specifically concerned, the existence of oppositions, and of their resolution, is a constant refrain in the culture

(Turnbull 1965). There are the obvious differences between the Mbuti and the villagers: tribally and ethnically distinct; their contrasting modes of subsistence and of social organisation; their physical and topographical differences; their beliefs in different gods and spirits. Yet, despite all this, they lived in a degree of symbiosis. The Mbuti supplied the villagers with forest foods, such as roots, berries, meat and honey, and with building materials. The villagers, unwittingly perhaps, provided the Mbuti with lootable cultivated foodstuffs. Their contradefinition was reconciled also through the great circumcision ritual of *Nkumbi*, which was held approximately every three years, and which federated many of the forest-dwelling peoples.

There are many other oppositions also: for example, between biological descent, and the classificatory kinship which makes the Mbuti individual so mobile. All males of one's father's generation, and all one's mother's female generational peers are classified, respectively, as one's fathers and mothers; similarly, ego's siblings' peers are ego's siblings, and the children of ego's children's generation are ego's children, with the consequence that one is always among kin, regardless of the band with which one lives and hunts. This kind of classificatory kinship and the mobility of band membership which goes with it, as well as the age-grade structure which complements it, suggests a pronounced egalitarianism. The equality is ruptured by marriage, but that contradiction is resolved in turn by the resumption of unrestricted sexual relations during the three years which follow the birth of a child. There is the contradiction between the principle of non-aggression and belief in the sanctity of life, and, on the other hand, the necessity for adults to hunt and kill game and meat – a contradiction which is resolved by the ritual purification of adults (who are polluted by their shedding of blood) through the agency of uncontaminated children. There is the contrast between the ideal of peace, *ekimi*, and the reality of noise or crisis, *akami*, resolved by the mediation of youths who bring the crisis out into the open and music it away with the sacred trumpet, the *molimo made*.

The metaphor of reflections – let us assume it *is* a metaphor – might itself be metaphorised as weights on either side of a set of scales. If they are unresolved, one pan will outweigh the other. The ideal of resolution is to bring them into balance, a concept we will pursue a little later. Mbuti make much of being in balance, the opposite condition being described by the KiNgwana (and Swahili) term, *waziwazi*. *Waziwazi* does not imply the unresolved tensions of individuality and social membership, or a movement from selfhood to society, it just means being disoriented. When the Mbuti refers to the 'real self', he can have in mind both the individual and the member of the wider collectivity. In this view, then, the mere fact of sociality does not compromise the idea of self. Rather, the balanced self, the essential Mbuti self, is fundamental to the ideals both of individuality and of society.

BALANCING THE SELF

If we take seriously Turnbull's account of the Mbuti's reflection, we have to accept that there is no *necessary* contradiction between the self and society; or, at least, we have to recognise that the Mbuti do not see any such contradiction. This rather sanguine view of social membership is uncommon in the ethnographic record, suggesting either that the Mbuti were unusually skilful in preempting the contradiction; or that Mbuti society, as Turnbull found it, was an aberration; or that anthropologists had somehow failed generally to do justice to the societies they purported to describe, when they emphasised the social at the expense of the individual, and even suggested that self consciousness and self-direction were unknown or were regarded in the society as aberrant.

The answer to this conundrum could be circumstantial: for example, that Mbuti enjoyed unusual freedom of movement, both geographically and socially, since they were not tied permanently to kin or hunting groups; and that this mobility itself suggests that society impinged to an unusually limited extent on the self, if at all (an answer which, incidentally, would provide a marked contrast to Rivière's account of individualism among potentially mobile Guianan peoples [1984: 94ff.]). But this is precisely the kind of argument which posits a 'society-driven' view of the individual, and which still directs us to limit our interpretation of individuals' mental processes to what can be documented in terms of 'social facts' (compare Needham 1981), or alternatively to generalised cultural models of the constitution of personhood (e.g. White and Kirkpatrick 1985; Heelas 1981b). If we were to allow the possibility that individuals are self-driven, the Mbuti case would not seem so discrepant.

The 'society-driven' view of the self sees the self being tugged in different directions by the competing claims and allegiances of the individual's social ties, each of which, as we have seen, implies a role with appropriate script. It is clear that the Mbuti theory of the harmonious self could not tolerate such subversion which must surely lead the individual off-balance, *waziwazi*. The Mbuti may therefore be able to help us understand the contrary view. Turnbull, again:

> One of the hunters cupped his hands into the form of a sphere and another pointed to a vaulted arch above us. From what followed it

seemed that the Mbuti live not in a linear world of time and space, not cyclical but, rather, spherical. Ideally, we should always be in the middle of our sphere. That is when there is *ekimi*. *Akami* comes from moving away from the centre of our sphere. This can be done by moving too fast, with violence, in body or mind. If we do that then we reach the edge of our sphere and it does not have time to catch up with us. Give it time, and it will, but meanwhile, in that world of time . . . we are *waziwazi*. . . . People who are *waziwazi* are best left well alone. Give them time, their spheres will catch up with them; they will be back in the centre of the world and they will be all right.

But if you are too violent or hasty (both among the most negative values for the Mbuti) you may pierce the wall of your sphere. And as you pass through, like walking right into a river, something will come in and take your place in this world, as you enter the 'other' world. That person will look like you, but will not be you. So if someone is *waziwazi* for more than a few days, it is probably not that person at all, but his or her other self. Then it is best to move the camp and suggest that that person go off and join some other hunting band. Perhaps the real self will find a way back, for neither self likes to be in the wrong world.

(Turnbull 1983: 123)

The Mbuti clearly make balance a precondition of authentic selfhood. Its distinguishing competence is its capacity to subordinate social associations to it. The self predominates over the social. It is not tied to collective groupings, and is not contingent on social relationships. It has about it the quality of absoluteness. Yet, the Mbuti are clearly neither asocial nor antisocial. They just have an enlightened theory that society does not depend for its integrity on intruding itself upon the selves of its members. To the contrary, the integrity of society depends on preserving that of its members. Selfhood and sociality are mutually implicated in a way which itself evokes the imagery of balance. Lest I be suspected of reinventing equilibrium theory, I will show that this imagery is grounded in ethnographic cases, rather than in a mere analytical device.

(i) Mbuti, again

It would seem unreasonable, and certainly uninteresting, to suppose that the Mbuti's use of the imagery of the sphere is merely gratuitous. But what can it mean? One possibility is that it is modelled on the forest itself, a definitely bounded and vaguely circular area. Turnbull remarks frequently that when he first went to the Ituri, and it was still relatively unscathed by the depredations both of the colonial and later independent governments, its hundred-feet-high trees rose wall-like out of the plain and formed an overarching canopy, standing out dramatically against the deforested clearings in which the Mbira villagers had built their settlements. As we have seen, the topographical contrast presaged fundamental social, cultural and ecological contrasts as well. The negative connotations of movement away from the centre of the sphere might therefore be read as analogous to the disorientation which, Turnbull says, the Mbuti experience when they are too long removed from their forest world. For example, we are told that although they quite liked visiting the villages, since they enjoyed plundering the fields and making fun of the villagers, they also fell ill if they stayed too long. This interpretation may also be bolstered by their imputation of *ekimi* to the centre (or forest?) and of *akami* to the village.

This seems to me at once too metaphorical and insufficiently metatheoretical. The sphere, of course, is not merely circular, but is all-encompassing. It has neither beginning nor end: it is a perfect organic unity. The empirical perfection of a sphere implies balance: first, so that, unlike a bowl, when projected along a line it will not be biased to one side; second, it perfectly reconciles centrifugal and centripetal forces in order that it does not collapse in on itself, nor fall apart outwards. In this respect, the sphere is a perfect resolution of contending forces. To be *waziwazi* is to be out of balance or disoriented. By contrast, to 'be spherical' is to have merged all dimensions into a perfect shape – just as the self, fully immersed in water, is a perfect unity. The sphere rotates on its own axis, through its mid-point. Therefore the Mbuti say, 'We should always be in the middle of our sphere. That is when there is *ekimi. Akami* comes from moving away from the centre of our sphere.' In a sense, the sphere *is* the forest, but only in that the forest symbolises the harmony and balance which is the ideal of Mbuti social life. It seems to have infused their view of their relationship to nature, and, more generally, to have informed their conceptualisation both of their inner selves and of their culture.[3]

The Mbuti's image lends itself well to the view of social membership presented earlier which sees the self being tugged in different directions by multiple claims and loyalties, some of which may be mutually antagonistic. If we are felt to have inadequately acknowledged any of the claims, we will be regarded as partial, and as egocentric if we attempt too obviously to subordinate them to our conception of ourselves. Against this view is one of a more authorial self (though one perhaps not so serene as the Mbuti) who somehow resolves these contending forces, and whose unique character as a member of society inheres in the nature and experience of their resolution. It would be absurd to suggest that everyone succeeds in this struggle. My argument is more modest: it is that most people make the effort (an effort which anthropology has largely neglected), and that most people succeed to a considerable extent. If they do not make the effort, or if they fail in it, we refer to them as 'unbalanced'.

(ii) The Utkuhiqhalingmiut Inuit

Like the Mbuti, the Utku Inuit of Chantrey Inlet, Northwest Territories, are hunters and gatherers (Briggs 1970). When Jean Briggs studied them during the 1960s they had declined to some thirty in number, spread among eight households. They lived in conditions the extremities of which were social as well as environmental. Depleted and isolated in the middle of the vast Canadian tundra, they lived in winter cheek-by-jowl with their neighbours. Entire families were crammed into the same few square feet of the *iglu* day in and day out, eking out rations of tea and tobacco, measuring each day's morsel of cardboard for the children to play with, against the all too finite supplies. When the tea was gone, they had to boil roots; when the flour was used up, there could be no more bannocks to relieve the dreary diet of fish. When the kerosene was finished, nothing could be cooked and no lamps could be lighted. Famines were within people's memories, and chronic illness was a source of perpetual anxiety.

These stressful circumstances provided the context (though I would not presume to say the *cause*) of the remarkable regime of emotional and personal control which Briggs describes as regulating Utku social life. Anger, temper, hurt, frustration are not shown. Attitudes such as those of resentment, dislike, envy and contempt are recognised but, again, must not be made apparent. To display these emotional reactions would be to demonstrate a lack of *isuma*, reason. *Isuma* is contrasted with every deplorable emotion as its opposite. To become an encultured Utku is to acquire *isuma*; indeed, maturation consists in coming to *isuma*. The Utku recognise that there are people who do not have it, such as very young children, and the entire non-Inuit world, but that, by definition, to be properly Utku is to have it, for acquiring *isuma* is tantamount to acquiring culture.

In her vivid account of the Utku, Briggs does not attempt to convey an impression of them as cultural automata. Far from it, it is a beautifully written ethnography, which bursts with life. The various members of the band live in her book as individuals: quirky, humorous, sullen, pompous, caring, humble. She shows us cultural delinquency (including her own) alongside virtuosity. *Isuma* seems to me less a monolithic discipline of selflessness, than a way of harmonising the emotional needs of the individual with their pragmatic need for society.

A child seems to be thoroughly indulged during infancy. Carried around in the mother's parka, sleeping with the mother under her quilts, the child is the object of everyone's affection. The recalcitrant infant is never scolded or punished, never threatened with deprivation or physical punishment, but is distracted by sweets and tallow, by being humoured and petted. Briggs gives in detail the example of Saarak, the three-year-old daughter of her adoptive household. 'It was immoral to deprive a child of Saarak's age of anything she set her heart on' (Briggs 1970: 113); so if Saarak screamed for Briggs' raisins, then raisins she must have: 'Saarak was convinced that if she screamed importunately enough, another box would materialize from some mysterious corner' (ibid.). The child's mother says, 'She hasn't enough sense (*ihuma*) not to ask for things she wants . . .' (ibid.).[4] There is no fear that a child might become 'spoiled' through being indulged in this fashion.

> She was merely expressing a childlike wish for affection, a wish in which her family happily acquiesced, nodding their heads at her lovingly. . . . Later, when she developed reason (*ihuma*), restraint and shyness, a wish to be properly inconspicuous, would, in their view, grow naturally.
>
> (Briggs 1970: 116)

It is from this condition of complete indulgence that the young child is torn without warning, usually following the birth of a sibling. The lesson is that self-control is the supreme value; and it is learned in the hardest of ways for a child: by giving way to another child. This does not only mean giving in to the other's whims, but also being apparently displaced by the other in one's parents' affections. The complaints of the child, however apparently justifiable, are ignored; the physical display of affection previously lavished on the child is suddenly withheld. She is simply left to cry, while the offending interloper in her mother's attentions is given the breast. Briggs describes in detail heart-searing scenes in which the lesson is driven home remorselessly to Saarak's six-year-old, mild-mannered sister, Raigili:

> It was difficult to tell how Raigili responded to this training in the use of reason. I often had to stifle pity as I watched her small figure

standing in motionless distress on her mother's side of the *iglu* or noted the dampness of her lowered face beside me on the *ikliq* (the sleeping area of the *iglu*). The demand for control, though clothed in the mildest voice, was so relentless, and Raigili was still so little.

(Briggs 1970: 144)

But, Briggs continues,

The lesson takes a remarkably short time to learn, judging from the almost infallible control of the children I knew who were ten years old or more.

(Briggs 1970: 144)

That the lesson is completely learned is evident in the vehemence with which children thus trained reject the playful petting of adults so soon after having delighted in it.

Acquiring *isuma* is a dramatic process, which may strike the reader as callous. Briggs herself suggests that 'the learning must entail suffering' (Briggs 1970: 144). Yet, the equanimity with which it seems quickly to be borne suggests that, just as it describes the necessary condition of balance between individual and society, so also it balances different aspects of the self to form a balanced individual. Indeed, she describes the acquisition of *isuma* as a condition of proper selfhood:

One consequence of – as well as evidence of – a well-developed *isuma* is the ability to act autonomously, self-sufficiently. . . . [O]ne who has *isuma* is an Adult.

(Briggs 1987: 10)

The contrary condition is one we prosaically describe in English as being 'maladjusted'. In the article cited immediately above, Briggs confesses to having previously underestimated the 'complexity' of Utku emotional theory because her approach was insufficiently self-conscious (ibid.: 15). She finds that the emotions she had identified earlier are qualified or multi-faceted; that far from regarding them as cultural 'givens', Utku continuously test them, and test themselves against them (Briggs 1982: 121–2). She elaborates on this compexity, arguing that, 'Not only do the behavioural values conflict, but the feelings underlying each value are themselves in conflict' (ibid.: 114); and, moreover, that commitment to values may depend for its motivation on such ambivalent, complex and even conflicting emotions (ibid.: 109): 'intrapsychic conflict about a value can create allegiance to it' (ibid.: 115).

Again, becoming adult, acquiring *isuma*, is not like graduating to a larger size set of clothes (to extend Gluckman's analogy), but is a recognition of the complex constitution of the self who has to be brought towards the goal of *isuma* rather like a complicated team of huskies: all must be kept in step, in rhythm, maintaining their position. It is an orchestration of the self in which harmony and balance are imperative, an image which itself implies the complexity of self and its problematic, non-mechanical relationship to the institutional and cultural structures of society.

(iii) The Huichol

The Huichol Indians studied by Barbara Myerhoff (1974) live in the mountains of the Sierra Madre Occidental in Mexico, and were some five thousand in number. They were poor even by Mexican rural standards. Formerly hunters and gatherers, they became small-scale agriculturalists attempting to cultivate maize in unpromising conditions, and supplemented their meagre livelihoods by selling craft work or by seasonal migration to the towns and cities in search of employment. They were regarded in Mexico as being of low status, anachronistic, and marginal to the concerns of a thrusting and developing oil-producing state. Through their religious beliefs and practices, and especially through the peyote pilgrimage which is the subject of Myerhoff's book, they transformed themselves in their own eyes from this lowly position to one of sacredness, even of deification. In the process, they should be seen not as trying to escape the reality of their condition, but as positing an alternative reality, one which was much closer to their own senses of themselves than to the image imposed on them by others.

The crucial figure who guides them through these transformations is Ramón, the *mara'akame*. A visionary and a shaman, he is their spiritual mentor and ritual courier. He is a man of exceptional powers, as he must be in order to convey his pilgrims safely on their journey from the mundane to the sacred and back again. He tells them repeatedly that their journey is fraught with ritual dangers, and successfully navigates their passage so that they exult in the incommunicable inner ecstasy of arrival in paradise, and find solace in the community of the pilgrimage.

Unlike some other North and Central American peyote cults, the Huichol do not venerate peyote *per se*, nor the state of mind which it induces. Rather, peyote (a mushroom containing mescalin) is an indissoluble element of the three-part symbolic complex which it forms with deer and maize. It is venerated as a symbol, rather than just for its hallucinogenic powers. Indeed, just as Azande deny toxicity to their poison *benge* until it has been ritually constituted as poison, so perhaps Huichols recognise the power of peyote to induce visions of the truth because of its use in ritual contexts. It is not its visionary power which makes peyote sacred, but its derivation from the ancient homeland, Wirikuta, to where the pilgrims journey under the direction of their *mara'akame*, partly to 'hunt' the peyote.

The metaphor of the hunt is deliberate. When the Huichol find peyote during their pilgrimage they 'shoot' it with arrows. What can explain the 'hunting' and 'killing' of a vegetable? The peyote symbolises the deer – specifically, the deer's hoof – and by shooting it, the deer is not killed but is fixed in place so that its powers can be bestowed on the hunter-pilgrims. The deer is sacred to the Huichol, evoking their earlier existence as hunter-gatherers. It is a provider: of peyote in its footprint; and of blood, which is the source of magical power. How can marginal Indians, who are shunned by the rest of society, think of themselves as having magical power? If they do have it, why are they propping up the entire status hierarchy of modern Mexico? Why are they so poor that they have to leave their homes to eke out a living elsewhere? It does seem rather paradoxical. Other adherents to religions of the oppressed may find God in their souls; but the Huichol *hikuritamete* (pilgrims) transform themselves into their gods. By virtue of their magical power, the geographical transposition from their stoney hillsides to Wirikuta, the realm of their gods and ancestors, is matched by their transformation from poor farmers and labourers into the gods. It is the pathway to perfection, illuminated by peyote. What does it all mean?

Ramón the *mara'akame* is given to leaping from rock to rock, across gaping ravines in the mountain peaks of the Sierra, risking life and limb with the appearance of extraordinary equanimity. He is being a bird, springing through space to land with consummate grace on one leg. But why? He says,

> the *mara'akame* must have superb equilibrium. . . . Otherwise he will not reach his destination, and will fall this way or that. . . . One crosses over; it is very narrow and, without balance, one is eaten by those animals waiting below.
>
> (Myerhoff 1974: 46)

Crossing over what? Mere space? No, it seems that he is crossing from one world to another. He crosses from the mundane, dull, day-to-day world of the Huichol smallholder to that of the Huichol supernatural, and thence again to that of the urban-industrial nation-state – and back again. What seem to be represented here are the multiple planes of reality on which the Huichol live. The bird signals their capacity to move among them; the *mara'akame*'s sense of balance signifies his virtuosity in balancing them, keeping them stable, moving between them with perfect poise rather than neurotically. Ramón's balance marks his knowledge of grace and the sacred, proof of his competence to lead the pilgrims on their journey to Wirikuta.

The virtues of balance in the physiology, nurture and psychological disposition of the person are to be found widely across cultures and across history. Its manifestation among the Huichol seems to be rather different to those emerging from oriental traditions which have become popular in the West. It deals less with the equilibration of contending forces than with the capacity to accommodate with comfort disparate personae or aspects of the self, which are oriented to different contexts of life, but which coalesce in the experience and selfhood of the individual. It is understandable that continuous movement between the tawdriness of their mundane lives and the mystical ecstasy of their encounters with their ancestors and the supernatural should require the Huichol to have stability in their selfhood. It may be significant that the trance-like introspection they experience in Wirikuta is caused by the ingestion of an extraneous agent, peyote, which contains the hallucinogen mescalin, rather than by the experience of psychosocial crisis or trauma which seems widely to be associated with trance and possession elsewhere (e.g. Vitebski 1993; Thin 1991). Under the influence of peyote, again taken only in ritual circumstances, the *hikuritamete* see 'the truth': of their sacredness, otherwise belied by their poverty and demeaned status, and of their relationship to their gods and ancestors. It may be helpful to exercise some interpretive licence and to compare the contemplative state in which they see the truth with the condition of prayerful repose which some Christians refer to as 'grace'. It is a moment clearly set apart in social time which is not assimilable to ordinary experience, and may not be recapturable in memory other than by repeating the act of pilgrimage.

It seems presumptuous (to say the least) for an anthropologist who could not claim to have had anything approaching a comparable experience to offer an interpretation of it. I offer this simply as a plausible reading. When the Huichol return to Wirikuta, the sacred homeland and pilgrimage destination, it is not to search for their pasts or to do a kind of historical tourism, but to discover their essential selves, their selves uncorrupted by the taints placed on them by the contemporary Mexican nation-state. Their notions of the 'sacred' themselves suggested an essentialism to Myerhoff:

> It seems to embrace above all the concept of attaining wholeness and harmony. To be in accord with one another, with oneself, with one's customs – this is the state of being a proper Huichol and is sacred. It is a dynamic condition of balance in which opposites exist without neutralizing each other, a tension between components that does not blur their essential separateness.
>
> (Myerhoff 1974: 74)

The suggestion is that this all-encompassing balance – with oneself, with others, with nature – is the distinctive and proper condition for a Huichol, and this condition itself is sacred: that is to say, provided one observes the imperatives and prescriptions of 'proper Huicholness', being a Huichol makes one sacred. Once again, we encounter the intriguing, but hardly unprecedented suggestion that people living in poverty, marginality and contempt can claim sacredness for themselves in terms which are credible at least to them. Again, the answer hinges on their spiritual mobility – between mortality and immortality, between worldly status and their incarnations as their own ancestor gods – for which they depend in turn on the *mara'akame*'s skill and wisdom. The mobility is demonstrated by the reconciliation of their selves, their wholeness, of which *his* balance and poise is symbolic.

Their personal integration is replicated at a higher social level by the solidarity of the pilgrimage group. This band of otherwise unconnected individuals is welded by their experience of the pilgrimage, and by some of its component rituals, into a strongly bonded entity. Even at its climax in Wirikuta, the 'hunt' oscillates gently between community – the *hikuritamete* having ritually knotted themselves together in unity – and the profound introspection of the peyote-induced repose into which no one else intrudes: it is not done to ask, 'What did you see? What did you think?' There is no ethic of individualism or of individuality in all this, but there does seem to be both a theory of the complexity of self and of its imperatives, and of the relationship between individual and society. Society and the individual are mutually implicated as concepts, not in the sense that society is reducible to its component members; but, rather, that the complexity of society cannot be grasped without understanding the complexity of individual selfhood which is its key. Just as the objective of selfhood is to keep its various elements in harmonious balance, so also the relationship of society and the individual is built on the aspiration to balance between them.

RHETORIC AND THE SELF

It is tempting to dwell on the accomplishment of peoples such as the Mbuti, the Utku and the Huichol who are represented to us as virtuosi of balance, and as having highly sophisticated theories of selfhood and its relationship to society which are capable of withstanding countervailing holistic pressures. Even acknowledging the possibility that their ethnographers have exaggerated their effectiveness in this respect, they do present one aspect of the creative, or proactive, self. Another mode of creativity which was more prominent in the anthropological literature was that of the performing self. I will discuss a manifestation of it here because, although it has become less fashionable in anthropology, it remains prominent in other social sciences and popular analyses of the public behaviour of individuals. It is analysis based on a view of the self as driven largely by a calculation of how to gain an advantage over others, rather than by the kind of idealistic or cosmological convictions we have seen above. The purpose of the present discussion is to show how this view can be moderated and assimilated to the paradigmatic view of the authorial self which is presented in this book.

The theoretical approach of 'strategising man' has a long pedigree, which it is unnecessary to rehearse here. In its more recent applications to political behaviour, it seems really to be built on an adversarial view of social interaction, in which ego and alter attempt to manoeuvre each other into positions favourable to themselves. Theoretical differences among the protagonists of this kind of approach concern the means employed and the extent to which individuals have discretion in their choice of objectives and tactics. I will illustrate this position by considering some work on political rhetoric, an issue appropriate to our present concerns since it involves the deliberate and persuasive projection of the self or of a contrived version of the self.

This kind of slant was cast by F.G. Bailey who extended its application from what we colloquially call political activity to interpersonal relations. Bailey's model constructs all behaviour as composed of tactical moves in the game of social life. In book after book, he piles on the examples of everyday point-scoring and manoeuvring, from the use by a Valloire housewife of an apron to signal her unavailability for gossip (1971), to the university committeeman's expedient loss of temper (1983). Individuals implicitly or explicitly convey their purposes by the intentional use of symbols, masks and emblems. They may employ 'hortatory' or 'deliberative' rhetorics, the one ignoring and the other appealing to reason (Bailey 1981: 27). They may try to preempt counter-argument or the use of evidence of any kind; they may appeal to the emotions rather than to the intellect; they may conjure up all sorts of undemonstrable consequences of a given course of action, and so on. This is Bailey's real stomping ground, most vividly illustrated in his portrayals of academic politics.

In his *Morality and Expediency* (1977), Bailey's topic is the university committeeman who employs tactic (or, his term, 'mask' or persona) to get his way:

> No effective politician presents his allies and his rivals with the rich indigestible confused complexity of his own true self: instead he uses a mask or affects a character. . . . It is not that *all* the world is a stage, but only that in the world of politics, no one ever wins without having at least some capacity to be a 'player'.
>
> (Bailey 1977: 127)

There is more to the player, then, than mere tactic (or rhetoric) (ibid.: 147 n.1), but tactic is an indispensable element in successful politics. Hence, the need for masks. So he gives us REASON, who

> 'displays the madness of the purely rational man' because he believes that every problem has a solution, that this solution will be discovered through reasoned debate and reasoned argument, and, once discovered, will be accepted and implemented by everyone capable of reason, which means, in REASON's view, anyone who deserves to be his colleague in the university.
>
> (Bailey 1977: 127)

He characterises REASON as 'a technician of the intellect' (ibid.: 128). By way of contrast, there is BUCK, who 'believes that anyone will do anything, if the price is right'. For BUCK, people are 'stomach writ large' (ibid.: 129). He gives us SERMON, 'the guardian of our eternal verities'. If

> REASON is expert in unraveling the chains that bind first principle to plan of action: SERMON deals exclusively in first principle . . . his discourse . . . is aimed at the heart rather than the head. 'It has long been our tradition that . . .'; 'The high standards which we have always maintained require . . .'; 'No decent person could contemplate . . .'; 'Others must share my great concern . . .' and so forth.
>
> (Bailey 1977: 130)

And he gives us BARON,

the man with moustaches, with testicles, who in every situation sees but two possibilities: to screw or be screwed. . . . (L)ife without a contest is no life at all – at least not for a real *man*.

(Bailey 1977: 134)

And so on.

In a later book, *The Tactical Uses of Passion* (1983), Bailey illustrates further kinds and 'codes' of rhetoric which seem (though he does not make this suggestion) to attempt to display the truths of propositions by associating the selves of the speaker and of his or her complicit audience with them: rhetorics of assertion, of compromise, of abomination. All of these manifest, what is for Bailey, one of the prime competences of rhetoric: the avoidance of reason. Rhetorics are 'postures': specifically, postures 'used for sealing a position' (Bailey 1983: 123), or 'devices that are directed to ensuring that only one side of the question gets a hearing' (ibid.: 124). The assertive rhetoric is peremptory, its truths 'inescapable'. Among his examples is Zola:

Dreyfus is innocent. I swear it! I stake my life on it – my honour! By the name I have made for myself . . . I swear that Dreyfus is innocent. May all that melt away, may my works perish, if Dreyfus be not innocent! He is innocent!

(Bailey 1983: 124)

And President Kenneth Kaunda to his party's National Council:

Comrades, in that cold winter of 1961 we committed ourselves to the total eradication of imperialism and colonialism from the Motherland. Because of that commitment, the revolution was successful.

(Bailey 1983: 125)

Not only is evidence not required; it is defined implicitly as inadmissible. In this vein, Bailey looks at the use of specific verbal devices to achieve the axiomatic quality of what would otherwise be extremely contentious statements. I give just one example, of Walter Reuther on racketeering in American trades unions:

I think we can all agree that the overwhelming majority of the leadership of the American movement is composed of decent, honest, dedicated people who have made a great contribution, involving great personal sacrifice. . . . We happen to believe that leadership in the American movement is a sacred trust. We happen to believe that this is no place for people who want to use the labour movement to make a fast buck.

(Bailey 1983: 134)

Here he alights on the repeated phrase, 'we happen to believe', as the device which converts a most dubious assertion into 'a self-evident undeniable value' (ibid.: 134). I cannot resist another: Lloyd-George, in his famous Limehouse speech. 'Why should I put burdens on the people? I am one of the children of the people' (ibid.: 136).

The 'rhetoric of compromise' invites open minds – but promptly sets about closing them, or, at the very least, opening them only to certain perspectives. And so it goes on. It is an elegant and aesthetically pleasing exegesis, but one which I find unconvincing. No doubt we could all identify these kinds of persuasive tactic in use among our colleagues; indeed, we could happily while away hours of committee meetings by slotting our colleagues into one or other of Bailey's masks – he describes more than twenty – and have some fun in the process. But we should not lose sight of Bailey's serious assertion that people have to adopt these rhetorical postures if they are to win. Now, what are we to do ethnographically, descriptively, with the man who, in spite of being portrayed by other people as 'political', as strategising, insists that he is not: that he has no plan, no intention to manipulate, he just *does*? Well, of course Bailey would have a mask for him. But that tells us nothing more than that we *could* depict the man as if he had some intentional programme. And, of course, we are able to make our interpretation persuasive by stringing together lists of incidents which appear to confirm it. Or, perhaps, incidents whose inclusion within our theoretical matrix *contrives* their confirmation of it? Our political theories and analytical models and devices are superimposed upon the speaker's meanings and intentions. The flaw in Bailey's compelling game-plan is that it is continually he who is masking the self, not the individual concerned.

He is doing theoretically what people may commonly do in social interaction: namely, interpret other people's behaviour by imposing on it a sense of their own making. This is what an audience does when it listens to rhetoric, especially to political rhetoric the meaning of which is clouded by the speaker's vagueness of expression or deficient command of language, but which nevertheless secures a response. The examples are legion as the articulacy of our leaders seems inexorably to decline. Here are two from Mrs Thatcher's speech to the annual conference of the Conservative Party, following the 1982 war with Argentina over the Malvinas. As a transcript will demonstrate, this oration was full of incoherent statements which were punctuated by applause following the speaker's pauses:

'Unemployment will not be an option . . . and we must, we have got to do it together.'

'Let all of us pause and reflect on what we who stayed at home owe to those who sailed and fought, and lived and died, and won.'

The pause may signal to the audience that they are expected to applaud. But they must surely believe that there is something to applaud, even though the speaker's intended meaning is elusive, to say the least. What happens, of course, is that the members of the audience supply the meaning, supply their *own* meanings, just as if they were supplying the actor with her mask. They all know what she meant: what she meant was what *they* individually mean. That is interesting: for the interpretation of rhetoric, in anthropology as in most disciplines, has almost always proceeded the other way around, assuming that the speaker achieves the audience's compliance with his/her intentions. What I am suggesting here is the reverse: that the audience constructs the speaker's intentions as being the same as theirs.

During the early 1980s, the sociologist Max Atkinson used various audio and video recording techniques in the attempt to discern how particularly successful speakers secured favourable responses from their audiences – laughter, applause, and so forth. He made especially detailed analyses of the speeches of Tony Benn, Arthur Scargill, Margaret Thatcher, John Kennedy and Martin Luther King. He did not suggest that they were good speakers, whatever that might mean, but was interested only in their rhetorical devices. One of Atkinson's most celebrated discoveries was 'the list of three'. Lists of three, he said, have the quality of completeness: they cue applause or other response; they do not invite interruption, as lists of two or four might; they produce effective emphasis. Gaitskell: 'We shall fight, fight and fight again to save the party we love.' Thatcher: 'This week has demonstrated that we are a party united in purpose, strategy and resolve' (Atkinson 1984: 60–1). Further, the point has been made after the first item in the list; making the audience wait for the next two, suggested Atkinson, builds up the pressure for applause:

> When members of an audience hear Mrs Thatcher start a sentence with the words 'Soviet marxism . . .', they can be confident in treating it as an announcement that some sort of attack or insult is about to be delivered. . . . 'Soviet Marxism is ideologically, politically and morally bankrupt.'
>
> (Atkinson 1984: 63)

Moreover, if they do start to applaud or to laugh after the first item, they have to respond ever more loudly as the speaker continues over their response. Tony Benn:

'If you have a veto those who oppose policies don't bother to argue with conference . . . they kill it, secretly, privately and without debate.'

(Atkinson 1984: 95)

This is the device Atkinson calls a 'claptrap'. The speaker's interruption of the applause so 'bottles up' the audience's enthusiasm that

everyone will be almost literally bursting to clap again at the next possible opportunity.

(Atkinson 1984: 104)

The advantage which Atkinson's analysis has over Bailey's is that it does not impute any particular intention or calculation to the speaker. It sticks more closely to what happens, describing what the speaker does. It may be a device which the speaker has found works well; it may be merely a speech habit, but nothing more than that needs to be claimed about the speaker's intentions. It takes the speaker at face value.

There have been other anthropological analyses of public speech which *do* assume deliberate manipulation, but in ways which differ significantly from Bailey's argument. Robert Paine applied to political rhetoric a long-standing interest in personal performance and the use of language, suggesting '"context", "strategy", "performance" and "persuasion" as key notions' (Paine 1981a: 2). Of all these I think it is fair to say that he places most attention on the last; and, like Bailey, he makes clear that persuasion is not to be confused with reason. Rather, it is a matter of securing the *complicity* of the audience, of making the audience 'go along with' the speaker. This does not so much signify the speaker's success in securing the audience's agreement with his/her choice of alternative arguments; rather, he suggests that it may be based on reducing 'people's perception of available choices': the persuasive power of rhetoric, he says, 'rests upon the ability to organise the experience' of the audience (ibid.: 10). His emphasis here is subtly different from Bailey's. His point is that rhetoric is not merely a tactical device to be employed in pursuit of some identifiable strategy: rather, the complicity being sought may itself be the objective. There may be nothing other than winning the audience's mind: it is a view of politics in which 'saying is doing', a view of 'politics as rhetoric' (ibid.: 11). The speaker aims to get the audience to 'swing along' – Burke's term – and uses all sorts of devices in the attempt.

Paine's explicit attempts to document this process were focused on electoral politics in Newfoundland (Paine 1981b); but it seems clear to me that it had its origins in earlier work of his which was concerned with the successful floating of innovative messages by an entrepreneur in a coastal community of north Norway (1970; also 1976). Although there is no podium or platform involved here, the tactical imperative is the same: to formulate and broadcast a message in such a way that you get the chosen target to 'go along' with you. Paine goes very much further than Bailey in attempting to 'document' ethnographically the intentions he imputes to his speakers. The sceptical reader may be disposed to see the difference between them as being between more or less informed theoretical guess-work. However, Paine's suggestion that 'saying' may be 'doing' is important. It does not imply merely the emptiness of words, or that there is nothing beyond the words. It can also acknowledge that the act of saying something may well commit the speaker to the truth of what has been said. This was precisely the competence which Robert Dahl attributed to, what he called, 'democratic ritual': acts, such as voting when the outcome is already a foregone conclusion, which may seem to other people like mere gestures, but which have the effect of creating or enhancing the convictions of their perpetrators (Dahl 1961: 112).

Bailey's self is a shallow manipulator; Atkinson's is a performer who acquires skill and effectiveness with experience; Paine's is a performer who tries to persuade, but may well also have been persuaded by his or her own efforts. In this respect there is less distance between Paine and an important interlocutor, Maurice Bloch, than the former may have supposed. In 1975, Maurice Bloch published an influential symposium, *Political Language and Oratory in Traditional Society,* which drew heavily on 'speech act' theory. Bloch saw politics as being about 'control', rather than persuasion. He therefore regarded political *speech* as a means by which control is exerted. He drew attention to 'codes' – really styles – of political speech, suggesting that it is these, rather than the content *per se*, which are coercive. His examples were drawn from his own study of the Merina of Madagascar, and led him to the assertion that a person's use of the appropriate code could oblige a Merina to do something or to agree to something to which he or she was really opposed:

> The speaker and hearer have slipped into a highly structured situation which contains the hierarchical situation which only allows for a one-way relationship.
>
> (Bloch 1975: 9)

Formalisation becomes power (ibid.: 13). Here Bloch compares the 'impoverished language' of formalisation to Bernstein's 'restricted code'. The formalisation of speech inhibits the creativity of the respondent (ibid.: 15). And,

It is because the formalisation of language is a way whereby one speaker can coerce the response of another, that it can be seen as a form of social control.

(Bloch 1975: 20)

Bloch was most certainly not alone in this view; nor was it restricted to those who might loosely be labelled as Marxist in theoretical orientation. Writing about interpersonal coercion among Trobriand Islanders, Annette Weiner described the use of 'hard words': a kind of pre-verbal tussle occurs in which one person tries to preempt the other's use of a 'hard word' which is tantamount to a curse or to an ominous, self-fulfilling prediction (Weiner 1983, *passim*). However, it is an essential part of Bloch's argument that the ability to use coercive speech effectively is less a matter of personal skill than one of social position and political status.

Formalisation is . . . a form of power for the powerful rather than simply a tool of coercion available to anybody.

(Bloch 1975: 23)

It excludes the kind of negotiation which is normally implied in dialogue, in which speakers adjust their responses to the others' statements which they also try to influence. Rather,

Continual renegotiation is ruled out by the arthritic nature of the features of articulation employed by formalisation. . . . (T)he formalised code contains within it the hierarchical relationship and it is therefore a tool of coercion.

(Bloch 1975: 24)

Its use 'springs from the forces of social power' (ibid.). If, for Paine, doing is in saying, then, for Bloch, saying is in being: what you say, and how you say it, depends on who you are. But for both of them, saying is an authentic expression of selfhood, rather than a gratuitous act or performance.

One of the principal criticisms advanced against Bloch's thesis is that it so exaggerates the dichotomy between formalised and non-formalised speech that it seriously misrepresents the nature of control which a speaker can exercise. Speakers adapt themselves to the situation as they see it: the demands and responses of the audience; the nature of the crisis, and so forth (see Werbner 1977). Parkin suggests that, rather than thinking of political language as stifling creativity and reinforcing control, it would be more accurate to suppose either a belief among people that a form of authority is formalised, 'or that we are dealing with the *appearance*, say for cere-monial purposes, of such oratory' (Parkin 1984: 351). Political speech, therefore, could be regarded as an expression of cultural values: more precisely, as the speaker's reading of the form of behaviour which he believes is culturally appropriate to him. Thus political speech is an expression of social selfhood: a discourse which may be contrived, may attempt to be manipulative, but is not *necessarily* so.

This position seems preferable to Bailey's. It puts politics back into culture, rather than making culture merely a political resource. It shows us 'political' actors belonging to cultural milieux much wider than those just of the political arena, from which they derive identities, ideologies, moralities, a sense of what *ought* to be accomplished and of what is accomplishable, in short, milieux in which they locate and express their selves rather than engage in a kind of selfless political puppetry.

I argued earlier that culture does not impose meaning on individuals. It provides *form* which individuals substantiate themselves. The same is true of the structures and contexts of public social behaviour. The imperatives of communication require people to use apparently shared forms: of exchange, of politics, of speech. These may provide broad limits on what an individual can do; but they do not determine *sub-stantively* what he or she will do within these limits. We can therefore specify the conditions of successful persuasion, of advocacy, within a culture, without suggesting that they materially compromise the dis-cretion which an individual has to be self-directing. The cultural rules of rhetoric and of politics may be regarded as a framework within which the individual acts; but they are themselves given meaning and point by the ways in which individuals use them. The rules of rhetoric as cultural products are nothing without their actualisation in the mouths of creative individuals. They are brought to life by the self. If they are treated by anthropologists merely as impositions on the self, as entailed in role theory, or 'theories of the state', or games theory, they are grotesquely parodied, and the importance of the self as the essential dynamo of social process is gratuitously ignored.

CULTURAL THEORIES OF THE SELF

This discussion of rhetoric focuses on the discretion which individuals may be judged to enjoy in their decisions about how to behave politic-ally. The theoretical positions reviewed above include those in which individuals are depicted as (i) constrained by the structural imperatives of their political roles (Goffman; Bailey); (ii) supported (or inhibited) by their structurally superior statuses (or lack of them) (Bloch); (iii) the agents of their own success, either because of their persuasiveness (Paine), their oratorical prowess (Atkinson) or their sensitivity to the use of appropriate cultural idioms (Parkin). If these positions were plotted on a scale of personal discretion, (i) and (ii) would be negative; (iii) would be positive. As we have seen already, anthropologists have been inclined in the past to see cultures as such being similarly graduated in the extent to which they recognise and license selfhood and self-directing behaviour. There seems to have frequently been a confusion here between two distinct matters: the cultural recognition of selfhood – that is, the existence within a culture of a concept which may be regarded as an approximation to 'self' – and the discretion allowed to an individual to be individualistic or even merely to be self conscious. The consequence of this confusion has been that anthropologists (and others) have mistaken cultural constraints on the expression of selfhood for the absence of any conceptual equivalence to 'selfhood'. For example, the philosopher John Mbiti argued that in East African pastoralist societies, individuals are so firmly embedded within their corporate groups or lineages that they simply have no consciousness of themselves apart from their membership of these larger social entities:

I am because we are, and because we are therefore I am.
(Mbiti 1970: 141)

This seems to me a misreading of the kind to which Finkelstein points when she suggests that to see a lack of selfhood in a person's adherence to the uniformities of fashion would be to suppose that

personality was available to us from the details and displays of personal affectations. It is as if the interior qualities of the individual, the essential self, were being exhibited through the contours of appearance.
(Finkelstein 1991: 6)

On the one hand, it would suggest that we have not got very far in attempting to overcome our philosophical difficulties with the relationship between action and belief. On the other, it suggests that the explication of cultural theories of selfhood requires us to look more deeply than at the merely superficial expression of individuality.

This view has been advanced with characteristic eloquence by Lienhardt[5] in respect of East and West Africa when, arguing against writers such as Lévy-Bruhl and Bastide, he distinguishes between the public expression of selfhood and the importance placed on its privacy:

one can lay too much one-sided stress on the collectivist orientation of African ideas of the person . . . the importance of an inner, mysterious *individual* activity, comparable to what is meant by speaking in English of 'what goes on inside' a person is attested by many proverbs.

(Lienhardt 1985: 145)

He gives examples of Fipa, Azande, Dinka, Fante and Congolese proverbs, all of which, he says, establish the importance of 'the private self' (ibid.: 146). So far as the Dinka are specifically concerned, he argues that membership in collectivities augments the self, rather than diminishes or curtails it (ibid.: 155) – precisely the view advanced above. His argument is based on, what might be termed, 'creative translation': the use of approximations, justified ethnographically, where easy verbal equivalences do not exist. For example, he suggests that the elusive notion of an 'inner' dimension to a person is sometimes implied by the Dinka term for 'heart', pwou, especially to connote the 'feeling' self, while the reflexive self may be expressed through a word for body, gwop. Lienhardt's subtle exegesis of 'the bodily matrix in Dinka notions of self' (ibid.: 151) prompts the thought that the denial by anthropologists to cultures of concepts equivalent to 'self' points less to 'selfless cultures' than to mistakes of, or a lack of imagination in, translation.

The bodily matrix appears again brilliantly in James' accounts of the Uduk 'whole person' (1979; 1988):

Among the Uduk I have no doubt of their strong sense of the moral autonomy of the individual person, a sense of 'I' and 'thou' as self-directed and responsive beings. The human being is the creature of no ruling god, no inner passion, nor are persons mere puppets of an external social order. . . . [The Uduk] view of the integrity of the individual is associated with a sense of responsibility and freedom more 'modern' than is often attributed to non-literate cultures.

(James 1988: 91)

A key notion in Uduk personal theory is *arum*, which may be rendered as spirit, destiny, god, ghost, a moving and guiding force which, though insubstantial, may even have the power of procreation (James 1979: 114, 118). The *arum* is personally embodied in the liver (where blood is concentrated), but is also circulated around the body in the blood and breath. But *Arum* is also rendered in another way to refer to the shade of a dead person which has become detached from the body, and which may invade a living person through the liver. In this second sense, it has to be regarded as an imposition on the individual. The site of resistance to this invasive and directing power is the stomach, *bwa*, which is associated with *ḵashira/*,

> the highest form of individual and receptive consciousness, the capacity I term the personal Genius.
>
> (James 1988: 7)

The stomach 'is the site of the will, reason, conscious reflection' (James: pers. comm.). The juxtaposition of the invasive *Arum* with the immanent *arum*, *ḵashira/* and *bwa* can be represented as the struggle between the lack of personal control (for example, over passion, invasive spirits or 'external powers'), and 'the exertion of reflective and deliberate will' (James 1988: 7). If the extraneous force predominates,

> The sense is that the human being is no longer a 'self'; there is no self-control, no himself or herself.
>
> (James 1988: 71)

The autonomy of the individual has been lost (ibid.). Its antithesis, the Genius (*ḵashira/*), the authorial individual, ceases with his or her death, and, unlike *Arum*, cannot survive in the realm of the spirits (ibid.: 82–3).

The 'bodily matrix' for the representation of vital forces appears cross-culturally throughout the ethnographic record, so its manifestation in North-east Africa is not surprising. However, in this case it does not signify a battle for the possession of a person by a malign social will (compare Favret-Saada 1980), or by invasive spiritual powers (e.g. Kapferer 1983), nor even the orientation of the person to society or to more intimate social relationships (e.g. Hsu 1985). Rather, it illuminates the tension within the individual between 'selfhood' (consciously authorial, self-directed behaviour) and obligation, curtailed autonomy or 'other-directed' behaviour – and thereby acknowledges the presence of selfhood (or of something very like it) against the insistence of other writers who deny its cultural presence. James is careful not to advocate 'self' as a translation of *ḵashira/* or of *arum* (which is said to be 'inside' the person [James 1988: 133]). But the subtlety of her exposition shows us how these concepts can inform our understanding of each of them. Indeed, she acknowledges the importance of self-scrutiny as a 'touchstone for understanding the world of others' (ibid.: 144). Hence her view, which anticipates the conclusion to this book, that

> Self-knowledge is intimately linked with the possibility of understanding others.
>
> (James 1988: 156)

CONCLUSION

In this chapter, I have attempted to show that the opposition of individual to society may well be a figment of the anthropological imagination, rather than a consequence of their irreconcilability. There seems
little reason to suppose that sociality and individuality must be mutually
exclusive, nor even that behaving in a 'social mode' requires a person to
mask his or her selfhood. The axiomatic juxtaposition of these
modalities might be seen to reveal an overemphasis on the superficial
dogmas of a cultural theory, neglecting the more substantial reality. I
suspect it also has a good deal to do with the disinclination of anthropologists to acknowledge that the people they study can bear much
resemblance to themselves, a disciplinary posture which has arguably
denied self consciousness to 'the other'.

But this is not to deny that society may use all sorts of devices in the
attempt to make the self in a social image. I turn to an examination of
some of these in the next two chapters.

Chapter 3

Initiating the self into society

CHILDHOOD

Family life provides the young child with the parameters of self consciousness. The child comes to consciousness with an idea of who constitutes his or her family, and uses this knowledge to formulate an initial sense of self. The idiom through which children with whom I am familiar do this is one of possession, by which they associate their relatives with themselves. A child refers to '*my* mum', '*my* brother', and so on: a sense of self which is anchored in possessiveness. Thus, an audacious inference: my first sense of self is one in which I associate other people with me. It may even be that I treat these associates, certainly my parents, as extensions of myself. Perhaps this may account for the devastating nature of the discoveries some of us make in adolescence that *we* are really different from *them*.

While we remain within the ambit of the family household, we may not really require a more independent sense of self than this. Of course, we do distinguish ourselves from our siblings, but do so still using the mediation of our ties to our parents. We know at some level of consciousness that we are siblings, and that our parents are *ours* rather than *theirs*. In this respect, we differ markedly from the Mbuti, whose ties to biological kin appear to be very weak (see p. 31). Not only are biological kin not semantically distinguished, but children passing through the two age-grades of pre-adulthood seem to spend most of their time in company with each other rather than with their natal families. When later they become classificatory adults, they move between groups as they judge expedient and as the need arises. One may suppose that the sense of an individual self (and of the self as a member of the non-familial collectivity) must develop earlier and more powerfully than in more family-oriented societies. As noted earlier, the Mbuti seem to view personal identity as being uncompromised and undiminished by social associations.

At the age of five or even earlier, we are thrust out of the secure womb of the family within which identity may be taken for granted, and suddenly have to fend for ourselves in identity terms. The Mbuti child enters the *bopi*, the children's enclosure, at the age of three, not necessarily any younger than our children attend nurseries or play groups, but is surrounded, of course, by its 'brothers' and 'sisters', and any adult who crosses its path is bound by definition to be its mother or father. I am not imputing to Mbuti kinship terminology a qualitative content equivalent to our own; but am merely drawing attention to the implications of being regarded as belonging to everyone, rather than as belonging to a very exclusive group. Our children's entry into the non-family world is an experience to which they have to become accustomed, for their lives will be punctuated by the need repeatedly to reformulate their identities and to convey them to other people. We become adept at it. At the very least, we become used to assimilating to our sense of self the succession of social categories through which we are forced to move. Let us recall Jean Briggs' trenchant description of the forcible socialisation of the Utku child (see pp. 36–7). At one moment the world is hers to command. She is totally indulged, humoured and pampered. She sleeps under her mother's quilts, spends her waking hours within her mother's parka, demands and is offered the breast whenever she feels so inclined, demands and must be given whatever object takes her fancy, regardless of who may be using it at the time. Suddenly, apparently without warning, she is displaced. Another infant has stolen her mother, has occupied her place in the parka and the blankets, is now the centre of the household's attention. The displaced child is no longer indulged, is not petted or kissed, is not comforted or humoured. She may cry for days on end with the shock of it all, but no one goes to her aid. Eventually, she appears to come to terms with her new status, seemingly with such completeness that she then stoutly resists her elders' attempts to tease her by indulging in the previously familiar and affectionate kinds of behaviour. She has made the transition from infancy to childhood. More than this, the ethnography suggests that she has augmented her former intensely family- and ego-centred sense of self with a sense of her self as Utku.

The development of the individual's self consciousness proceeds with the acquisition of experience. Indeed, we may say that social experience augments and enhances the sense of self. Ironically, part of that experience will concern the tension between selfhood (the substance of 'me' of which I am aware) and personhood, the definition of me as a social entity which society imposes. There is an experiential tension between them. Experience expands my sense of who I am, a sense which may well be frustrated when social process requires that it should be subordinated to my personhood. For example, consider a registration form for admission to hospital, or for matriculation at the university. All that it demands of me is my name, gender, next of kin, address, course choices or treatment required, and so forth. Nothing else seems to be relevant. These items are my credentials for admission or for membership. It is a stark diminution of self and continues to characterise the process of my relationship with the institution. The nurse treats me as a patient with a given condition, anonymises me as 'Sunshine' or, more prosaically, 'the patient in bed 3', and strives to press me into the hospital's routine. I resist, at the cost of being pushed into a further typification, 'a "difficult" patient'. The person who is being treated does not seem to have much to do with 'me'. My personhood is a cipher of me; it debases, certainly undervalues me. It may not be 'not-me', but it is a very selective version of me, and in its very selectivity may seem to me to be a falsification of me. I will return to this matter later in this chapter. For the moment it will be sufficient to note that the individual's developing sense of self, and the processes through which society presses that self into a matrix of its making, are often contemporaneous.

The significance of their contemporaneity is such that anthropologists and sociologists seem frequently to have been led to overestimate the efficacy of society's efforts, and to underestimate the resilience of the self. The view is that the social construction of the person has to be achieved at the cost of the authorial self. My argument will be that the self assimilates personhood, is affected, but not subordinated by it. Much of this discussion will focus on those processes categorised as 'initiation' and 'socialisation'.

INITIATION

The classic studies in anthropology of young male and female initiation, such as Audrey Richards' *Chisungu* (1956) and Victor Turner's *Mukanda* (1967), focus considerable attention on the competence for society as such of the ritual passage of young people to their new statuses. These rites of initiation transform individuals by investing them with socialness. In doing so, they also enable the society to reproduce itself culturally. The picture which is presented shows the neophyte individual being reclaimed for society, by being drawn

towards, and then inducted into, it. Individuality is replaced by socialness in the person; selfhood is replaced by society in the form of
personhood. But another interpretation may also be available: that
initiation provides social experience which augments, rather than
diminishes and displaces, the neophyte's self.

Rituals which initiate children into adulthood emphasise the gendering of the social world and of those aspects of nature which are culturally appropriated. In so far as they involve more or less radical surgery,
the gendering theme also entails the imposition of culture on nature, the
transformation of the natural body according to specific and distinctive
social conventions. Drastic and irrevocable though it may be, the
surgery is not usually an end in itself, but is one of the fugue-like
variations on the textual theme of the ritual, a text which grows increasingly complex in the course of its enactment, calling for ever more
specialised ritual knowledge among the participants and exegetes. But it
is the aspect of the ritual which can be regarded as impressing society
most intimately and insistently on the individual's mind and body. The
question is, does it transform the individual into a replicate of the larger
social whole? Or does it provide initiates with a text which they assimilate, and thereby transform, to their own experience?

The texts are dogmatic, and may well be delivered with considerable
force, even violence. Yet, they still require to be made sense of by the
individual, perhaps more so the more traumatic the mode of their
delivery. One of the most brutal male initiations in the ethnographic
record is the *ais am*, the first stage of the cycle of initiation undergone
over a period of between ten and fifteen years by the Bimin-Kuskusmin
of the West Sepik Province, Papua New Guinea, described by Fitz John
Porter Poole (1982). His study offers a particularly apposite illustration
because it is explicitly concerned with the dialectic of selfhood and
personhood; and because, unlike most anthropological writers on initiation, Poole makes a deliberate attempt to address the *experience* of the
ritual for the initiate, rather than just its sociological significance. He
suggests that the point of the ritual is to impress 'cultural constructs of
personhood' (Poole 1982: 103) on the self through the sheer intensity of
its experience.

These countervailing ideas of selfhood and personhood are expressed
through two different kinds of energising spirit: the *finiik*, which
governs 'the person' (an idea to which 'role' is an approximation); and
the *khaapkhabuurien*, which pertains to the essentially individualistic
self. The ritual retrieves the boys from the female domain, and places
them firmly in the male domain, definitively gendering them. It

accomplishes this by the emphatic denigration of everything with female associations, to express their inferiority, indeed their repugnance, to Bimin males. Like other Melanesian and Amazonian peoples, the Bimin-Kuskusmin manifest the separateness of the sexes in social life by the presence in the village of men's and women's houses, domains of solidarity and collective life exclusive to each sex. The withdrawal of boys from one, and their transfer to the other, is more than a figurative transformation, but one which has immediate and pervasive repercussions in daily social life. For example, taro is a male crop; sweet potato, a women's crop. Therefore taro has ritual significance, whereas sweet potato is simply a consumable. Taro gardens are enhanced by the strategic placement in them of tubes of semen, believed to strengthen *finiik* spirit which is nurtured by taro, indicating the direct relationship between taro and Bimin-Kuskusmin personhood.

The gendered dimension of initiation is apparent also in the depiction of uninitiated men as 'essentially female in character and bodily substance', a view consonant with people's opinions of them as 'weak, irrational, vulnerable' (Poole 1982: 107). Overall,

> The successive stages of the cycle exhibit a progression from a negative emphasis on the female nature of boys to an increasingly positive concern with masculinity and then to a sustained focus on male ritual control of female substance and procreative power.
>
> (Poole 1982: 109)

Male substances, such as semen and agnatic blood, are positively valued and are associated with strength and knowledge. Female substances (breast milk; menstrual blood) are seen as inferior versions of male counterparts, or as being responsible for less important parts of the body. Males produce the forehead, the avenue of powerful knowledge; females are responsible for the navel which admits inferior female knowledge.

An *ais am* group is given the name of one of four ancestors, a name which cannot then recur until three further *ais am*'s have taken place. In this way, the ritual theoretically links the novices to their ancestors, reproducing the presence of the ancestors in Bimin-Kuskusmin society, and reasserting the continuity of the social present with its ancestral past. Each stage and element of the ritual is said to have been ordained by the ancestors and to parallel rites which 'occur simultaneously in the ancestral underworld'. It is because of the ancestral provenance of the ritual that its meanings are said to be elusive: they are 'secret', and if discoverable at all, only at successive stages of the ritual cycle. They are rendered ever more elusive and mysterious. But if the meanings of the rites cannot be explained, they can be conveyed by intense experience. Thus, Poole says, the revelation of these meanings is a consequence of

one's participatory experience: experience cannot entirely be communicated, it must be undergone. In the *ais am*, a myriad of verbal and nonverbal communicative acts converge to shape the novices' experience by enhancing the intensity of participation. Indeed, the intellectual opaqueness of messages only seems to reinforce the aura of mystery and power in the *ais am*.

(Poole 1982: 110)

Hence the drama and immediacy of the ritual acts.

The *ais am*, as the first stage of initiation, deals principally with retrieving the boys from the female domain, and transforming them into 'becoming new men'. The progress of this transformation is reflected in their treatment. In the opening phases of the ritual, when the boys are still 'people of women's houses', their treatment is at its harshest, and mimics the treatment of women. Apart from the sheer physical depradations and the consequent mental stresses which they are made to suffer, they are fed only with female foods, especially raw sweet potato. In the latter phases, the brutality decreases, marking the diminution of their female substance, and they are fed with male foods, especially taro.

Before the ritual proper begins, the boys have received some instruction on the matter of bodily substance, but have little if any idea of the ordeals they are about to undergo. Apart from post-menstrual women who are involved in the initiation, and pre-menstrual girls who provide other assistance, the area is purged of female influence. These female participants might perhaps be regarded as more gender neutral than female, given their respectives stages in the life-cycle (especially since the paramount female initiators are transvestite; and the ancestors appear in androgynous form). The presence of these 'sexless' women and girls marks, by contrast, the emphatically gendered men, without risking the contamination of the sacralised ritual site by female substance. The male-ness of the area is emphasised, and perhaps guaranteed, by the strategic concealment throughout it of boars' genitalia.

The women are implicated as agents of their own denigration in the first rite proper. They humiliate the boys by stripping and washing them, and then, having daubed them with yellow funerary mud, mimicking the preparation of corpses, they become complicit in the boys' terror by alluding to the rumour that they are to be killed by the men. Poole comments that 'This female complicity in *ais am* ordeals will be remembered' (Poole 1982: 121). The ritual is supposed not just to move

the boys from the female to the male domains, but to turn them definitively against women. In the first stage of the ritual, the boys are lined
up to confront their mothers who, they are told, have so polluted and
weakened them that they (the boys) must be killed. They are drenched
in sows' blood (believing it to be human), beaten, and then instructed
that they must henceforth refrain from eating female foods. They are
incarcerated in a ritual lodge and harangued by hidden speakers:

> The speeches are vivid in their portrayal of the filth, putrefaction, and
> moral degeneracy of female substance and behavior.
>
> (Poole 1982: 122)

As if to rub in their depravity, they are then fed female food by the
women initiators. During the next four days, the boys are continuously
reviled, humiliated and terrorised by the men. Forced to punch their
heads through a screen of boughs known as the 'vomit house', they are
daubed with female pigment, forced to eat in rapid succession female
foods: frogs' eggs, tadpoles, black mushrooms, crayfish, punctuated by
ginger and sweet potato. They are then scourged with stinging nettles,
and made to vomit by drinking pig's blood and urine. In the next rite,
they are made to ingest female parts of slaughtered sows and have their
own 'female parts' smeared with sows' blood. In the succeeding stage,
the ancestors (Afek, the cassowary, and Yomnok, the spiny anteater)
appear from the underworld, and are witness to further beating and
cursing, the bleeding of female parts, and humiliation. The boys now
observably attempt to fend away female objects.

In the presence of the androgynous cassowary ancestress, the boys
are seized by their mothers' brothers who pierce their nasal septums
with cassowary bone daggers. Poole writes:

> The psychological and physical shock is staggering; and many boys,
> with blood cascading down their bodies, faint or become quite
> hysterical.
>
> (Poole 1982: 127)

Told that they are dying, 'the boys are now in a most wretched condition' (ibid.). On the following night, they are burned by having boiling
marsupial fat applied to their inner forearms. They listen to a sacred
myth which recounts the gradual ascendancy of men over women. They
are given secret male names and told that they are about to become 'new
men', are then burned again, made to inject the pus from their lanced
blisters to fortify their male substance; and, as if to complete their
agony, have their nasal septum pierced yet again by their ritual fathers.

Now the recipients of the male ancestor's strength, they are exhorted to be stoic.

Gradually the tenor of the ritual changes. The suggestion that they are 'becoming new men' is reinforced by the more 'reconstructive' and positive character of the proceedings. The emphasis has switched from the destruction and extrusion of their female substance, to the strengthening of their male substance. The sexual imagery focuses increasingly on the male, and therefore propitious, parts of the body: the forehead, the penis and the hip; and the colours with which they are daubed change accordingly, from the female black to the male red. The boys are treated with greater consideration and sympathy. While it is recognised that they feel angry and resentful, they are required to manifest a rigorous control. The succeeding rites reverse the polarities of the opening stages: they are fed with male foods, rubbed with anodyne leaves, beat their male tormentors and feed them female foods before incarcerating them. Finally, they are physically reconciled with their fathers, embracing them publicly for the first time in their lives.

During the ritual, there is no detailed exegesis of its symbolism and meanings. Indeed, the meanings repose with the ancestors and are thus acknowledged to be profoundly complex. The ritual makes its impact in the boys through the sheer intensity of their experience which cannot be put into 'discursive language' (Poole 1982: 139). It fosters the unity of the senses and, thus, an awareness of selfhood, of the self reflecting outwards like a crystal (which is itself a sacred ritual object). Poole emphasises the traumas which the boys suffer, as they are subjected repeatedly and over this prolonged period to physical assault, mental cruelty and emotional distress (ibid.: 143–4).

Poole says that the intention is to map the Bimin-Kuskusmin ideology of personhood on to the boys' selfhood. Such a reconciliation of the social and the individual is a commonly reported rationale of initiation. But it prompts more questions than it answers. Does the brutality of the ritual suggest that this reconciliation is regarded as particularly difficult to effect? And why does the gendering of the initiates' consciousnesses have to be accomplished by such deliberately and unusually misogynistic means? The denigration of women which is evident in the *ais am* would appear to go beyond the general disadvantage and marginality of women elsewhere in Papua New Guinea and Melanesia; and looks remarkable compared to other societies which have similarly elaborate theories of physiological change, such as the Merina of Madagascar (Bloch 1986, 1987).

Ambiguity is a striking theme in the Bimin-Kuskusmin ethnography. Uninitiated males are formally masculine but substantively feminine and require initiation to render them definitively male. The ancestors who participate in the ritual are androgynous:

> Believed to be highly androgynous, but more female than male, Afek [the ancestress] is married to her hermaphroditic sibling Yomnok, who is more male than female. Possessing a vagina in each buttock and a 'penis-clitoris', Afek gave birth to the human and totemic clan ancestors.
>
> (Poole 1982: 127)

There is much anthropological literature which addresses the importance of unambiguous classification, and the unpropitious character of blurred categories. The Bimin-Kuskusmin ancestors would appear to be an aberration, unless we take androgyny to suggest either gender neutrality, or to imply a kind of collaboration, a mutual dependency of the sexes in which male and female complete and complement each other. In this respect, the slight gender bias of each of these ancestors may be interesting as a comment on the cognatic nature of descent among some New Guinea peoples, acknowledging that descent rests both on men and women, although there may be biases in given circumstances.[1]

Amid this apparent egalitarianism is found the marked inequality of men and women: 'hierarchical relations', says Strathern, 'are most visibly constituted on the basis of gender itself' (1987a: 3). From what does this inequality arise? There does not appear to be a sociological reason outside the fact of gendered inequality itself. Strathern again:

> inequalities between men and women seem to be 'about' themselves. Gender symbolism turns in on itself.
>
> (Strathern 1987a: 3)

This, she says, is illustrated most dramatically in rituals in which each sex separates itself from the other to 'elaborate its own internal distinctions in exclusive cult practice' (ibid.). That very largely describes what we have been seeing, except that women of a kind, 'neuter women', are present and active in the ritual, but in an obviously inferior, even servile, role. The point is that where elsewhere gender may be one among many or several significant dimensions of inequality and/or difference, here it appears to predominate. Sex does all the hierarchical work for the Bimin-Kuskusmin which elsewhere may be done by class, kinship and descent, sect, property and so forth. It is surely this paramount importance attributed to gender differentiation which accounts for the apparent gendering of everything: the forehead and the elbow, taro and the sweet potato, black and red, different sides of the 'root house' (one of the initiates' lodges). For the Bimin-Kuskusmin, gender constitutes the world.

Strathern observes that because of this cognitive matrix, gender does not explain inequality merely between the sexes, but also within them. One is not merely older, more skilled, more ritually specialised than another, but, rather, is an older *woman*; a *male* elder; a better *man* with a bow. Within the society, gender is all. Or is it?

Poole insists that the *ais am* attempts to reconcile selfhood and person-hood by making them focus on identical qualities of the person: stoicism, bravery, emotional control, obedience and discipline, and so on. Rather than seeing person and self as dimensions of the individual which are bound to be in opposition, the Bimin-Kuskusmin seem to attempt to forestall the opposition by forcibly impressing 'proper personhood' on to the indivi-dual's self-awareness. His gender must be an aspect of both. Male person-hood must be defined by the values of masculinity inculcated by the ritual which, if Poole is correct, transforms the individual's selfhood by making him aware of his transformation from his formerly ambiguous gender to his new (unambiguous) manhood.

We can surely accept that the *ais am* presents the individual with circumstances and conditions which change him mentally: he learns to despise women, to distrust everyone, to value resilience, to control anger. But this is not to say very much. Does he learn to think *as a Bimin man* or just to think some of the same things as other Bimin men? The difference is crucial: the first suggests that his experience of the ritual clones his consciousness; the second, only that it gives him some things to be conscious of. We may grant that the boy sees his self and others differently than previously; but is he conscious of this perspective as distinctively Bimin-Kuskusmin, or as distinctively his? We do not know; perhaps we cannot know. But is conjecture so undesirable that we must continue conventional anthropological practice and opt for the fiction of socially directed transformation? The choice may amount to accepting that the newly initiated boy now sees himself as a Bimin male and a virtuous (or otherwise) instance of the species, or that he sees himself as a member of the Bimin-Kuskusmin who happens to be male, in virtue of which he has just been through a particularly nasty experi-ence which has left him regarding himself and others differently than he did previously.

Poole gives us a sensitive and detailed account of initiation and strives to bring us as close as our imaginations will allow to the boys' experience of the ritual. My reservations really amount to saying that he does not go quite far enough in exploring the dimension of selfhood. It seems unreasonable to doubt that the boys' consciousness is affected; but, while selfhood entails consciousness, it goes beyond it. The idea must capture the awareness of an individual *as an individual*: as someone who can reflect on her or his experience of and position in society, of 'being oneself'. I cannot see this condition in the sort of 'selfhood' which Poole postulates as the objective of Bimin-Kuskusmin strategy. Rather, it is a consciousness, of oneself as a Bimin male. The term 'consciousness' seems closer to his intention than 'self' and, indeed, his very thesis is that the *ais am* is intended to map the indigenous ideology of personhood on to the boys' consciousness (and, hence, the consumption in the later stages of the *finiik*-nurturing taro).

This may be a useful way of regarding rites of passage generally. It is another dimension to the transformation which ritual effects. Bloch has recently argued that, apart from rehearsing a kind of fantasy on the nature of society, the process of initiation rituals (as of all religious experience) accomplishes a sociological transformation as well, linking the individual and mortal initiate into the transcendental and eternal values of society.[2] It turns the consumable into the consumer, 'prey into hunter' (Bloch 1992). Bloch's thesis is motivated by his intention to show that, and how, all social process is informed by the same basic logic, and to portray this structural homology as a universal feature of human society. Apart from being curiously atavistic, this argument still implies that we cannot get any closer to individual consciousness than to assume that it is modelled by and on this organising social logic, one which may not even have the virtue of existing in the indigenous collective consciousness (as Geertz [1975 (1972)] claims for the Balinese cockfight), but which is instead the contrived product of comparative analysis – not just of initiation rituals, but of everything!

By initiation the status of the individual is changed sociologically: that is to say, the *person* is changed. But also the individual as an aware being, with a mind, a self, is transformed. We must suppose that in an event so powerful as the *ais am* the consciousness *is* changed, but whether in quite the ways the Bimin-Kuskusmin suppose is another matter. The experiences of victims of terror and torture, such as concentration camp internees and hostages, suggest that the self may be resilient even in the face of an assault such as the Bimin-Kuskusmin men mount on their successors.[3]

BECOMING SOCIAL

My argument above, as throughout this book, is to acknowledge individuals' consciousness of their difference from each other, of their distinctive identities, even though these may be masked by the social glosses of stereotype, orthodoxy, category or collectively imposed identity. In a remarkable series of studies made among children, Allison James has shown that within each age-group, from four to six year olds up to adolescents, there is a striving for conformity to, what is perceived as, the norm for that age cohort. At the very least, unflattering attention is drawn to manifest difference. For example:

> complaints adolescents make about their own bodies are always through reference to excess: too tall, too short, too fat, too thin. Bodies must not deviate from a *median* upon which they themselves have tacitly agreed. Those who are perceived to differ *too* much from this symbolic mean are ruthlessly identified and named. . . .
>
> (James 1986: 162)

Young children aspire to the virtues of 'bigness'. The failure to achieve it at the appropriate time stigmatises the child as 'little' and associates her or him with the inadequacies of 'little children', such as ineffective control of bodily functions. But it also represents a failure to achieve 'sameness' on which, she says, children place considerable value (James 1993: 141). In addition to 'proper' size – a quality which she shows often to be confused with age and status – children also aspire to proper gendering, constituted by a range of stereotypic qualities and models. The salient point for us to note is that the aspiration to 'sameness' or to 'normalcy' *must* proceed from the awareness of difference, of distinctiveness.

These aspirations are the product of adults' treatment of young children, of the children's own perceptions of social models (for example, through the media), and of the pressure they exert on each other through what may be loosely described as 'play', processes through which, as James trenchantly observes, children socialise each other, as well as socialise with each other. In all of this, the dialectic between selfhood and socialness is apparent. Perhaps what especially characterises childhood and, even more so, adolescence, is uncertainty about or discomfort with the self which the child perceives in himself or herself. From the juvenile Ego's point of view, there is a world 'out there', which can perhaps be largely taken for granted; but 'in here', what? The body as the physical referent of his or her selfhood changes continuously and rapidly, although Ego may be unaware of this until prompted by the observations and comments of other people (James 1993: 93–100). And the mind, consciousness, changes continuously through the successive phases of childhood, youth and adolescence.

There is perhaps the sense that the years leading to adulthood are simply that: a preparation for something which is to come, rather than a stage and status with its own integrity. This may be particularly so of adolescence, a phase which James regards as comparable to that of ritual liminality. In her view, the liminality of youth is not just an adult perspective, but is one which the youngsters themselves hold, seeing themselves as marginal to the larger social scheme of things, as 'nobodies' (James 1986: 167). They counter this insecurity by attempting to anchor themselves in style and in behaviour which they may regard as conventional to their generation, however iconoclastic it may seem to members of older generations:

> Adolescents are very much people in the process of becoming and their lack of a structured place in society makes the restructuring of their own liminality the more critical for it is here that knowledge of the self is gained.
>
> (James 1986: 158)

In this process of restructuring, adolescents may use style as their compass points, just as younger children may use gender role models. But it is surely incorrect to suppose that style – a mode of social discourse – somehow displaces or replaces the self. It should rather be seen as an accretion to the self. The youth in question is therefore not just a 'raver' or a 'punk' or whatever, but is a particular exponent of the style. Is it just a happy accident that, to describe his activity on the pitch or in the ring, the professional sportsman has adopted the cliché of 'expressing myself'? We should perhaps take this sometimes jarring expression seriously and grant that, what to the spectator is just another footballer having a good match, is to the footballer in question a young man fulfilling his vision of his self in the most accomplished way that he can. It would be nonsense to limit one's description of him to 'a footballer' or even 'a centre forward', although it is not unusual to find 'style' or age-grade used descriptively in this way to gloss over the individual to whom these labels are applied. But what may be acceptable in tabloid journalism should surely not be currency in ethnographic description. Yet, if we ignore self in accounts of the efficacy of initiation and socialisation, that is precisely what we risk.

I do not presume to offer any new insights into childhood socialisation, nor into the complex symbolic structures of initiation rituals, and there is an obvious risk in paddling in waters so rich in scholarship and argument. I have exploited (uninvited) the work of Poole and James because, in my limited experience of the specialisms within which each works, they seem to me to go significantly further than others have done in redeeming ethnographically the conventional neglect of the self, and, thereby, in offering us more complete accounts of the social processes with which they deal.

INSTITUTIONS AND SELVES

Of course 'becoming social' is not accomplished with the achievement of adulthood, whether or not marked by ritual. It continues throughout one's social career, as new milieux are broached and new *social* experiences accrue to the self. The self provides experiential continuity throughout a life which would otherwise be a series of disjunctions of the kind depicted by the structural functionalist role theorists referred to earlier. The notion of selfhood as an essential and continuous core of experience does not exclude the application to it of the concept of role. For example, while Goffman's 'performing self' is basically a role-player, she or he clearly exploits the accumulated experience of a lifetime in the performance of any one role: that is to say that *general* experience is applied to *particular* facets of the self. One therefore becomes increasingly experienced as a performer. My disagreement with Goffman is really with his contention that selfhood does not extend beyond the skills and imperatives of performance.

It was said of Laurence Olivier that his entire life became a performance: that his own sense of identity became irredeemably confused with the characters he portrayed on stage and screen. I am not convinced that this is a plausible claim to make about anyone; but if it is, would plead that a consummate actor who had spent the best part of eight decades flitting from role to role hardly makes a convincing paradigm for the rest of humanity. Social roles are grafted on to, inform and substantiate the self. They are not discarded in quite the way that the actor wipes off the make-up and reaches for the next script, although this itself does less than justice as an account of the actor's craft. Her experience accumulates. Having played Desdemona, she has experience of interpretation, stagecraft, of insight into character, of performance itself, which she will bring to her portrayal of Lady Macbeth. If this is true of the theatre, it is surely even more so of social life. The self is the repository of this experience. This seems so obvious as to be hardly worth saying. Why have social anthropologists neglected it for so long?

Part of the answer is, of course, that it was much easier to deal with structures, with institutions, and to make inferences *from* them *to* people than to proceed in the reverse order. Modern social anthropology was founded on Maine's and Morgan's encyclopaedic comparisons of systems of law and kinship which charted the course for the kind of inferential procedures which Radcliffe-Brown elaborated as 'the comparative method' and which remained for so long essentially unchallenged philosophically, although considerably refined by the increasing sophistication of ethnography and of regional analysis. Throughout this phase of anthropology's growth, which lasted into the 1970s, the behaviour and identities of individuals continued to be related to and derived from their institutional contexts, whether these were conceptualised as 'social structure' or as 'culture'.

Anthropology was not peculiar in this respect. The social sciences generally were gripped by modernist theories of determinism of one kind or another. Developmental psychology was fascinated by behaviourism; the mainstream of sociology and political science was divided among Marxism, structural functionalism and positivistic empiricism. But on the fringe of sociology and social psychology in North America there were other kinds of theoretical enquiry too: experimental, rather than iconoclastic. Symbolic interactionism refocused attention on the self and on the symbolic means by which individual and society are related. Interactionism spawned a variety of mutually antagonistic movements: phenomenology (of various kinds); ethnomethodology; a general interest in hermeneutics and in, what came to be called, human 'agency'. It did not really have a prominent analogue in anthropology until the 'interpretivism' of Clifford Geertz and his school began to appear during the 1960s and 1970s. It was a more complex theoretical position than interactionism, not only because its intellectual influences were more various (ranging from Weber to Lévi-Strauss), but because its problematic was subtly different. Symbolic interactionism focused on the cognising 'I'; interpretivism focused on culture as the means by which individuals engaged with society.[4] It was a posture which explicitly recognised the 'inner' and 'outer' (private/public; self/person) facets of the individual, often by making reference to analogous ethnographic discriminations – see e.g. Geertz's description (1983 [1974]) of the distinction made in Java discourse between *alus* and *kasar*. But, having done so, it then continued to turn away from the self, on the grounds that if the anthropological concept of 'culture' had any integrity, it identified what was shared among people, and maintained that this marked the bounds of anthropology's competence. By this device, the self was excluded from the anthropological agenda.

There is, of course, a fundamental flaw in this posture: it must either deny *cultural* properties to the self or must deny its own competence to address such a fundamental aspect of culture. Neither of these reservations would do much to establish the credibility of anthropology's claim to expertise in cultural exegesis. Its feebleness was eventually recognised explicitly in the post-Geertzian turn to 'reflexivity', in which ethnographers 'reflected' on the ways in which their own selves intruded upon their definition of issues in, and their conduct of, their fieldwork. Seminal work, such as Rabinow's *Reflections on Fieldwork in Morocco* (1977), brought the ethnographer's self-consciousness firmly into the frame. It seems but an obvious step from there to use this self consciousness as a means of focusing on other people's selves.

We will return to reflexivity later in the book. For the moment, I simply offer tentatively the ethnographer's self consciousness as a (philosophically fraught) medium for testing the plausibility of the kinds of claim we have been inclined to make about other people's self consciousness or their lack of it. I have previously argued that this is a description of what anthropologists actually do anyway, notwithstanding our denials and canonical exhortations to the contrary (Cohen 1992c). If we apply our own experience to the notion that transformations of social status are accompanied by fundamental alterations (rather than accretions) to the self, I suggest it must appear implausible.

Goffman formulated the 'total institution' as an ideal typical model of the transformable self. He had in mind institutions the totality of which was marked by their separation from the mainstream of society in terms of both geography and culture. Their physical boundaries also marked different worlds of discourse and conduct, and were impermeable. He had in mind such closed entities as asylums, prisons and monasteries. Aubert later suggested the ship at sea as another example (1965).

The institutions imposed their regimes upon inmates by a combination of discipline and the engineering of institutional personalities. The individual's self was stripped away at the portals of the institution. The given name was replaced by another, or by a number; the clothes through which personality and identity were expressed were discarded to be replaced by uniform. Hair was shorn to a conventional length and style; and the individual was divested of other personal accoutrements. Daily routines were utterly different from those 'outside', and were marked by measures of time unique to the type of institution (for example, 'slopping out', matins, the four-hour deck watch, and so on). The institutional regime attempted to fabricate an absolute disjunction between the inside and the outside in order to remake the institutionalised self. The individual who entered was the same as the inmate in body only.

Goffman himself recognised that institutional regimes could not sustain their absolute power, and would be subverted in one way or another: perhaps by the creation of informal codes which were beyond their control. Inmates may be endlessly subtle and ingenious in creating and maintaining these subversive devices. But they are aided immeasurably by the permeability of the institution's boundaries: by culture, and by selfhood. The walls do not block memory. Individuals demonstrate remarkable powers of resistance to the destruction of their selves, even when they are attacked with drugs and other forms of physical intervention. As I remarked earlier, the testimonies of concentration camp survivors and of the victims of kidnapping and torture show the extraordinary resilience of the self when it can contrive to grasp even the flimsiest of lifelines. Of course, these are extraordinary cases and I would not be so foolish as to suggest that people do not succumb or that they are not profoundly damaged by such experiences. But the 'total-itarian' nature of these contexts, and the pressures they exert on the resisting self, are also extraordinary – far outside common experience. If they are resistible, even in a few cases, we may be entitled to suppose that the less extreme forms of pressure which are entailed in processes of socialisation are resistible and are resisted more thoroughly.

Societies do *not* determine the selves of their members. They may construct models of personhood; they may, as the Bimin-Kuskusmin evidently do, *attempt* to reconcile selfhood to personhood. But they have no absolute powers in this regard, and almost certainly have an exaggerated view of the extent to which they can clone their members. I think of society and the self as dancing an improvised *pas de deux*: each tries to cover the moves of the other; sometimes they merge, at others they separate. Their combination may be harmonious; or it may be awkward in the extreme. Society creates the illusion (which social science has perpetuated) that it ultimately controls the dance, for it provides the music and the stage. But, to coin a phrase, it takes two to tango. To focus on only one of the partners is to take a very skewed look indeed.

NAMING

I wish to illustrate the dance, and the privileged position in it which is appropriated by (and analytically accorded to) society, by briefly considering the anthropology of naming.

The anthropological literature on naming is very extensive.[5] I will do no more than skim its surface in making the elementary observation that its explanations of naming as a ritual means of initiating the person into an identity almost invariably privilege the social definition of the individual over his/her self-concept. In drawing on widespread examples somewhat out of context, I indulge in an old-fashioned and probably flawed mode of comparison. However, I do so in order to draw attention to the extent to which anthropologists have masked the diversity of cultural contexts by the orthodox manner in which they have treated theoretically naming and initiation: admitting sociological explanation, to the virtual exclusion of personal meanings and experience. Despite their supposed cultural specificity, their accounts of naming practices have in common the virtual absence from them of self-aware individuals.

An obvious first question to ask is why naming seems so frequently to be accomplished through ritual? Having been schooled in analyses of *rites de passages* and in the cross-cultural study of classification systems, social anthropologists may well be inclined to answer that the ritual of naming terminates the dangerously ambiguous condition of liminality – of being, in Turner's phrase, 'betwixt and between', neither one thing, nor the other: biologically, but not yet socially constituted; a presence, but not yet a member. Lévi-Strauss has pointed out that naming is a mode of classification, and that classification is a necessary precondition of possession (1966). His logic would lead us to the conclusion that naming is required for society to possess a person, that is, to make that person a member. It does not often confer full membership, which is left to be accomplished through future rites of initiation. Rather, it confers socialness (see Alford 1987: 29), possibly in ways which signal some conventions of social organisation. One aspect of this minimal socialness may be the propitiation of ancestors or of spirits who are themselves integral elements of the society, or of a God, gods, or other religious precepts which are major referents or icons of the society's identity.

This kind of answer to our opening question suggests that the point of such rituals is to confer socialness rather than selfhood: the performance of ritual which sacralises the conferment of a *social* identity also minimises the mystery of the self either by concealing it, or by making the self in a social image, or both. In concentrating on the social construction of the self, this conventional anthropological answer utterly ignores self consciousness, and thereby leads us to deny to cultural others intellectual capacities and proclivities which we so value in ourselves. The recent 'reflexivity' and 'writing culture' critiques have sensitised us to the ethnocentric biases in these expository devices. Perhaps more substantially, the development of symbolic anthropology has revealed the personal discretion which individuals exercise in their interpretation of symbols – to the extent that, as argued above, we can no longer get away with rendering the self as the mere replicate in miniature of society or social group. We should now be able to perceive in rites of naming not just the *socialisation* of the individual, but the tensions which inhere in the relationship of individual to society, tensions which we trivialise if we continue to regard them as capable of a kind of mechanical resolution through ritual. These tensions arise over fundamental issues of identity. Who has the right to determine who a person is: the person in question, or those with whom the person interacts? In treating the self as socially constituted, social science has denied 'authorship' to the individual, seeing identity either as imposed by an other, or as formulated by the individual in relation to an other. Both views imply the insubstantial nature of selfhood.

Yet they are also at odds with – here I dare to generalise from my personal experience – *our* views of our own selves, which are based on the possibility of distinguishing conceptually and experientially between the characterisations of ourselves made by others and expressed in our social identities, and our self-concepts. The distinction to be made here parallels one which we have now come to accept in symbol theory between the socially propagated *forms* of symbols, and their *meanings* which are the products of individuals' interpretations. With the advent of this approach, we have been able to recognise that individuals make meaning, using shared cultural devices. Seen in this light, naming and initiation rites tell different kinds of story than in earlier ethnographic accounts. We may now have to deal with as many texts of the ritual as there are participants, for we are theoretically bound to acknowledge each of them as authors.

As with the ethnography of initiation rites generally, there is notably absent from the literature on naming work which deals substantially and descriptively with people's experience of being named and with the meanings they impute to their names as symbols or icons of themselves. Many writers have drawn attention to the ways in which naming practices reflect the nature of the societies in which they occur. For example, we find ubiquitously the use of ancestors' names to stress continuity and the primacy of affiliation to the descent group, or, conversely, of the parent's choice of an affinal forebear's name to express the importance of the child's *bi*lateral descent (Rossi 1965). Léon has described the French requirement to use an officially approved saint's name as a means of indicating allegiance to the state, rather than to the saint or the Church (Léon 1976). Segalen has shown how name-sharing in nineteenth-century Brittany demonstrated the practical importance of godparenthood (Segalen 1980: 69), and the bonds implied by name-sharing have been noted in such other widely dispersed instances as the Saunik system of Qiqiktamiut Inuit (Guemple 1965) and the Hispanic *compadrazgo* tradition.

As a social instrument, the name can be coercive. It is usually bestowed by others and obligates the individual in its use (Zonabend 1980: 7, 15). It may express the subordination of an individual or of a class of persons. Black American slaves in the southern states were named by their owners, rather than by their kin; in the Anglo-Saxon (but, note, not the Scottish) tradition, women give up their own family names on marriage. The demeaned status of the Sarakatsani bride is evident in her obligation to adopt every element of her husband's name in place of her own (Campbell 1964: 186).

In Western societies, the instrumentality of names as means of address and reference is obvious, but is also limited by the attenuated nature of the naming forms which prevail: one or more personal names (not chosen by the person), one or two surnames indicating direct descent, and, possibly, one or more nicknames (to which I shall return shortly). Apart from the question of the attitude of named persons to their names, the matter is uncomplicated, and may even reflect a tacit social notion that the identity of the individual is normally un-complicated because of the unambiguous means by which individuals are subordinated by and attached to society. Elsewhere, we find much more complex naming forms and practices which, I believe, encode more complex assumptions about the relationship of individual and society. Maybury-Lewis recalled the consternation he caused with his naïve question to the Akwe-Savante headman in whose village he had just arrived (Maybury-Lewis 1984). Thinking he was just making polite conversation, he asked, 'What is your daughter's name?' Frantic con-sultations followed prompted first by the multiplicity of possible answers to the question, and, second, by its impoliteness. Work among other Amazonian peoples confirms that they too find such direct ques-tioning about names to be unacceptable.[6]

In other societies, a distinction is made between names as terms of address and of reference. Among the Moslem Kandayan of North-west Borneo (Maxwell 1984: 35–6), and the Nigerian Oru-Igbo (Jell-Bahlsen 1988: 203), the discourtesy of addressing people by their given names is avoided by the use of 'greeting names'. Evans-Pritchard described the variety of greeting terms available to Nuer, of which the best-known is the ox name, after the person's favourite beast (Evans-Pritchard 1964). Antoun noted that in the Jordanian village of Kufr al-Ma, the use of names as terms of address was deprecated because it ignored the several modes of address available as means of indicating respect (1968). Nicknaming presents another option to the use of formal names. In Lewis (in the Scottish Western Isles) (Mewett 1982) and East Sutherland (Dorian 1970) the coincidence of given name, surname and patronym is so frequent that other means are required to distinguish among individuals. Segalen found a similar issue of homonymy in Bigoudensud. Hence, the 'substitute naming systems' (Dorian 1970), 'by-names', popular names, *surnoms*, nicknames which are so characteristic of Celtic societies, perhaps referring to physical characteristics, place of birth or residence, personal idiosyncrasy or whatever. For similar reasons, nicknames appear to have been in widespread use in Barbados and Bermuda among all but the élite and the elect, and were supplemented by the owner's car registration number, even in public anouncements of marriage and death (Manning 1974). In some societies, these descriptive informal names became formalised with the passage of time into family names.[7] In southern Italy, nicknames were applied to mafiosi by the police to bias public judgements of the individuals thus named (Jacquemet 1992), an extreme, but telling instance of the social fabrication of identities.

A further dimension to the intrusion of society on to the individual through naming is to be found in the practice of routine name-changing. The Borneo Penan change and/or add names as their children are born or as significant kin die (Needham 1954; 1965). Writing about the Ilongot, Rosaldo argued quite explicitly that their name changes are indicative of social relationships (Rosaldo 1984). They are used by 'significant others' to manipulate an individual's identity in a comparable way to the Moroccan *nisbah*, the identity tag which is affixed to a person by others and which refers to what they regard as the person's salient social associations (Rosen 1984, also Geertz 1983 [1974]: 65ff). Ilongot names often have the quality of play and teasing about them, the bestowing of names being tantamount to a process of initiation, and Rosaldo argued that such jousting is an elementary means of constituting the person.

In similar theoretical vein, Brewer has shown how the naming system of Bimanese islanders encodes information about individuals and their social relationships. All given names are modulated by 'common' and 'respect' forms, the use of which depends on the relative seniority of the person addressing and the person addressed. They also connote the primacy of kinship for, on becoming a parent, a person assumes a teknonym; and on becoming a grandparent he or she replaces the teknonym with a 'paidonym', referring to the name of the first grand-child (Brewer 1981: 206). Lopes da Silva reported that, after initiation, a Xavanté boy is given the name of his mother's brother; but since adult homonymy is proscribed, the adult has simultaneously to divest himself of his old name and take a new one (Lopes da Silva 1989: 384). Far from being personal, Xavanté names are public and corporate property, intended for distribution rather than for private hoarding (ibid.: 336).

All of this is customarily explained as means of imprinting society on the initiate's blank consciousness, of ways in which society attempts to make the self. Even when this is done through ostensibly supernatural devices, the ritual is nevertheless given *social* reference, to the exclusion of the personal. Two examples may illustrate the point. The Sanumá Indians, Amazonian hunter-gatherers, name their children after forest animals (Ramos 1974). An animal of the chosen species is ritually hunted and killed by the father. The choice is not random, for the child will be invested with the spirit of the animal which will enter through his or her lumbar spine. This does not indicate an ideology of human–animal symbiosis, nor even a form of totemic belief. Grafted on to it through the ritual sequences of naming are practical and pragmatic statements about social balance: between kinship and affinity; between agnatic and non-agnatic kinship, statements which correct the biases of formal social organisation. So, the child who is supposedly named for an eponymous coccyx spirit is actually an ambulant depiction of the Sanumá ideal of social normality.

The second example concerns conventions of Jewish naming. In the pre-exilic biblical era, it was conventional to avoid strictly the repetition of forebears' names, since not to do so would have traduced the unique-ness of the original holder and questioned 'the absolute identity of the person with the name' (Lauterbach 1970: 30). In post-exilic times, such repetition, referring to grandparents, became normal. In the post-Talmudic period, conventions changed again. Sephardic Jews estab-lished the practice which they still routinely follow of naming children after living relatives. Askenazim were more squeamish. Tormented by the suspicion that the spirits, perhaps especially the Angel of Death, were fallible, they assiduously avoided repeating the name of a living relative for fear that the spirit might mistakenly take the wrong person (ibid.: 52–3). There is also here an echo of the mystical belief which associates the name with the soul, so that to give one person's name to another would cause the soul of the first to migrate, thus killing him or her. Rabbi Lauterbach could not find any theological rationales in these practices or in their transformations. He concluded that they were entirely circumstantial. It does not take an excess of imagination to see why historically Jewish emphasis on the uniqueness of the individual should give way to a stress on continuity, to such an extent that individuality becomes so masked that even the Angel of Death could be misled. But this broad historical view utterly ignores the self-perception of the named individual, and, as in the Sanumá case, simply assumes that this would be congruent with a social logic.

There does not appear to be much room for the 'authorial self' in these views of selfhood and naming. In almost all of them, naming is a means of placing the individual in the social matrix. Where is the individual's exercise of his or her own discretion? Where is the discretionary self anything more than the dependent variable of social structure and historical circumstance?

The final example I will introduce into this discussion is one of the most noted in the literature: Ward Goodenough's famous comparison of naming in two Oceanic societies, Truk (in the Caroline Islands) and Lakalai (on the north coast of New Britain) (Goodenough 1965). Among the 793 inhabitants of Truk, people are addressed by their personal names rather than by kin terms, and there is virtually no duplication of names. By contrast, on Lakalai almost everyone shares at least one name with others; the use of teknonyms and kin terms is common, and names do not even discriminate gender. Naming is strictly regulated and codified. So, while Truk naming would seem to emphasise individuality, Lakalai naming appears to stress the social order (ibid.: 271). However, the seemingly obvious inferences to be drawn about the relative rights to individuality in each society would be quite incorrect. Truk social organisation is firmly based on matrilineal descent groups whose lineage elders exercise near-absolute authority over the decisions of their juniors and sustain the primacy of solidarity within the lineage, even to the extent of obliging a woman to take her brother's side in any dispute he might have with her husband. Lineage ideology and authority thus frustrates a desire for individuality (ibid.: 272). According to Goodenough, one of the more prosaic ways in which Truk islanders relieve their frustration is in naming. Individuality exists, quite literally, in nothing more than name (ibid.: 273).

Lakalai presents the obverse case. Public values emphasise individual achievement; lineages have few corporate functions; and leadership, like that of the Melanesian Big Men, is sustained tactically, rather than based on seniority. While in Truk personal virtue elicits no reward, in Lakalai it is all important. The people of Lakalai are rugged individualists, and their apparently contradictory naming conventions are to be understood as 'continual reminders that people are, after all, part of a social order' (Goodenough 1965: 274).

Goodenough concluded that names communicate ideas of the self and of self–other relationships (1965: 275). His account clearly reveals the conventional *modus operandi* in the anthropology of naming and, more generally, of identity: the assumption of an isomorphism between the anthropo-logic of interpretation, and the ways in which the persons thus named made sense of and supplied meaning to their selfhood and their experience of being named. We constructed cultures in the images of our own intellectual consciousness, and then derived selves from them: 'ethnocentric intellectual gymnastics', as Turnbull so pointedly put it (1990: 50).

This brings us to the second large question which we have to ask of this body of scholarship. In presenting naming and initiation rituals as formal means by which societies attempt to socialise their neophyte members, are anthropologists merely conveying what societies actually do and what their members actually believe? Or, are they conveying what societies *say* they do and believe? (The distinction between these possibilities is obviously important.) Or, are they imposing on their 'data' a theoretical matrix which emphasises society at the expense of the self and, in so doing, advocates one kind of anthropology rather than another. I suggest that the answer does not lie in a choice between these, but probably entails all of them to varying degrees. The theoretical posture which treats society and self as mutually exclusive entities seems unconvincing and unnecessary. They *coexist* within our own consciousnesses, even if uneasily. It is perfectly plausible to attach to these naming and initiation practices a socio-logic which does not preempt the self's own experience and interpretation of them.

It so happens that my forenames do not convey to me any message about myself. Yet we routinely presume that for the bearers of 'other cultures' their names must be meaningful. Because their naming forms differed from ours, we seem to have supposed that they must be sociologically significant, and to have further supposed that individuals would think alike about the social significance of their names and naming practices.[8] We are led to this error because we deny selves and self consciousness to them; at the very least, we construct and supply selves to them, and then assume that there is no dissonance between our invention of their selves, and their own sense of their selves. In making the kinds of assumption which we have witnessed about the social and personal significance of names and their meanings, we neglect people's self consciousness or dismiss it as irrelevant. The ways in which we have rendered naming rituals attributes to the societies we describe the denial of selfhood to their novice members. The ethnographic literature on initiation is full of accounts of socially scripted personhood from which the authorial self is entirely absent, and which treats rites of initiation (including those of naming) as processes which establish society's rights over the individual. To acknowledge self consciousness is to recognise another competence of ritual: that it provides a means through which individuals construct the terms of their membership, establish the meanings of selfhood and society to them, and rehearse their rights to their selves.

Chapter 4

Social transformations of the self

'If I should be someone else, who would be me?'

(Myerhoff 1978: 64)

MAKING THE 'I' INTO 'WE'

The studies of initiation which we reviewed in the last chapter clearly suggest that social membership, and induction into a new kind of membership, somehow 'remakes' the self, discarding the previous version or reformulating it in terms which will make it more obviously pertinent to the group it is now joining. This ostensible reformulation of the self appears to be required in circumstances other than just those of joining a new group of people, such as an individual's change of social status, or passage into a different category of social membership. Bearing in mind the distinction for which I have argued above between ostensible (or prescribed) and actual (or accomplished) changes to the self, it might be helpful to characterise this transformation as one which is directed to 'socially scripted personhood', leaving open the empirical question of whether, and the extent to which, the self really is changed. We are therefore concerned here with *assumptions* which people feel entitled to make about the changed selfhood of an individual following from some change in his or her social circumstances, assumptions which inform their conduct towards the individual concerned.

(i) Greek marriage

I refer first in some detail to John Campbell's classic study of the Greek Sarakatsani, *Honour, Family and Patronage* (Campbell 1964). Among other often-noted features of this book, one cannot help but observe the dispassionate manner in which Campbell deals with the attitudes of

Sarakatsani men to their womenfolk. So far as this latter point is concerned, it had for long been a reasonable assumption that this was due in part to the exceptionally difficult political circumstances of his fieldwork which obliged him to cut short his research, and which combined with the pervasively gendered ethos of Sarakatsani society to restrict Campbell's access exclusively to men. However, in a recent *mémoire*, he makes clear that he did have access to women through his wife, Sheila; and that, accompanying her, he was frequently present at women's gatherings and was able to talk to them about 'their acceptance of women's subordinate position' (Campbell 1992: 159). It seems that we have to locate his book firmly within the tradition of male-biased ethnography – a tradition which, having been recognised, is now being increasingly corrected by anthropological studies of Greece which cast gender relations in a very different light.

The Sarakatsani were a transhumant shepherding community of some four thousand people, based in Zagori, a district of the Pindus mountains in the Greek province of Epirus. Each family had grazing rights in the grasslands around the Zagori villages. During the winter, they moved down to the coastal plain, extending quite far to the south, in which the climate was less severe, but where they had to rent pasture since they did not have grazing rights. Winter was regarded as a kind of exile. Campbell's account of Sarakatsani life unmistakably recalls the manner in which Evans-Pritchard related Nuer social structure to the ecological imperatives of their transhumant pastoralism, and derived Nuer culture from the logic of their social structure.

Campbell portrayed the ethos of Sarakatsani society as being intensely agonistic and familistic:

> It is believed by the Sarakatsani that the interests of unrelated families are opposed and, indeed, mutually destructive.
>
> (Campbell 1964: 9)

It was a competitiveness among families (rather than individuals) which appears to have bred rivalry, envy and a continual concern to place others at a disadvantage. Fortune was seen in zero-sum terms: the failure of others was your success; and, conversely, their success must be to your detriment. The object of competition was honour, a more complicated matter than mere wealth, or superior grazing, or the best prices at market, although all of these may have been implicated in it. Each family strove to preserve, protect and defend its honour, preferably at the cost of another family's dishonour. The dynamic of social life thus resided in the pressure to display

right ways of acting in family and kinship roles and the sex-linked
moral characteristics which a man or woman ought to exhibit when
he, or she, stands forward as the protagonist of the family and the
guardian of its honour.

(Campbell 1964: 9)

The 'intrinsic principles' of honour are discriminated on gender lines
which

distinguish the ideal moral characters of men and women: these are
the manliness of men, and the sexual shame of women.

(Campbell 1964: 269)

Honour consisted in the capacity of men and women to discipline their
respective 'flaws of nature': cowardice, and sensuality (ibid.). Campbell
went so far as to suggest that the competition for honour implied a
'hierarchy of prestige', and bound the Sarakatsani together as a
community.

Honour (like social identity) was imputed by others. It was a necessary criterion for attributing integrity to a family. Without it, the family
was regarded as 'of no account'. If the family's honour was impugned,
their only recourse was to revenge, usually violent revenge (Campbell
1964: 269). Honour was what distinguished humans from animals. It
was demanded continuously from men. The quality demanded of
women, shame, was inextricably related to it, for if the woman was
shown to be wanting in shame, this inevitably detracted from the honour
of her husband and his family. Shame, specifically sexual shame, should
be manifest in

an instinctive revulsion from sexual activity, an attempt in dress,
movement, and attitude to disguise the fact that she possesses the
physical attributes of her sex.

(Campbell 1964: 270)

A woman who failed in this respect revealed her animality and thereby
forfeited her right to respect. But although the shame was the woman's,
it was detrimental to the honour of the men associated with her:

The woman is soiled, and blackened, and she marks with her dishonour all those who are close to her through kinship or marriage.

(Campbell 1964: 271)

Such dishonouring triggered revenge, but this did not erase the woman's
stigma. Even if she was the noncompliant victim of rape, question marks

would remain over her integrity, and her men remained dishonoured since they had failed to protect and preserve her virtue.

Honour seems to have informed the conduct of every aspect of social life, from the organisation of sheep husbandry to relations between the sexes and, certainly, between husband and wife. Women, being regarded as generally unpropitious, were classed with goats, in contrast to men and sheep. Because by nature women were vulnerable to the will of the devil (see also Du Boulay 1974: 102ff.), they did not work with the sheep, although in an extension of their maternal roles they cared for sick sheep or orphan lambs. Women who were menstruating or who were sexually active would avoid walking in front of sheep, to which, said the Sarakatsani, their presence would be offensive. They bore the brunt of the heaviest manual labour: building houses, carrying water from the well, managing all the domestic work which included the gathering of firewood, spinning and making the clothes.

Because relations among the constituent entities of Sarakatsani society (families and the *stani*, collaborative herding units) were so hostile, and because women were regarded as so corruptible, the contracting of marriage presented a grave problem. It might have been to a family's advantage to trick a suitor into marrying one of their daughters who was not a virgin in order to sully his family's honour. Using the kindred, exhaustive enquiries were made about a potential bride and her family. For the bride, marriage entailed the virtual severance of ties to her natal family. Residence after marriage was strictly virilocal. Her family did not even attend the wedding. The ritual enactment of the separation, and of the bride's induction into the affinal family, was arduous and elaborate. It involved the continuous exchange of gifts, and the incessant display by the bride of respect to her husband's kinsmen. She was obliged to stand in their presence, to kiss their hands, and to prepare ritual foods for them. Throughout these proceedings, wrote Campbell,

> there is symbolized the initial pattern of their relations, submission and respect on her part, and acceptance and protection on theirs.
>
> (Campbell 1964: 61)

In the later stages of the ceremonial, and following the consummation of the marriage, the bride was introduced ritually to her wifely tasks: collecting water, washing, spinning and so forth. Campbell explained the protracted ritual, and the domestic regime which followed it immediately, in this way:

The ceremonial induction into the family of the groom during and immediately after the wedding, the symbolic acts which she must perform, and the exchange of gifts with her close affines, all indicate the quality of her initial status within the extended family. The essential fact is that the new bride is subordinate to all other adults in the extended family. Even the five-year-olds try with varying success to boss the new 'bride'. As a worker, her services belong to the whole group. She is, as they often say, 'our bride'. Not only does she care for the comfort of her own husband but she is responsible for washing, mending, and darning the clothes of all his unmarried brothers. In general, it can be said that any hard or unpleasant work will be delegated to her. A mule to be rounded up, water to be carried – the new bride is certain to be sent. 'She must learn our ways,' the other women explain, 'and must take root in her new family . . .'

(Campbell 1964: 64)

Such an apparently heartless initiation suggests an attempt similar to those we saw earlier to strip the self, and to fabricate another in its place. The bride's self was to be remade in the image of her husband's family. The other side of this coin is that the bride was regarded as a full (if junior) member of the group: '"She is one of us", they say' (ibid.). Every feature of the bride's induction, from the ceremonial exchange of gifts to her display of humility and abject subservience, which even included the surrender of her own name, seem logically related to the task of incorporating her fully into the affinal group. The strongly functionalist orientation of Campbell's ethnography implies that the agonistic character of Sarakatsani social life demanded absolute solidarity within the family and their kindred. The inmarrying bride had therefore to be transformed rapidly from outsider with loyalties elsewhere into a dependant whose absolute loyalty would be matched by protection and membership rights.

The picture Campbell painted was of a society in which group membership (in the form of the family) entailed the strictest compromise of the self. The authorial self was replaced by a compulsion on both men and women to subjugate themselves to the inflexible disciplines of maintaining the family's honour. The individualistic girl became the constrained bride, a compliant appendage to her husband, a woman who must be vigilant about her reputation lest she bring dishonour to her husband and his family. The man, whether he was by nature aggressive or retiring, reflective or extrovert, must strut the social stage, crowing his machismo and *eghoismos*, and wresting revenge when appropriate. We are told nothing about the introspective dimension of these people's lives; they perform continuously on a remorselessly public stage, playing roles which have been scripted for them, and which apparently do not permit any discretion to them. Even within the privacy of their own homes, they must ape their role-models in striving to make the closest possible approximation to the holy family (Campbell 1964: 37).

For the woman, this means that she is defined, and is required to define herself, strictly as wife and mother, roles which should help to inoculate her against the corruption of her sexuality, and which have the virginal Mary as their apotheosis (cf. Greger 1988: 127). A woman did not corrupt her household by building their hut, by collecting their firewood, by carrying their water, by preparing their food, by making and washing their clothes because these were wifely and maternal tasks. She did not harm or offend sheep by building sheepfolds or by tending sick ewes, because these again were expressions of her motherhood. The vulnerability of women was 'contained' by the family as a spiritual and a social entity. Their very subjugation could be seen as divinely ordained, since the struggles for material benefit and honour, and for virtue, were mutually implicated:

> The family and the flock are both forms divinely confirmed, the earthly family being a refraction of the Holy archetype Family, while the sheep is a sacred animal blessed by God. These things have always been so, they always will be so. Life is sheep, children, and honour. . . . The family is the form in which these three elements are fused. . . .
>
> (Campbell 1964: 34–5)

Campbell's somewhat docile reiteration of Sarakatsani doctrine rendered almost bland their harsh, even brutal lives. It is a nice symmetry; but in its presumption of the silence of the self, it is frankly implausible and, as we saw above, leads (or misleads) him to assert that women 'accepted' their inferiority and the denigration of their sex. Recent studies of gender in rural Greece have given considerable attention to reflexivity both among men and women, and to the mental stress and strain which is caused by the pressure to conform publicly to expectations and social stereotypes, while experiencing privately their contradiction (Cowan 1990; Greger 1988). Women are increasingly portrayed as the authoritative decision-makers, whilst men are shown to be dependent on their wives' labour and neurotically obliged to pretend publicly to an unconvincing superiority.

Juliet du Boulay, a student of Campbell's, largely concurred with his depiction of gender inequality, although she suggested that it was a partly pragmatic hierarchy. In her beautifully written study of Ambéli, a Greek mountain village of olive growers, she echoed Campbell's suggestion that public life involves a subordination of the self. Indeed, she said:

> the structure of social relations in the village encourages the development in the individual of qualities which, although they are a necessary part of family integrity, act against a certain type of self-awareness. This is by no means to say that the individual has no personal integrity, nor that he is totally lacking in self-awareness; it is to redefine the concepts of integrity and self-awareness in terms which relate to village culture rather than to more introspective types of thinking. . . . He acts more as the protagonist of the family group than as a person with his own individual moral existence.
>
> (Du Boulay 1974: 74–5)

In her view, then, the culture of social life required the individual to subordinate his self to a regime of social convention. Individuality was subordinated to conformity (Du Boulay 1974: 80). In so far as it existed at all, personal reflexivity was restricted to the terms of public performance. She referred to a 'lack of self-examination' (ibid.: 81). Even with respect to one's spouse, reflection is not on 'deepening awareness and knowledge of self and other', but on 'a focus always outwards to the material, social, economic, and religious world' (ibid.: 90).

However, there was relief at home from the pressure to perform:

> In the house, *egoismós* disappears. But outside the house everyone tries to make himself out a bit larger than he really is.
>
> (Du Boulay 1974: 75)

Marriage was a relationship of interdependence, albeit one built on a pronounced inequality of authority. This interdependence was clearly manifest in the domestic division of labour, in the man's need of his wife to procreate, and the wife's need of her husband to subdue 'relentlessly her own nature' in order to

> conquer the evil elements in her nature. . . . If she does this, she can achieve a state in which, though subordinate, she is not inferior, and may become perfect in her own domain.
>
> (Du Boulay 1974: 135)

Du Boulay chose the idiom of 'partnership' to describe marriage in Ambéli, a relationship in which the harmony of the household was entirely dependent on the wife, whom

I once heard referred to, by a man, as 'a second God'.

(Du Boulay 1974: 135)

Sonia Greger, writing of Magoulas, a village on the Cretan Lasithi Plateau, goes considerably further than Du Boulay in developing this notion of complementarity. She suggests that women rightly see themselves as the energising force in the relationship. She quotes approvingly 'A male ecclesiastical speaker' at a conference of Cretan country women as saying:

The man is the head, but the woman is the neck that moves the head.

(Greger 1988: 135)

Greger thus rejects Campbell's view of women's acceptance of their subordination. To the contrary, she says, women

do not have, nor do they seem to have a sense of, relatively low status in their society.

(Greger 1988: 135)

And she continues,

We should beware of making the superficial judgement that Greek peasant women have a status inferior to men's. Regarded as very different to men they are, nevertheless, economically, affectively and socially indispensable. The community, as well as the household, would fall apart without them.

(Greger 1988: 136)

This suggestion of equality and complementarity makes even more implausible the Campbell–Du Boulay assertion of selflessness. On the one hand, we have an image of men desporting themselves in public as the all-powerful, totally authoritative figures in their relationships with their wives yet, in reality, being dependent on them (Du Boulay 1974: 134). Greger says that Lasithiot men 'are afraid of their wives and mothers' (Greger 1988: 127). On the other hand, we are told that women are utterly compliant, forever dancing to the tunes of their husbands and their mothers-in-law, yet knowing that they are the motivators and enablers of their households' activities. Is it conceivable that people can live with these contradictions *without* reflexivity? What other agency of reflexivity can there be but the self?

Michael Herzfeld also used the metaphor of performance to describe the presentation of selfhood by men from the Cretan village of Glendi. This combines the assertion of 'personal excellence' (Herzfeld 1985:

11) and the identification of the individual with his male forebears (ibid.: 10). Indeed, he writes of 'The entailment of the self in the agnatic ideology' (ibid.: 53), an association reflected in a naming convention which combines the individual's baptismal name with that of an apical ancestor. A man may also take on the *paratsoukli* (nickname) of his father or grandfather (ibid.: 234 ff.). Like Du Boulay, Herzfeld reports the use of the word *eghoismos* to connote the performing self: 'a *social* rather than a psychological phenomenon' (ibid.). The putative social-ness of *eghoismos* rests on a variety of bases, including the merging of an individual into his patriline,[1] and the manner in which it is performed. Cowan writes that it is 'socially configured and involves a highly conventionalized posture' (Cowan 1990: 173).

All of these authors accept the gloss of 'self-regard' which Campbell put on *eghoismos*. However, as we have seen, in their various ways they then distance the object of this regard from the selfhood of the indivi-dual. It is the male rampant; or it is the patriline manifest; or it is the performance of aggressive male personhood. The *individuality*, the I-ness, of the man seems hardly to enter this picture. Du Boulay suggests that 'individualism' in Ambéli is tantamount to a 'loss of identity' – that is, behaviour which is so far outside of the acceptable idiom that it is dimissed as bizarre, a view reiterated by the Macedonian villagers of Sohos when confronted with 'an excess of *kefi*' (exuberance) (Cowan 1990: 111). For Herzfeld, it seems to refer to little more than the style or virtuosity of the individual man's performance. Among these authors, consciousness of individuality is addressed explicitly only by Cowan, and, perhaps significantly, in respect of women rather than of men. It is in their demand to men to recognise them *as* individuals, rather than just as objects. She describes two young women who 'draw upon the rhetoric of individualism to argue for a different conception of female personhood':

> *this* is what we want to do. To make it so that a man doesn't look at a woman as an object no matter what place she walks into. Why should he see her as an object? We want to get to the level where the man looks at the woman as a person.
>
> (Cowan 1990: 86)

Cowan expresses a puzzlement similar to mine at the apparent lack of reflexivity, and wonders whether the conventions of performance and beliefs about gender are not so deeply embedded that, in Bourdieu's phrase, they 'are placed beyond the grasp of consciousness' (ibid.: 130, quoting Bourdieu 1977: 94). She suggests that while they may not be verbalised, they are certainly not beyond consciousness. They are embodied:

> the very panache with which a young man drapes his jacket over his shoulder . . . and the very thoughtfulness with which the bride assumes a pose of modest dignity in her walk to the church testify to a practical awareness of the power and manipulability of the bodily insignia of gender.
>
> (Cowan 1990: 131)

Yet, as in Du Boulay's and Herzfeld's accounts, the consciousness is of *performance* (ibid.) – that is, of the presentation to others of a desired image; and we still know little or nothing about what is thought, felt, experienced or meant. Cowan argues that the ideology of gender in Sohos (presumably the other anthropologists of Greece referred to above would say the same of their fields) so pervades every aspect of life, from the organisational to the aesthetic and the sensual, that it precludes the possibility of becoming conscious of it in other than its own terms.

One cannot but be impressed by the consensus of views to be found in the literature on Greece. After all, surely what is being described is the reality of culture, and why should an anthropologist of all people doubt it? My scepticism lacks the elementary virtue of being based on evidence; it is purely intuitive. It seems to me that what we have before us is the reasonable assumption that performances which are so compelling and apparently so orthodox must express a uniformity of thought, of consciousness. I wonder if we may not be confusing appearance and reality a little: confusing common vocabularies of gender relations and of membership with shared messages. There is no reason to doubt the cultural forms of posture and gesture which Herzfeld and Cowan so sharply observe and to which they attribute so much significance. They are means by which Glendiots and Sohoians express themselves. But express what? Their terms are *eghoismos, kefi, dropi* (shame, modesty); but in searching for ways to make these meaningful, do we not constitute them as having more concreteness, more orthodoxy, less fuzziness and diversity in their meaning and use than might actually be the case?

I find myself having to ask the same question about the Glendiot man as about the young Bimin-Kuskusmin initiate. Do his provenance and his culture mean that he must think certain things, and about things in a certain way? Or do they, rather, provide him with the means to think about them, and the terms in which to express approximately what he thinks? Have the anthropological Hellenists adequately considered the latter possibility? Its implications are substantial. It could certainly construe marital relations in a very different way than the 'hierarchical complementarity' which is the most these authors, with the exception of Greger, seem willing to concede. Rather than seeing men and women fatalistically going into marriage knowing that it entails roles which are so prescriptive as to exclude personal discretion or direction, it would mean seeing marital roles as *frameworks* which the individuals themselves substantiate and negotiate through their own agency and creativity. In the first case, marriage would essentially imply the loss of self; in the second, its modulation. We come back here to a problem raised earlier with respect to ethnographically 'accessing' the self. It is one thing to say that Sarakatsani and Ambéli villagers do not disclose what they think about how they are constrained by public expectations and norms, but quite another to suppose that, therefore, they do not think about these things. The absence of obvious and explicit concern about the self does not entitle one to deny that individuals do commonly have such concerns.

In Europe, the public supervision of marital roles and relations was by no means limited to rural Greece. Using ethnological data, including surveys made by Van Gennep, Segalen has ingeniously created a picture of the nature of domestic relationships in nineteenth-century rural France (1983). One of the most intriguing conclusions to emerge from her study is that, rather than just transforming them into the statuses of bride and groom, marriage subordinated individuals to the regime of the community. In so doing, we may suppose that communities sought to limit, perhaps even to eliminate, authorial discretion over personal behaviour – that is, to attenuate selfhood.

Many of the marriage rites which she reconstructs appear to state and celebrate normative forms of authority within the marital household. For example,

> Arrived at the altar, the future couple kneels, and at Fours, near Barcelonette, 'the young woman spreads out her skirt or apron in such a way that the knee of her husband rests upon it, in sign of the superiority of the husband and of the amiable deference due from a wife to her husband'.
>
> (Segalen 1983: 25–6, quoting Bérenger-Féraud 1971: 194)

This is interpreted as signifying male authority, the subordination of the wife to her husband in their working partnership – the apron being emblematic of labour – and also of the husband's sexual rights over his wife since, as Segalen asks, 'who should not remove her apron except for him?' (Segalen 1983: 26).

Other elements of the wedding rite are similarly seen as statements and auguries of authority:

> If the groom slips the ring on to his bride's finger, it is said that he will be the dominant authority in the household, whereas if the bride resists, and he cannot get the ring past the second joint, it is said that she will be the mistress of the household.
>
> (Segalen 1983: 27)

These practices reveal obvious sexual symbolism, but are also divinatory procedures concerning the outcome of the marriage.

> 'In the Haute-Saône, when the couple returned to the house, the cook presented the husband with a wooden spoon containing an egg. He had to throw the egg over the house; if he threw it well he would dominate his wife.' In Mâcon tradition, it is a sign of feminine authority if the bridegroom, on the wedding-night, has difficulty in removing his wife's bridal crown. The act of going to bed is also accompanied by omens predicting both authority and death. In Brittany, 'whoever gets into bed first will die first, and whichever one of the couple sleeps at the front of the bed will be in charge'.
>
> (Segalen 1983: 29, quoting Sébillot 1886: 133)

Segalen emphasises not just the symbolism of the rites, but the fact of their *public* performance. She argues that this implies that the community

> will oversee relations between man and wife, watching to see that the social order is not disturbed by a complaisant or weak husband, or by a shrewish or idle wife.
>
> (Segalen 1983: 37)

The community sought to impose a matrix on the selves of bride and groom. Indeed, she goes on to show in detail that, 'The intrusion of the community into every aspect of family life' was obvious, even to the point of constituting a 'right of control' (Segalen 1983: 41–2). So, for example, women who were perceived to be dilatory or delinquent in their gardening would be publicly identified by having a straw man placed in their gardens. A proposed marriage which was publicly regarded as being unsuitable would be mocked and denigrated. A husband who beat his wife too severely, or who allowed himself to be beaten by her, or the discovery of adultery would all be marked by the charivari or by some other satirical event. So a husband who had been beaten by his wife might be made to ride on a donkey, mounted backwards and holding its tail. The symbolism is not hard to penetrate: the culpable behaviour is a reversal of the norm. Its perpetrator would be seen not just as a ridiculous individual, but as 'a danger to the whole social order of the village' (ibid.: 47). Comparable examples of the public policing of social standards are widespread and would include, in Britain, 'rough music' (Thompson 1991) and the satirical vigilance of Welsh 'corner boys' (Peters 1972).

The logic of these rites seems transparent. The self is depicted as pliable, and its plasticity and subjugation to the conventions of the group as normative. There is the strong implication that resistance by the individual would have been regarded as pathological. Perhaps the kindest term available to describe such resistance would have been 'eccentric'; it would more likely have been treated as 'anti-social'. But what status should we accord to these rituals: were they symbolic expressions of what people believed actually to be the case? Or were they ritualised fantasies which acknowledged the difference between ideal and actuality, principle and practice, and, in so doing, made it tolerable? It is just this kind of difference which lies behind Geertz's distinctions between 'ethos' and 'world view', 'models of' and 'models for', and which is widely documented across every area of social life from kinship to politics. We have long recognised ritual (and other practices) of this kind to be necessary means of dealing with the intractable difficulties and the otherwise unresolvable tensions and contradictions of social life. To mistake them as statements of fact, or as descriptions of social reality, would surely be unacceptably naïve. It seems to me appropriate to apply the same reservation to the depiction of self-less individuals in marriage.

(ii) Organisational membership

Notwithstanding its naïveté, it is a fallacy which seems to inform organisational and management theory to a considerable extent.[2] Throughout the various theoretical traditions which have dominated organisational theory, the individual is assumed to be plastic, to be modelled by the logic and imperatives of the organisation's structure. This view was plain in the 'scientific management' and 'human relations' approaches, was perpetuated in structural-functionalist analyses, and survives in contemporary theoretical models which portray organisations as 'cultures' which shape their members' behaviour. It is a conception of the organisation as a 'psychic prison' (Morgan 1986: 199ff.), in which the deterministic power of the organisation is regarded as inhering not in any penal sanctions which it may be able to impose, but in the organisation's assumed capacity to confer identity on its members. Indeed, it is arguably the case that contemporary management strategies attempt to entice the member into identifying with the organisation so completely as to create an identity of aspiration and absolute loyalty.

For anthropologists, there are parallels to be drawn between such models of complex organisation and those of segmentary lineage structures (which were identified most famously among pastoral societies with unilineal descent systems). Studies of these segmentary systems showed complex social aggregates to be broken down into units to which ideological charters could be attached. To some extent the charters masked the functional and pragmatic nature of the segmentary units which made them useful for such purposes as grazing herds, feuding, contracting marriages, making war, and so on. The classic anthropological theory of segmentation, which linked Evans-Pritchard with Dumont, depicted the segments as being progressively included in the whole structure. In his seminal analysis of caste in India, Dumont (1980) used the term 'encompassment' to suggest the idea of smaller units nesting within larger ones. These early theorists, as well as more recent authors such as Holy (1979), Galaty (1981) and Combs-Schilling (1985), were so finely focused on the organisational implications of segmentation that they neglected to elaborate on its significance as a theory of social identity. A person identifies with different entities, and with different levels of society for different purposes.

The idea of segmentary structure offers a powerful metaphor for complex organisations. But segmentation also has a non-structural dimension which leads to an analogy no less compelling. This may be described as 'the culture of segmentation', and refers to the ways in which people conceptualise, symbolise and transform their sectional associations. We come back here to one of our original questions, raised in Chapter 1. Are individuals the creatures of their social relationships or are they their orchestrators? Are individuals created in the images of the segments (tribal or organisational) to which they belong, or do they assimilate their membership of these entities to their own interests and identities? Sectional or segmentary associations extend beyond formal structures; they are ideas rather than mechanisms, social relations rather than operational systems. They are made meaningful through being marked symbolically by their members, in the same way that individuals and groups process the claims made on them by those with whom they have relationships so that they can be acknowledged and managed appropriately. In addressing their social commitments, including their membership of organisations, individuals may be regarded as speaking in the active voice, rather than as having behaviour determined by structures which are imposed on them. The boundaries of segments, although possibly structural in form, are substantiated – made meaningful – by members themselves through these symbolic means. For example, segmentary boundaries which are formally constituted by such diacritica as dialect, knowledge, sectarian identity or organisational specialism are sufficiently plastic to leave members with enough scope for interpretative manoeuvre that they can construct them symbolically to express their own particular interests and attitudes. It follows that membership of such a group does not entail in *fact*, rather than *form*, discarding a previous self in favour of one which is modelled on the group's distinctive character.

If we consider specifically the use of organisational symbols, as do such writers as Dandridge (1976), Feldman and March (1981) and, most notably, Pondy *et al.* (1983), it will be clear these are not monolithic in character: they do not convey uniform meanings. Management may propagate a symbol (for example, the company 'hero', or the ideal of 'service'), in the hope that it will convey to the organisation's members a shared meaning; but there is no such orthodoxy. Members process symbols, if not as wholly free agents then, at the very least, as interpreters. Moreover, just as they manipulate the symbols which mark their organisational membership and environment, so they also negotiate the relationships among the organisation and their many other social commitments. In so doing, they reveal as vacuous the management's assumption that *they* control the terms on which the individual relates to the organisation.

Over the last decade or more, organisation theorists have ransacked the social sciences and humanities to find theories and concepts with which to try to make sense of complex organisations. Anthropology has been a favourite nest to plunder, from which they have purloined and perverted the concept of 'culture' (see Pettigrew 1979; Allaire and Firsimotu 1984) to fabricate the neologisms 'organisational culture' and 'corporate culture'. I say 'perverted' because the manner in which they use the concept – to convey a compelling ideology – has long been discredited in anthropology itself. For example, in their instructively titled book, *Corporate Cultures: the Rites and Rituals of Corporate Life*, Deal and Kennedy say,

A strong culture is a system of informal rules that spells out how people are to behave most of the time,

(Deal and Kennedy 1982: 15)

and refer to 'strong' and 'weak culture' companies. (See also, Bate 1984; Lee and Lawrence 1985; Schein 1986.) Linda Smircich has to go back to Benedict in order to vindicate her view of culture as a concept of order and orderliness (Smircich 1983: 341).

A penetrating discussion of the use of the 'culture' concept in this literature discerned two tendencies: those of the 'pop-culture magician and the honest grappler' (Turner 1986: 104). The first sees culture simply as an ensemble of stories and beliefs, and applies the metaphor mechanically. The second critically examines the applicability of theories of culture to organisations.[3] Turner himself concludes that organisations are not 'well-integrated mechanisms' and that they cannot be considered as societies. To this extent, there is no reason to suppose that they are informed by a singular culture – indeed, quite the contrary (ibid.: 110). If one is to take seriously and faithfully the application of 'culture' to complex organisations, this really can only be done by recognising that culture reposes in individuals, who bring it to the organisation. That is to say, individuals, rather than organisations, are the agents of culture; and their agency is constituted by their continuous experience of their own selfhood (cf. Giddens 1991: 53). The complex organisation is an aggregation of disparate selves rather than a dismal battery of uniform automatons. That is why they are so difficult to manage. The observation seems so obvious as to be banal, but it hardly seems to have found its way into organisational theory and analysis. Yet the literature is replete with descriptions of ruses by which obviously desperate managerial minds attempt to contrive both commitment and identity. Deal and Kennedy offer us the 'attaboy', a plaque awarded for commercial success:

All work comes to a halt as a manager marches out into the hallway and rings a bell. Everyone files down from the executive suite and other offices. . . . With a great flourish, the manager announces that another 'attaboy' is to be awarded.

(Deal and Kennedy 1982: 61)

Five attaboys earn their recipient a 'gotcha'. Culture? The self may respond to an attractive stimulus, but it surely does not thereby become a slavering Pavlovian pup.

It would be a travesty to suggest that all of this work is a similarly naïve rendition of stimulus–response theory. However, the concept of 'corporate culture' does not seem to be formulated by management practitioners and analysts in much more sophisticated terms than those of a compelling ideology which integrates the discrepant interests, functions and proclivities of the organisation's many members so that they focus on the single goal of the organisation's objectives – as if their selves could simply be assimilated to the greater organism of the organisation itself. It is a notion which recalls the structural-functionalist view of culture as the means by which the members of a society were integrated by their common participation in, and sharing of, specific modes of behaviour. In contemporary anthropology, 'culture' has now to be used in a significantly different manner, to refer to the manifold activities and experiences of the *diverse* people whom it *aggregates*. Culture is the framework of meaning, of concepts and ideas, within which different aspects of a person's life can be related to each other without imposing arbitrary categorical boundaries between them. The ingenuity and social skill of the individual is tested by the degree to which she or he can reconcile these various activities and interests, a reconciliation which implies that, while engaged in any one activity, individuals are nevertheless repositories of all their other commitments and experiences. That is what makes them unique. However, the notion of organisational culture implies the very opposite: that the front door of the company office also marks a boundary between the individual's life inside and outside it. In this view, individuals are seen as bits of the organisational structure and are assumed to be activated by its system needs. It seems likely that this misappropriation of the concept of culture may have led organisational analysts and practitioners to misunderstand the extent to which formal structures can determine the behaviour of people, by misinforming them about the agency of the individual (the authorial self) with respect to social formations.

As aggregates of selves, complex organisations are conglomerates of widely differing kinds of activity. They subsume not only different kinds of skill, but also different interests the reconciliation of which may be extremely difficult, if not impossible. Differences of interest and of philosophy divide from each other people within the same structural niche of the organisation, as well as from those in its other sections or on different levels of the hierarchy. For example, consider the general hospital, working within a regime of scarce resources and increasing demands which exacerbates divisions between medical staff and administrators, among doctors, nurses, technicians and ancillary workers; between consultants and junior doctors, among medical specialties; between different philosophies within the same speciality – say, conservative as opposed to radical or invasive therapies – and so on.

Let us think about the complexity of a symphony orchestra, a complexity belied by its relatively small size: say, one hundred musicians (and perhaps a dozen administrators). This supposedly coherent entity is divided into discrete instrumental sections, all playing the 'same' score but playing different notes and playing at different musical moments; each observes the disciplines of, and is informed by, the distinctive traditions which pertain to their particular instruments. This diversity is held together (or not, as the case may be) in performance with a degree of actual or figurative harmony by the conductor as manager. Even within the same orchestral section, there are quite different activities in progress simultaneously: the principal cellist concentrates on tone, while her platform neighbour worries about knocking the score off the music stand as he turns its pages; his neighbour's mind wanders from the conductor to the lessons he has to give on the following day, or to his child's impending exam. The players may have quite different opinions about the music they are playing. To say that all the players are 'doing the same thing' is to draw a very thin veil over a diversity of behaviour. The success of the masking depends on the skills of the conductor, leader and principals, and on the professional discipline and commitment of the players. It is obviously not determined either by the score itself or by the players' orchestral roles. Perhaps the pressures of public performance also assist the drawing of the veil.

There is no obviously comparable discipline to hold together the commercial or industrial corporation, composed of separate and, possibly, competing companies, and discrete sectors within companies – marketing, production, finance, research – with their own hierarchical strata, and competition for promotion on any one level. If we add to these plausible divisions in each of these organisations the complications of extra-organisational factors which inevitably intrude routinely in a person's life – matters of personality, friendship, family, social relationships which cut across organisational commitments, personal anxieties, competing interests and preoccupations – it becomes clear that the organisation bears little resemblance to the neatly arranged and methodical flow charts on the chief executive's office wall.

Organisation theorists over the last fifty years or more have supposed that the complexity of organisations derived from the multiplicity of functions they served and the plurality and diversity of skills required to perform them. This overly structural view neglects the real source of complexity: that the organisation is constituted not by *roles* but by *self conscious individuals* who have somehow to be led to make their behaviour approximate to the idealised profiles of their organisational roles. Organisations are perverse institutions. They are superimposed on the personalities, personal identities and other social allegiances of their members, whose wider social lives they thereby contradict. Individuals cope with this contradiction by managing it: rather than permitting themselves to be assimilated to the demands of the organisation, they do exactly the opposite and strive to assimilate their organisational commitments to their own circumstances. As we saw in discussing Goffman's total institutions (p. 70–1), organisations are culture-permeable. Individuals bring culture, *their* cultures to the organisation, the management of which responds with ideology, rather than with culture. The organisational regime is prescriptive and deterministic, culture is not. The organisation prescribes action through its procedures, its imperatives of accountability. Culture has none of this rigidity; rather, it is indefinitely readable and interpretable, and is continuously remade through people's behaviour.

It is this essential difference which accounts for the inevitable failure of organisational plans which are formulated in the abstract – that is, in isolation from what the members of the organisation actually do. Most British university staff now have painful experience of the inability of their institutions' management consultants to distinguish between a university and, say, a bakery or a chemical factory. There appears to be a confusion in much of the organisational literature between the ideal and the actual. The ideal seems to be regarded as attainable by the creation of appropriate organisational structures (e.g. Lee and Lawrence 1985). Individuality can be accommodated within the system if it can be subsumed under such labels as 'innovativeness' or 'entrepreneurialism' (Kanter 1983). If it is manifest as a philosophical dispute with the organisation's ideology, it is regarded as pathological or deviant. The continuous reinforcement of uniformity is attempted through the application of standard tests for the purposes of recruitment and assessment which measure individuals for their approximation to an organisational norm.

Whatever the source of these norms may be – they are often depicted in the literature as traditional or adventitious – they do not seem to be modelled on a sensitive appreciation of selfhood. This also means that organisations are insensitive to personal links which cross organisational boundaries and which may well be more compelling than those intended to bind people within an organisation (see *inter alia* Salaman 1986). Ironically, modern information technology links individuals in ways which cannot be constrained by organisational structure. The aptly named 'personal' computer may be recognised as precisely that: a device which, subject to any security systems which may be in force, is capable of freeing the individual from the constraints of a highly specialised organisational role and niche.

The notion of the organisation as an encompassing world which transforms the individuals who join it, and which is implicit in its characterisation as a bounded entity, seems quite implausible because it depicts individuals in isolation from their social contexts. Indeed, it abstracts out the organisational persona from the individual's self. The acknowledgement of the self as authorial inverts this relationship. Instead of seeing the member as being drawn by the organisation out of his or her self, we would see the organisation as incorporated into the individual's social world. We need to re-humanise our view of organisations (whether segmentary lineage systems or multinational corporations) by recognising that they are composed of individuals as active agents, who process their relationships and determine their movements through different social milieux. They are not merely acted upon. Organisational routines, however dictatorial, should not obscure our view of organisations as aggregations of selves speaking in the active voice.

HOLDING ON TO THE SELF, AND RESISTING THE CLAIMS OF OTHERS

So far in this chapter, I have argued that assumptions made about the transformation of the self on marriage and on entry to organisational membership are unwarranted, and derive from the failure to accord to the self the authorial power of agency, the capacity to be self-directing. The corollary of this failing is the overestimation of the power of structure to determine the self, a matter to which I shall return in Chapter 5 when I discuss the need to distinguish between principle and practice. To conclude the present chapter, I wish to look in a fairly cursory way at some instances of the self's resistance to attacks made on its integrity. If marriage and membership might be considered as points on the upward curve of the social career, old age is very definitely on the downward curve. I shall draw attention to the subversion of the self which seems often to be entailed in the social processing of the elderly.[4]

The fallacy of Goffman's 'total institutions' thesis may have originated in a confusion between individuals' loss of their capacity or right to control their lives, and their loss of self. The assumption here would be that as you come under the control of others, a control exercised by consigning you utterly to a category, the self is neutralised and then destroyed by being made irrelevant. The elderly become simply that: people who can be categorised in these ways, and who are therefore regarded simply as requiring certain kinds of care or as having entitlements to stipulated kinds of benefit. This is indeed the nature of public discourse about such categories of persons, and doubtless insinuates itself into the ways in which other people perceive them and relate to them. As everyone else commits category on them, the elderly cling to an earlier – pre-retirement – version of their selves in which they had a more satisfying identity:

> One of the fearful developments in the consciousness of many old people is that, in the eyes of society, they have become another species. Ironically, an intensive caring and concern for their welfare is frequently more likely to suggest this relegation than indifference and neglect. The growing bureaucracy, amateur and professional, voluntary and state, for dealing with geriatrics, makes some old folk feel that they no longer *quite* belong to the human race any more. They want those who really knew them as fully operative human beings to speak up for them.
>
> (Blythe 1979: 114)

Elderly people enter our consciousness as manifestations of a problem: ageing. This process of anonymising categorisation belongs as much to the discourse of compassion as to that of bureaucracy. Jerrome observes that even in church prayer, old age is presented as a categorisable affliction:

> the elderly join the 'needy and suffering in the world', who include the hungry and thirsty, the homeless, the unemployed and unemployable, alcoholics and drug users, the sick and the lonely.
>
> (Jerrome 1992: 133)

Hazan, who studied a Jewish day care centre for the elderly and handicapped in North London, refers tellingly to the effects of this relentless categorisation as amounting to 'self-degradation' (Hazan 1980: 20). He remarks that it implies

> an unmistakable insinuation that this marks the end of any significant involvement and participation in making decisions. . . . One way of relating to old people is by obliterating their life history and social identity, and reducing them to their physical and mental disabilities.
>
> (Hazan 1980: 30; see also 76)

It is therefore hardly surprising that the testimony of elderly and unemployed people, as revealed through ethnographic and other interpretative accounts, emphasises their experience of having their selves
degraded, and the enormous effort which, as a consequence, they put
into self-maintenance. Jerrome refers to this laborious self-defence as
'the strong face of ageing' (Jerrome 1992: 198), and finds it done
collaboratively in organised groups. Similarly, Jennie Keith notes the
contrivance of community as a necessary condition for the maintenance
and exercise of selfhood among the residents of a French retirement
residence (Keith 1980). The Japanese historian Sakei Tsunoyama has
described the growth in urban Japan of networking among the retired
elderly, 'the wet fallen leaves', as being partly a defence against the
neglect which is implied by categorisation (Tsunoyama 1993). In
Jennifer Hockey's view, the very fact of entry into a residential home for
the elderly in a north of England town posed a crisis of identity for the
residents. For men, it marked the definitive break with their occu-
pational pasts; for women, it signified the end of their caring and
domestic selves. She thus finds that those who remain physically and
mentally able deliberately set out to *re*create identities for themselves
within the home (Hockey 1989).

Among the most celebrated of recent ethnographic accounts was
Myerhoff's *Number our Days*, a study of very elderly East European
Jewish immigrants who formed the membership of a day centre in the
Californian coastal resort of Venice (1978).[5] These old Jews, most of
them in their eighties or older and living in considerable if genteel
poverty, spoke Yiddish as their favoured and first language, but were
also fluent in Russian or Polish, many knew the classical Hebrew of the
Old Testament, and all spoke English. Many had lapsed from the orthodox practice of Judaism even before they left the *shtetl*, indeed some
professed atheism; they had behind them lifetimes of left-wing politics,
having been revolutionary Marxists and union activists. The culture in
which they participated was that of *Yiddishkeit*, a moral and ethical
Judaism which was essentially secular despite its inextricable relationship to religious practice, and which had recently come to focus also on
committed support for Zionist causes.

The picture Myerhoff paints is one of barely contained anarchy. The
interpersonal conflicts become so intense that the centre's Director
desperately calls in a behavioural therapist, the hapless Dr Cohen, who
is chewed up, spat out, and rapidly sent on his way by his putative
clients. The tension is articulated with the barbed and biting wit which
is the peculiar genius of *shtetl* folklore, through the *bobbe-myseh*

(grandmothers' tales) and the satirical poems and songs composed by the old people themselves. Myerhoff brilliantly resisted the temptation to depict this milieu as one in which the stereotypical characteristics of Ashkenazi Diaspora Judaism are given full rein, and exploited as a licence for cantankerous, self-indulgent, especially loud and voluble Jewish*ness*. Instead, she presents their behaviour as means by which they cling on to their selfhood by demanding that others should be aware of it: it is an expression of their 'acute need for visibility and attention' (Myerhoff 1978: 10). And, again,

> More afraid of oblivion than of pain or death, they always sought opportunities to become visible.
>
> (Myerhoff 1978: 33)

> the opposite of honor was not shame but invisibility. Being neglected was more unbearable than disgrace.
>
> (Myerhoff 1978: 144)

One of the members had painted and hung a sign over the front door:

> 'To the extent that here at the Center we are able to be ourselves and to that extent Self feels good to us.'
>
> (Myerhoff 1978: 13)

Selfhood is for them a tenacious reassertion of their individuality against the dreary homogeneity of their categorisation as elderly, even as elderly Jews. One of Myerhoff's principal informants, a didactic and forceful retired tailor, responds aggressively with a Yiddish saying to her enquiry about why he conducts himself socially in so different a manner to his wife, to whom he is devoted:

> 'If I should be someone else, who would be me?'
>
> (Myerhoff 1978: 64)

Obviously, their individuality did not consist just in audibility and visibility, but in the demonstration of continuity with their past lives in which their identities rested on the more secure bases of occupation, parenting, and place and family of origin. This concern with continuity echoes the problem which Giddens sees as posed for the self by 'modernity', to which he sees the self responding by its authorship of a narrative project which connects the past and future lives of the individual. It differs in this respect: as I argued in Chapter 1, Giddens sees the self as having continuously to react to the institutional regime of modern society. The elderly of Venice seem rather more proactive in the authorship of their agendas. Their creativity, adaptability and syncretistic skills enable them to contrive an alternative institutional order. It could be argued, with some justification, that this is their mode of reaction; but it seems clear that in their *own* consciousness, they, rather than circumstances, are the authors of their own selfhood. They always

> sought evidence that they were still the same people now that they had once been, however transformed. The sense of constancy and recognizability, the integrity of the person over time was their essential quest.
>
> (Myerhoff 1978: 37)

If they felt that their identities rested on fragile bases, it would be easy enough to understand why. Paid occupation was only their most recent loss. They had lost their natal homes by emigration; their parents and other members of their families of origin had perished in the Nazi gas chambers; their children were long since independent of them – indeed, many kept them at a continent's distance. Each of them therefore had a lifetime's experience of having to forge a new life trajectory based on their *own* sense of their selves. Now in their late old age, their demand is for acknowledgement that their selfhood did not lose its integrity when they retired (ibid.: 222). Blythe reported a similar insistence among the English village elderly he describes in *The View in Winter* (1979):

> Constantly, as one talked to the aged, one felt this struggle to say who they *are*, not just who and what they have been.
>
> (Blythe 1979: 15; see also 23; 263)

Indeed, the London centre's 'participants' whom Hazan describes were inclined to dismiss the past as irrelevant, because irredeemable, and to demand that conversation and discussion should focus exclusively on their present circumstances.

The Venice Center's Jews provide an exemplary illustration of the skills of *bricolage* which people deploy to create and maintain their selfhood. They use their polyglot talents, especially their command of Yiddish; they make (invariably contested) claims about their skills as cooks, writers, singers, philosophers, dressmakers, Talmudists, as *menschen*; they use the visibility of their charitable works, especially with regard to Israel. They find means of contriving plausible connections between the present and the past, particularly by the adaptation or invention of rituals and ceremonies (see also Myerhoff 1984). For example, a new enthusiast concludes a series of meetings by inventing a graduation for his cohort, ostensibly modelled on the *siyum*, a celebration held by religious Jewish men to mark their completion of a programme of scholarship. The ceremony, like much of their syncretism, offended some of the purists. Yet Myerhoff was convinced of its efficacy, arguing that the sense of personal continuity has to be achieved rather than merely assumed, and requires mnemonics and other means of evoking past experience. The older the referent of experience, the more likely it is to be effective (Myerhoff 1978: 108).

The impression is conveyed that the *Yiddishkeit* which has been transposed from the *shtetl* to the Californian beach community is an artifice, a culture which has been constructed to provide a stage for the rehearsal of insistent selfhood. These old people do not fetishise the self; it is the medium of their consciousness, an explicit feature of their knowledge of the world and of themselves. 'Knowledge of self', says Myerhoff,

> is requisite to complete consciousness; consciousness requires reflecting surfaces,
>
> (Myerhoff 1978: 148; also 222)

a notion which eloquently directs us back to the self's authorship of the individual's behaviour and which, in turn, explains the tenacity with which individuals resist the subordination-by-categorisation of their selves. Blythe draws attention to the refusal of the elderly to conform to the expectation of their asexuality which younger people impute to them (Blythe 1979: 16; also Hazan 1980: 36). Jerrome decries the misunderstanding of the elderly which derives from the professionals' failure to consider and comprehend elderly people's own views of themselves (Jerrome 1992: 4):

> The strong face of ageing is the weak front of gerontology.
>
> (Jerrome 1992: 198)

In a study of the social relations of the elderly in rural England, Michaud showed that professionalism intruded upon the basic rights of the elderly to have views of their selves and their needs to such an extent that it became at least as much of a problem of ageing as are physical and mental infirmity (Michaud 1986). The old lady who insists on her rights to her self is dismissed by the professional carers as 'difficult', even as dotty. This phenomenon will not be unfamiliar to those who have had occasion to tangle with professionals, whether as patients or parents. The counterpoint to this professional attitude is the anguished demand of an old lady, whose poem was discovered after she died in a geriatric ward:

So open your eyes nurses, open and see,
Not a crabbit old woman, look closer – see *me*.

(Hazan 1980: 29)

These various accounts all lead to the conclusion that the reassertion of selfhood against its social subversion is an essential element of the life work of the elderly, the labour which Myerhoff, among others, refers to as the 'aging career', and which evokes Wadel's compelling notion of 'the hidden work of everyday life': the unremarked, taken-for-granted toil through which relationships are maintained and which is required to sustain the values on which these relationships are predicated (Wadel 1979). I find wholly persuasive the suggestion made by Hazan, with which these other writers concur, of the degradation which inheres in the subordination of selfhood to category. In this regard, the elderly present a stark illustration of the dehumanisation implied by generalisation, not to mention the elementary factual mistakes which generalisation both perpetrates and then masks (cf. Okely 1990: 194–5). In their case, it has obvious and profound practical consequences, which do not follow from the relatively detached pursuit of anthropological analysis. But it serves as yet another reminder of the extent to which the denial of self consciousness misleads us into a fundamental misreading of those who we otherwise claim to understand and to represent in our texts.

Wadel's 'hidden work' concept originated in his dissatisfaction with the definitional restriction of the concept of 'work' to economistic, market-oriented notions of paid employment. Quite apart from the semantic nicety of acknowledging as 'work' the labour entailed in the maintenance of such fundamental social institutions as family, friend-ships and community (Wadel 1979), it also responds to that most insidious aspect of post-industrial social change which has made the expectation of *un*employment a feature of the normal adult career. Wadel's early anthropological experience was gained in a society, Newfoundland, to which high rates of unemployment were endemic. Nevertheless, to be unemployed over the long term, even in rural New-foundland where seasonal unemployment among able-bodied men of working age might be as high as 25 per cent, was to have a 'spoiled identity'. Wadel's portrait of such a stigmatised individual showed perceptively and sympathetically the tactical devices he used in the attempt to fit the persona of 'the working man' and to escape thereby the stigma of being *out of work* (Wadel 1973). I think it is significant that Wadel saw the imperative need of the chronically unemployed as being, as the subtitle of his book puts it, to 'struggle for self-esteem'.

Ironically, part of the stigma of being able-bodied and unemployed is that one is put into a dependent category similar to that of the elderly; and, as the recipient of statutory 'benefits', one's rights, including the right to self-regulation, are considerably diminished. As with the elderly, one's self becomes the object of attack, submerged in the publication of monthly unemployment statistics and in the proliferation of impersonal categories: unemployed, unemployed and claiming benefit, long-term unemployed, unskilled unemployed, unemployed school-leavers, and so on. In another significant phrase, Howe refers to the failure to avoid or divest oneself of the stigma as 'self-defeat' (Howe 1990: 181). Yet, as with the elderly, studies of unemployed people, as of other bearers of stigmatised identities, reveal the enduring nature of the battle to assert self against its subversion. In the last resort, it is all there is to hold on to, which makes all the more peculiar its neglect by social scientists.

Chapter 5

The primacy of the self?

MODELS AND MUDDLES OF PRINCIPLE AND PRACTICE

The historical neglect of the self in anthropology clearly derives from paradigmatic views of what anthropology is, and how it should contribute to the project of social science. Over time, these views have focused on 'institutions', 'social relations', social and cognitive structures and culture. In part, these foci represented contemporary theoretical and normative statements about the possibilities of a social science, whether modelled on its essential similarity to, or inevitable difference from, natural science. In part, they were ways of imaging society and the relationship of the individual to society. These theories and images were complicated by sectarian disciplinary interests – immortalised by Gluckman and Devons as 'closed systems' and 'the limits of naïveté' (1964) – and by methodological dogmas, both of which produced orthodoxies laden with ideological and/or professional values. These made attention to the self and its relation to society a particularly fraught matter, sometimes a dialogue of the wilfully deaf. At different times to have been accused of 'holism' or of methodological individualism was tantamount to the accusation of a definitely deviant failing. Even now we seem to reserve less sympathy for structural-functionalists than for flat earthers, and 'positivism' remains a term of abuse.

I do not intend to rehearse any of these positions here, but just to draw attention to how this contest of frailties has complicated the inclusion of the self within our disciplinary charter. In the Introduction to his *Political Systems of Highland Burma* (1954), arguably among the most important seventeen pages of theoretical argument published in British anthropology, Leach propounded the virtues of the 'as if' model. Social structures, he insisted, are really ideas about the distribution of power, ideas which differ among individuals but which they can express through their shared cultural forms, especially ritual (Leach 1954: 4). Now, the relationship of idea to 'reality' was hardly a novel philosophical issue. But what was novel in Leach's argument was its explicit acknowledgement of ethnography as a second-order idealism, in which the putative social structure (body of ideas) described by the anthropologist is itself an idealised construct of her or his own making. Of course, Weber had advocated the use of such models as a desirable analytical device for historical and sociological explanation. For Leach, the desirability or otherwise of such models was hardly the point. Their construction and use were inevitable features of human cognition; the virtue of anthropological models rested on the theoretical sophistication with which they approximated to and explained the models in use among the people under study.

Leach referred to the anthropological model as an 'as if system of ideas' (1954: ix), clearly intending to emphasise the problematic relationship between an empirical phenomenon and its description. The substance of his study is the depiction of the substantiation and transformation of such models among the Kachin communities, focusing especially on forms of political order, marriage and ritual. The argument touched explicitly on the failure of other anthropologists (inter alia, Radcliffe-Brown, Fortes, Evans-Pritchard and Gluckman) to recognise that their interpretative models skewed the data which they ordered to the extent that their essentially hypothetical character masqueraded as 'reality'. Leach's critique was aimed most trenchantly at the use of equilibrium models, and led him to argue for the historical contextualisation of ethnographic accounts. However, he did not show generally how analysts could avoid the problem of 'as if' models validating themselves by constituting the very data which they were intended to explain.

It is a familiar problem in social anthropology and cognate subjects. It has an added piquancy in anthropological studies for one frequently finds, as among the Kachin, that people describe their society as being ordered by an 'as if' principle, when this principle is consistently subverted in practice, or when the principle provides a convenient gloss over the subtleties and complexities of differing practices. This juxtaposition of principle and practice has been observed in a number of culture areas, perhaps most often in Mediterranean societies (e.g. Pitt-Rivers 1972; Peters 1967, 1976; Khuri 1970; Holy 1989), and I shall offer some further instances shortly. It is a matter which is particularly relevant to our present concerns for the juxtaposition may often be translated into one of society and individual, in which the putative doctrine of society disguises the empirical reality of individuality, constituting an indigenous 'as if' model which fools the anthropologist into supposing that individuality in such a society is aberrant, and that selfhood is simply culturally alien. That is to say, we (the analysts) construct the society's rules in accordance with the publicly expressed and affirmed *principles* in a way which excludes the *practices* of self-hood, and then we attribute the absence of selfhood to the society rather than to our own 'as if' models.

Whether our fallacies are the consequence of our credulity, of our theoretical prejudices or of the complexities of translation, the consequence has been the same. The societies we have constructed have been overordered, implausibly systematised, bloodlessly regimented by organisational principles; and we therefore have good reason to doubt their veracity. I offer the following ethnographic example as an instance both of the difference between principle and practice, and of how individuals' exercise of their ingenuity can resolve these dialectics without subverting the principled bases of social structure.

DESCENT AND MARRIAGE ON TORY ISLAND

It is hardly novel to suggest that social life is peppered with contradictions, with the tensions which they can create if they are not satisfactorily resolved, and by the rich variety of cultural devices which are dedicated to their resolution or management. It is a theme to which anthropology has long been sensitive, and has been approached from many theoretical perspectives. It underlay Malinowski's theory of the charter function of myth. Malinowski argued that the purpose of myth was to situate and thereby to legitimate an event, a decision or some historical process in order to contrive the appearance of its consistency with tradition: to endow it with the sacredness of tradition. The tactical logic is compelling: 'our forefathers treated these principles as sacrosanct: therefore, they must be appropriate for us too.' It was precisely this competence which Malinowski imputed to myth as the invocation of a charter.

Although his *mythologiques* proceeded from different theoretical premises, Lévi-Strauss also acknowledged that myth resolves contradictions. Of course his analysis is built upon the identification of oppositions within myths, the point of the myth being to achieve a mediation or synthesis between them. Nor would he dissociate himself from the functionalist proposition that the resolution of such contradictions is necessary in order to forestall or relieve the crises which might follow a failure to reconcile them.[1] Leach insisted that Lévi-Strauss lived quite happily with Malinowski's charter functionalism (Leach 1967b: xvii).

The point is that an alternative to viewing structure as the determinant of behaviour is to see it instead as providing a framework of principles which is so all-encompassing that it can even accommodate their very subversion. People act within the framework of, and in the knowledge of, principles, but not necessarily in strict accordance with them. Indeed, their behaviour may well seem to contradict the principles, but to do so without causing critical disorder or revolution. As Robin Fox trenchantly remarked (with Geertz clearly in his sights),

> most of 'culture' consists not in 'values of and for behaviour' . . . but in the fantasies we weave to explain away our inability to keep even the simplest of our self-made rules, to say nothing of those handed down from heaven.

> (Fox 1982: 51)

His studies of Tory Island kinship have provided us with some fascinating examples (*inter alia*, Fox 1978 and 1982).

Tory is a small island lying some nine miles off the coast of Donegal, Ireland. During the period of Fox's fieldwork in the late 1950s and early 1960s, its population numbered about three hundred Gaelic speakers who subsisted on a combination of small-scale agriculture, seasonal fishing, and government subsidies of various kinds. There was a strong tradition of locally endogamous marriage, and islanders frequently commented to him on the universality of their interrelationships. Fox was able to trace relationships of blood and/or marriage between any two islanders. However, in circumstances such as these where most people could be said technically to be related to each other, without the addition of some extra quality or criterion, kinship loses its meaning and utility as a means of discriminating kin from non-kin. One therefore finds pragmatic and somewhat arbitrary discriminations being made. Two people may be related to Ego in the same degree, but Ego will acknowledge only one as a kinsman. This was precisely what I found in Whalsay (Cohen 1987). It would appear that the discrimination of kin was a little more systematic than this on Tory Island, or was at least made to look more systematic, and, therefore, to create the illusion of responding in practice to a structural principle.

One of the principles was that descent should be traceable back to an ancestor at least four generations removed from one's oldest living relative. In practice, this meant seven generations removed from Ego. In a community with such a small population and in which local endogamy had been the near-invariable rule, it would hardly be surprising to find the entire population to be interrelated, and to be able to trace multiple links between any two people. However, genealogical memory is always incomplete:

> What they know are the exact links for varying generations of every islander to a select group of focal ancestors who lived in the latter half of the eighteenth century.

(Fox 1982: 54)

Exact links between ancestors further removed than this were incomplete and imprecise. To cover this imprecision, there had emerged the term *clann* (progeny) to signify relationship. *Clann* was really a conceptual resource: people who could be claimed as kin, even by specifying a hypothetical degree of 'grandchildship', or, alternatively, whose kinship could be disowned, or who could be treated as less significant kin, because the relationship was not known precisely.

In principle, descent on Tory was cognatic. Therefore, if the four-generation rule was applied, Ego would have had available a minimum of eight lines through which she or he could have claimed descent. But to complicate matters still further, Tory genealogies were not reckoned from ego upwards (cognatic systems usually being thought of as ego-focused) but, because of the *clann* principle, from the ancestors downwards.[2] In this system it is obvious that any one descendant would belong to a number of different *clanna*. Therefore, the local Tory Island genealogists established four major genealogies which, with overlapping memberships, were always rendered in full. Seventy per cent of the islanders could be reckoned as belonging to these four *clanna*. Added to their originators were five 'independent ancestors', to make a total of twenty-three 'original' ancestors from whom all Tory Islanders should be able to claim descent. In practice, the reckoning of descent is a less precise matter than this theory would suggest, for the simple reason that the spouses of lineal descendants were frequently forgotten, unidentified or unknown in the system, and might be lumped together into a residual category, perhaps 'outsider', or treated as belonging to another *clann*.

How did practice compromise these principles? Tory Islanders were known by their personal names, rather than by their surnames, and these constituted a string: personal name, mother's name, father's name (for this *was* a cognatic system), and possibly the grandparents' names. Suppose the question had been the relationship between Willie-Hannah-Tom and Kitty-Mary-William. The genealogist would have said that they were both members of the *clann* Rory, and would have recited, 'Willie-Hannah-Tom-Jimmy-Séamus-Rory', and 'Kitty-Mary-

William-Annie-Willie-Rory' (Fox 1982: 58). But people were not referred to in this kind of depth; and, in any case, descent could not have been so unambiguous as portrayed in this formulation: everyone potentially had as many strings of names as they had ancestors in any generation, and obviously no articulation of descent could include all the possibilities. So Fox observed that

> from all the theoretical strings of names a person might have, he will only in fact have a few of these 'activated' on his behalf. . . .
>
> (Fox 1982: 58)

So, the *principle* was that each individual was descended from one of the twenty-three original ancestors. But in genealogical *practice* the principle was subverted and became, 'anyone ought to be able to trace descent, through such naming, back to one of the ancestors'. There is a clear difference between them. The principle states that everyone has a fixed place in the system; the pragmatic qualifier suggests that it ought to be *possible* to contrive a niche for everyone within the system. Fox pointed to a corollary: 'any people who claim an ancestor in common should find their names converge on that ancestor' (Fox 1982: 59). But, of course, because of overlapping *clann* memberships, one would always be able to contrive such a convergence, or, if one chose, to avoid it, and in either case to produce a genealogical reckoning as a validation in a similar way to that in which Malinowski saw the use of charter myths as legitimations.

What was the point of all this contrivance and fiddling? One of the answers is to be found in the pragmatics of marriage and inheritance. The immediate heirs of a landowner had an equal entitlement to inherit. But Tory is a small island and the supply of land is all too finite. If everyone had actually inherited equally, the land would have been divided and subdivided continuously in a process of infinite fragmentation. Entitlement to land was crucial for reasons other than the subsistence it might generate – which, in truth, was very little for most of the island:

> Without at least a cow's grass, one has no stake in the island, no place in the social scheme of things.
>
> (Fox 1978: 85)

Above all, without land one could not marry. Paradoxically, the average size of landholdings remained fairly constant between the mid-nineteenth and mid-twentieth centuries. How could this be? The principle was that every heir of a landholder had an entitlement to an equal share of his land. In practice, the principle was circumvented: 'owner-ship' was vested not in the occupant, but in the *clann* of the original recognised owner (ibid.: 124). Because of the ancestor-downward principle of descent, everyone retained a residual *claim* to the land, regardless of who was occupying and using it at any time. The rights of occupancy did not include the right of disposal, because that would infringe the rights of all those who retained a legitimate claim to the land. In effect, it was held in usufruct (Fox 1982: 61). The problem posed by the limited supply of land for those with potentially competing claims was alleviated by the ability to activate a residual claim by engaging in one of these genealogical manoeuvres. If one *clann* did not offer an available holding, the person in need could activate one of his other *clann* memberships, and place himself as a would-be claimant in another line of descent pertinent to a holding which just happened to be available.

The individual pragmatically articulated genealogy with marital necessity. The result, says Fox,

> is a rational distribution of land that is perhaps the best solution for this particular terrain and population.
>
> (Fox 1978: 126)

It is a nice case of the individual piloting himself around the navigational hazards of structural principles, which he reinterprets and re-configures as his ingenuity permits. Tory Island men exercised this pragmatic ingenuity as well in the ways in which they justified their recruitment of seasonal herring fishing crews. Because of the number of men required, they had to go beyond the *clann*, yet also had to be able to present recruitment as principled rather than merely arbitrary. The principle was: 'all people are related'; its expedient modification: 'but some are more related than others'. To get round the problem of numbers, ties of affinity were invoked to complement those of descent. Recruitment was then displayed in terms of relationship to the core members of the crew, moving outwards. Fox's examples are interesting for the way in which they move freely across affinal boundaries: the owner's FaBroSo, then his FaBroSoSoHuMoBro, and so forth. Obviously, such routes would have been almost inexhaustible, and were so tortuous that they could not actually have motivated recruitment. Rather, they made an ego-focused network look as if it was articulated by the logics of descent and affinity (Fox 1978: 136ff.; 1982: 66ff.).

Perhaps the most intriguing instance of the dialectic of principle and practice on Tory was the peculiar incidence of married couples who did not cohabit. The principle expressed the holiness of marriage, using the Holy Family as its archetype: the nuclear family under its own roof. But the *practice* was that the intending marriage of children was disliked and resisted by the parents. It activated a child's claim to inheritance; it broke the coresident nuclear family; and it deprived ageing parents of domestic labour and support. In practice, therefore, marriage tended to be contracted at a late and often post-childbearing age. They used a variety of expedient devices to reconcile principle and practice. Illegitimacy was tolerated as preferable to an unwelcome marriage. And cohabitation was frequently postponed until the last dependent parent had died, despite the fact that the couple may have acquired a marital home when they married (Fox 1978: 163–85).

The eccentricities of Tory Island ingenuity aside, it must be clear that the survival of any society over time requires a conviction among its members that the regime of social life allows them creative and interpretative space to fashion its organising principles. The social determination of individuals simply cannot be sustained in the long run. To take Weber's ideal typical forms of authority: traditional hegemonies wilt; charismatic regimes become routinised; and bureaucratic structures are subordinated by the informal social processes created by their members. The most totalitarian, self-denying autocracies seem eventually to collapse in on themselves. As I argued in the last chapter, the relationship of formal organisational structures to actual practice is problematic.

It is undeniably the case that many people, perhaps most, do feel the constraints of society; some – many – feel powerless in the larger scheme of things. Yet, in other than extreme circumstances, people do exercise considerable discretion, even some autonomy, in the conduct of important aspects of their lives, to an extent of which they may not always be aware. I am not invoking here, far less defending, philosophies of possessive, political or market individualism. Rather, my concern is with how people see and make sense of the world and their position in it. What I am suggesting is that these are *their* perceptions. People may suppose that they are shared by others, but they nevertheless claim ownership of them, even though they may lack confidence in their correctness. They may be hedged around with disclaimers of competence: 'I may be wrong, but I think that. . .' but the pronoun is significant. It puts their selves at the centre of their worlds. The self has primacy.

WORDS AND WORLD-MAKERS

What might such a claim mean? Certainly not that the self is auto-nomous – such a claim would be facile. Selves are acted upon; they *are* social. They are also cultural. But the self is not passive as a subject of society and of culture; it has agency, is active, proactive and creative. Constituted by society and made competent by culture, individuals make their worlds through their acts of perception and interpretation. The external world is filtered and, in the process, remade, by the self. It is in this sense that the self is the centre and the premise of the individual's world. Rorty calls this primacy 'contingency', and also recognises the individual self as world-maker:

> Since truth is a property of sentences, since sentences are dependent for their existence upon vocabularies, and since vocabularies are made by human beings, so are truths.
>
> (Rorty 1989: 21)

Rorty's argument is based on his juxtaposition of such individual creativity to a philosophical tradition which posits an absolute reality (or truth) external to the individual by whom it must be discovered. This clearly parallels paradigmatic oppositions in the social sciences, but also focuses on the more subtle distinction between 'forms' and 'meanings' on which I touched earlier. As we have already seen in this chapter, societies contrive masking devices which may conceal for certain purposes the differences between appearance and reality. For example, there is no suggestion in Fox's exposition that Tory Islanders are deliberately duplicitous in their genealogical constructions. Rather, they attempt to formulate their necessarily pragmatic decisions in a principled idiom. It is not just a cosmetic exercise undertaken for the benefit of the outside world, but may also be required by the disciplines of local discourse. To revert to Rorty's terms, culture is articulated by vocabularies and sentences to which particular value is given. The words may exist and be used elsewhere in other cultures, in which they are not valued similarly.

But a valued word does not a shared meaning make. It is an item of currency, available to the various parties to a transaction who may all acknowledge its exchange value; but it does not dictate to them how they must use it, or what its relative value shall be to each of them. Variability of meaning and value is not peculiar to complex and heterogeneous cultures. It is a characteristic of the self-centred interpretative process as such and therefore occurs everywhere. That anthropologists have neglected it or have failed to recognise it is a consequence of their theoretical inclination to generalise, rather than of the kinds of social and cultural milieux which they have studied.

A notable departure from these assumptions of culturally induced uniformity is to be found in the work of Nigel Rapport. His *Diverse Worldviews in an English Village* (1993) is a microscopic study of interpretative differences, concealed by a shared vocabulary, among a handful of closely related individuals in the remote English upland village of Wanet. Rapport shows how each of them spins the common verbal currency into individually distinctive 'loops' of meaning which constitute their respective 'world views'. These individuals believe that they share the meanings of the words they transact with each other, just as they believe that they think alike about their principal ideological compass points. They resent 'offcomers' (outsiders), despise intrusive officialdom, and seem generally to regard themselves as the last repositories of whatever may still be worth preserving of the English heritage. They are self-made, hard-working yeomen, struggling to preserve the integrity of their culture against a debased world full of intellectuals, urbanites, immigrants and bureaucrats which they see as pressing in upon them ever more insistently.

Yet, notwithstanding their broadly similar orientations to the world and despite their long and intimate associations with each other – the two central characters are affines and had been friends since childhood – they are engaged in a dialogue of the deaf. They use familiar words, but talk straight past each other, since each imputes to these shared verbal forms significantly different meanings based upon their *personal* experience, on which their selfhood rests. The meanings do not just differ but, as Rapport skilfully shows, they are mutually antagonistic. Indeed, rather like picking at scabs, he unravels a kitchen table conversation among parents and their adolescent children to expose them all as being, apparently unknowingly, at odds with each other.

Rapport's point in this somewhat dispiriting excavation is not to show merely that shared cultural forms conceal a multitude of substantive differences, but, perhaps more importantly, that it is by appropriating these forms in their individually distinctive ways that individuals constitute their selves – and, thereby, make their worlds:

> To talk through a self . . . is to bring it to life, for saying is doing. . . .
> (Rapport 1993: 152)

Individuals order their worlds by applying their world views to them:

Through language, individuals become origins of action upon the universe and centres of experience within it.

(Rapport 1993: 152)

The people of Wanet are revealed as habitual users of 'as if' models who find in them precisely the self-validating competence that we noted earlier when discussing Leach's advocacy of them. It will not do to dismiss Rapport's ethnography as an expression of English individualism, for Kondo makes a similar argument with respect to individuals in Japan, showing how 'selves are constructed variously in specific situations', and that 'these constructions can be fragmented by multiplicity, contradiction, and ambiguity . . .' (Kondo 1992: 41).

One would not have to go all the way with Rapport in order to acknowledge the proposition that 'speaking is self-actualising'. Regardless of what 'saying' actually 'does', saying is manifestly *being*. By assimilating the world to their characteristic world views, these individuals continuously confirm themselves by contriving to find that the world inevitably conforms to their expectations of it:

We find them seeing what they expect to see . . . their worldviews acting as self-fulfilling prophecies whose meanings are self-sustaining.

(Rapport 1993: 153)

It is important to stress that these processes (poetics, for Rorty) which eventuate in highly diverse selves are conducted within the shared idiomatic forms of a given culture. It is precisely by attending to individuals' diversities and discrepancies of meaning (which are the expressions of their selves) that Rapport shows how the self can be made competent by culture without being subjugated by it. Although he does not remark on it, it is perhaps not insignificant that the differences of interpetation which he sketches so graphically are largely judgemental, or are cast in judgemental mode. In his argument with Geertz, Rorty explicitly associates self-consciousness with the capacity to take moral positions. An excessive concern to avoid ethnocentrism risks the loss of 'any capacity for moral indignation, any capacity to feel contempt' (Rorty 1991: 203). In this condition of non-judgemental liberalism,

We (would) have become so open-minded that our brains (would) have fallen out

(Rorty 1991: 203)

and our sense of selfhood would have dissolved. Perhaps it is truistic to remark on the capacity for thought as the essential property of the self;

but it does underline the inadequacy of those more conventional anthropological views of the individual as a mechanical regurgitator of social doctrine and as the culture writ small.

The implications of this argument for the architecture of anthropological argument would seem to be quite serious. They indicate that the relationship between culture and society on the one hand, and the individual on the other, must be regarded as problematic. They suggest that the dynamic of society must be sought among individuals as well as at the collective, institutional and structural levels. They clearly call into question the facile generalisation of individuals into 'cultures', and require us to address the thorny issue of quite where culture is located.

CULTURE, BOUNDARY, CONSCIOUSNESS

It would surely be both presumptuous and unnecessary to rehearse here the shifts which the concept of culture has undergone in Western scholarship.[3] Suffice it to say that it remains the key concept, both as the explanatory referent of social behaviour, and as the paradigmatic template for anthropological explanation. Not surprisingly, our concepts of culture have tracked prevailing developments in social science theory and methodology. For example, structural-functionalism rested on the proposition that the major institutional domains of social life – the economy, polity and legal system – could be separated from each other analytically and, therefore (this being an 'as if' model), empirically. Culture was defined as the functional subsystem which integrated them and made them consistent with each other. It was because of this integrative emphasis that the encultured person was depicted as a conformist, as the embodiment of the normality which is logically entailed in the concept of function. Culture provided the shared values, the common ways of behaving, which underpinned and valorised the structural mechanisms by which the person was bound to society. Durkheim's view that the unintegrated *individual* indicated the existence of a social pathology persisted throughout the history of this sociological approach, even if anomic and other antisocial behaviours were conceptually softened into 'subcultures'. Society was composed of 'individuals' integrated by culture and thus transformed into 'persons' whose behaviour was determined by it. The various deterministic theories which have appeared in twentieth-century social science have operated in similar fashion, whether the significant variable has been relations of production, ecology, technology, or culture itself. In all of them, the individual was treated as a micro-replicate of the larger social and cultural entity.

With the demise of these modernistic grand theories and the advent of 'the interpretative turn' in its various guises, the tendency has been to treat culture much more loosely, as that which *aggregates* people and processes, rather than integrates them. As noted in the last chapter, this distinction is important, for aggregation implies *difference* among people rather than similarity. If we think of culture as aggregation, it is entirely plausible to conceive of Rapport's Wanet villagers as participants in the same culture who nevertheless manifest pronounced differences from each other of which they may be quite unaware. Notwithstanding the misuse of the word in lay speech, to speak of a culture is not to postulate a large number of people who are merely clones of each other and of some organising principle.

Moreover, if culture is not *sui generis*, exercising a determining power over people, then it must be regarded as the product of something else: if not the logical replicate of other social processes – for example, relations of production – then of social interaction itself. In this perspective, we have come to see culture as the outcome and product of social interaction, or, to put it another way, to see people as active in the creation of culture, rather than passive in receiving it. Therefore our ethnographic constructions and anthropological explanations cannot now derive the behaviour of individuals from the axiomatic premise of culture. It is precisely this relationship between the individual and the collective that has to be recognised as problematic. I turn to the topics of ethnic identity and of boundary to illustrate this further.

Rather like the word 'culture', ethnicity suffers from the confusion of being a technical term which has been imported into ordinary language use and abuse in which it can signify anything from racial difference to sectarianism. It can be appropriated to signify denigration or valorisation. In anthropology itself, having passed through a number of theoretical transformations which need not detain us here, the term has settled on a faintly neutral application. Ethnicity has come to be regarded as a mode of action and of representation: it refers to a decision people make to depict themselves or others symbolically as the bearers of a certain cultural identity. The symbols used for this purpose are usually mundane, drawn from everyday life, rather than from elaborate ritual or ceremonial occasions. In effect, ethnicity has become the politicisation of culture (cf. Paine 1984: 212). In part, therefore, it is a claim to a particular culture, with all that such claims entail. They are rarely neutral. The statement made in Ethiopia, 'I am Oromo' (or in Northern Ireland, 'he's a Prod'), is clearly not merely descriptive: it has an added negative or positive value, depending on who is speaking and to whom.

One aspect of the charged nature of cultural identity is that in claiming one, you do not merely associate yourself with a set of characteristics: you also distance yourself from others. This is not to say that contrast is necessarily the *conscious* motivation for such claims as some writers have argued (a matter we shall come to shortly), but it is implicit and is understood, the more so the more highly charged the situation may be. It is certainly the case that anthropology was long dominated by the view, primarily associated with Fredrik Barth, that ethnicity (politicised cultural identity) was merely contrastive: that it is invoked primarily to draw a real or conceptual boundary.

The argument pursued in the present book suggests that this view must be unsatisfactory, since it rests on the assumption that ethnicity is simply generalised to the members of a group, and is not implicated in their self-perceptions other than as bearers of a given ethnic identity. In treating ethnicity only as a tactical posture, it ignored both self consciousness and the symbolic expression of ethnic identity. When we consult ourselves about who we are, that entails something more than the rather negative reflection on 'who we are *not*'. It is also a matter of autobiography: of things we know about ourselves, of the persons we believe ourselves to be. The symbolic expression of ethnicity renders it multivocal. Suppose that I identify myself as Tamil rather than as Sri Lankan, I do not necessarily mean to suggest that I am just like every other Sri Lankan Tamil. I do not have to sublimate myself in an anonymising 'Tamilness' in order to suggest that Tamils have something significant in common which distinguishes them from Sinhalese. But because ethnic identity *is* expressed through symbols, it is possible for this internal heterogeneity to be preserved, even while masked by common symbolic forms.

I put these two matters together – the self-consciousness of ethnicity, and the symbolic form of ethnic identity – to suggest that the political expression of cultural identity has two distinctive registers to which we should attend. The first is used for apparently dogmatic statements of more or less objective doctrine: 'I am a Palestinian' – and certain things will be understood as following from that. The second is for contentious statements which treat ethnicity as the context of, or as an aspect of, identity with very *un*certain implications: 'I am a *particular* Palestinian'. The apparently monolithic or generalised character of ethnicity at the collective level thus does not preempt the continual reconstruction of ethnicity at the personal level. Ethnicity is not a dogma, although in certain circumstances political leaders and others may attempt to politicise it to the point at which they can enforce it dogmatically

(Apter 1963). But this is comparatively rare, since ethnicity is so frequently a matter of dispute and cannot often command consensus for longer than the brief period of a specific campaign. Ethnicity has a definite appearance but rather indefinite substance.

This same discrimination of appearance from reality, of substance from insubstantiality, is pertinent to the related idea of 'boundary'. This most topical of terms, or the entity which it expresses, seems recently to have preoccupied the social sciences, prompted by the development of supranational entities such as the European Union, and by the collapse of the central European state socialist empires. In the attempt to shed some conceptual light on a categorical morass, the political scientist Malcolm Anderson attempts to distinguish among 'frontier', 'boundary' and 'border':[4]

> Frontier is the word with the widest meaning. . . . In contemporary usage, it can mean the precise line at which jurisdictions meet, usually demarcated on the ground with posts, stones or fences and controlled by customs, police and military personnel. Frontier can also refer to a region. . . . Even more broadly, frontier is used in specific cases to refer to the vast interior of a continent. . . . The term border can be applied to a zone, usually a narrow one, or it can be the line of demarcation. . . . The word boundary is always used to refer to the line of delimitation or demarcation and is thus the narrowest of the three terms.
>
> (Anderson n.d.: 7, fn. 14)

His usage is similar to that proposed by Coakley:

> Political geographers conventionally distinguish between *boundaries*, which have a precise, linear quality, and *frontiers*, which have more diffuse, zonal connotations. The concept of frontier has a broader social significance than the more restrictive legal concept of boundary.
>
> (Coakley 1982: 36)

The confusions among these words, all of which express the condition of contiguity, are those of ordinary usage rather than of science. It might be helpful to think less in terms of discriminating among them on the grounds of their putative referents – since ordinary language will not honour such precision – than in terms of how they are used and what they are used for. In the discourse of anthropology, such a taxonomy of concepts and attitudes (rather than of concrete empirical referents) would suggest almost the opposite of Anderson's and Coakley's surveys: that 'boundary' is the word with the most general application (since, in anthropology, it has been used to signify such diverse things); whereas border seems situationally specific, and frontier has come to be reserved to fairly strictly limited geo-political and legal applications.

In an essay on the implications for the Irish border of the European Union's 'internal market', Thomas Wilson (1993) sets out a rather different definitional schema to Anderson's. He treats the 'frontier' as a barrier: in effect, as the statutory point at which the free flow of goods is halted and is permitted to continue only on payment of a tax or by permission of an official gatekeeper of some kind. The 'border' and the 'boundary' both suggest to him hazier kinds of dividing line which may be matters of symbolic construction and which are different from, although related to, *The Border*. *The Border* clearly designates a statutory or historical division which, despite its political specificity, does not contain meaning unambiguously. Its meaning is a matter for construction and elaboration (as is also the case with the [mere] border or boundary).

The application to contiguous social units of a distinction between material and symbolic divisions is uncontentious. Anderson acknowledges its persuasiveness. One of Wilson's points is to draw attention to The Border as a concrete referent of social organisation and identity, and to the border as an idea. But this discrimination requires him to make 'border' and 'boundary' synonymous. The distinction between Border and border is cumbersome (and vulnerable to mistakes of typesetting and proof-reading!). The distinction can be accomplished simply by regarding frontiers and borders as matters of fact, whereas boundaries are the subjects of claim based on a perception by at least one of the parties of certain features which distinguish it from others. Whether it refers to a collective condition, such as ethnic group identity, or to something as ephemeral as 'personal space', boundary suggests contestability, and is predicated on consciousness of a diacritical property.[5]

There is a tendency among anthropologists (and, indeed, among other social scientists who write about ethnicity) to credit the concept of boundary to Barth's seminal symposium, *Ethnic Groups and Boundaries* (1969), and, by implication, to associate it with ethnicity (or, as the subtitle of Barth's book put it, with the social organisation of cultural difference). But the concept is really much more fundamental to the discipline and to the nature of our enquiry. When anthropologists defined the subject as tne study of other cultures, they necessarily (if unwittingly) placed 'boundary' at the very centre of their concerns. The relativism of anthropologist/anthropologised, us/them, self/other, clearly implies boundary. The early modern British ethnographers may have been innocent or unaware of this implication, for they were clearly distanced hierarchically from those they studied. There is no reason to infer from anything they wrote that Malinowski and Evans-Pritchard regarded the barriers between themselves and their subjects as being mutually negotiable. To apply the concept of boundary to the division between people may not necessarily imply their equality, but it does suggest the possibility of being crossed, *from both sides*, a movement which these scholars would have regarded as improper, even if they granted its feasibility. Other people were divided by boundaries; but *we* were separated from *them* by the intractable differences of type.

This view has changed radically as anthropology has developed. Ethnographers have increasingly aspired to equality with the people they have studied, and some have certainly toyed with the ambition to cross boundaries. The recent widespread preoccupation in the discipline with the relationship of self and other has provided evidence of this ambition, and much of our recent theoretical and methodological debate has been concerned with the question of how, and the extent to which, it may be realisable. It is essentially an ambition to connect consciousnesses.

However, this ambition has to be tempered by an increased awareness of its audacity and of the degree to which it risks subverting the very enterprise of anthropology itself. Less ethnocentric than his predecessors, Evans-Pritchard was sensitive to the problems of moving cognitively across boundaries: the languages of either side could not be regarded as simply equivalent to each other, since they were born of cultures which might well be incongruent. Hence the difficulty, as he presented it, of bridging the conceptual gap between Western rationalism and Azande mysticism. He saw it as a problem of translation which could be settled only by invoking the device of relativism. Flawed though his position may have been, it still seems rather more sophisticated than the arguments which emerged contemporaneously from phenomenological philosophy and from symbolic interactionist sociology which seemed to assume the routine feasibility of, what was portentously referred to as, 'intersubjectivity'. Perhaps I do an injustice here to writers such as Schutz and Blumer, but anthropologists do seem to have recognised more quickly that the possibility of a meeting of minds depended largely on their compatibility. My caveat is that they did not take this reservation far enough.

The problem became fixed as one inhering in the distance between *cultures* rather than between *minds*. Anthropology has been preoccupied with the boundaries between cultures. As we have seen earlier in this book, it has preferred to avoid the boundaries between minds, between consciousnesses, either because these have been regarded as too difficult to cross (e.g. Needham 1981), or because such a refocusing of enquiry would have subverted the disciplinary practice of generalisation and its conceptual bases. This more fundamental problem has been shoved aside simply by predicating consciousness on culture, which is itself anthropologically constructed as being different from, and therefore 'relative to', *other* cultures. In doing this, anthropologists have replicated the lay practice of cultural exaggeration which Boon saw as the *raison d'être* and necessary condition for culture (Boon 1982).

One consequence of this has been that anthropologists have been largely content to assume the existence and integrity of collective boundaries. Rather than questioning their existence, or questioning the extent to which they might reasonably be generalised (*whose* boundaries are they?), they have been concerned almost exclusively with the ways in which boundaries are marked. There have been significant theoretical debates concerning the differences among the ways in which they have done this, and concerning the nature of the boundary-marking devices and processes which they have attributed to people. But there is little room for doubt that their concern has not extended to the more fundamental question. It has been so central an ethnographic preoccupation that examples would be somewhat gratuitous, but to give just an idea of their range: it could be found among Leach's 'aesthetic frills', those non-technical aspects of ritual which express collective identity by emphasising cultural possession (1954: 12). It was explicitly at the heart of Schwartz's depiction of the 'ethnognomomic' activities of Admiralty Islanders (Schwartz 1975). It was strikingly and movingly present in Eidheim's famous account of the reaction of Norwegian Saami to the stigma they supposedly perceived as attaching to them (Eidheim 1969); and it provided the material for the reformulation of migrant West Indian identities among the Notting Hill carnival participants described by Abner Cohen (1980, 1992).

So ubiquitous has this kind of work been, especially in studies of ethnicity and social identity, that we have taken for granted the integrity of its central concerns: to show how individuals are constructed in the images of their collective representations. It has imputed boundary-consciousness to people without pausing to enquire quite what it is that they are supposed to be conscious of. Appadurai has recently argued that boundary-consciousness in the form of 'the production of locality' may be contrived and constrained by operating within the matrices of global forms – which, however, do not necessarily diminish their localness (Appadurai 1993). This notion of the commoditisation of local identity, and of the boundary as its referent, may be useful. But it still does not ask what the individual is conscious of when she or he invokes a boundary as a means or source of social identity. In the ethnographic literature, people have been constructed in terms of putative boundaries (localities), and in terms of anthropologists' consciousness of boundaries, without adequately interrogating these notions.

Clearly, this is a criticism which could be made generally of anthropology, and not just of anthropologists' specialised attention to boundary. However, I suggested above that the concept of boundary must be regarded as central to anthropology, precisely because it addresses the essence of our task: to extend our own limited consciousness in order to comprehend another's. The argument throughout this book has been that self-consciousness provides a paradigm for this kind of interpretative endeavour. The centrality of this concern to the subject makes the discrimination of 'boundary' from cognate terms more than a matter of semantic nicety. The terms 'frontier' and 'border' (and boundary, if it is not distinguished from them) alert us to lines which mark the extent of contiguous societies, or to meeting points between supposedly discrete social groups. We have barely glanced at those more amorphous divisions which appear routinely, not just between cultures nor even within them, but between intimates who share culture. It is his attempt to repair this omission which makes Rapport's work so striking. As suggested above, we have shied away from, have even denied any interest in, the boundedness of the mind, the limits of consciousness which separate one self from another. We have excused ourselves from such an enquiry on the grounds that it would be too difficult, and that our concept of culture enables us to invent people who are similar to each other. Instead of dealing with the individual, we have restrained our ambition and addressed ourselves instead to whole societies or to substantial parts of them.

Once more we find that as soon as we begin to formulate questions about the self, the integrity of our customary generalisations appears doubtful. The adequacy of the simplistic ways in which we have tried to derive selfhood from culture has been powerfully questioned in work on Japan. In her study of craftsmen, Kondo argues that it is a fallacy to see individuality as being predicated on a cultural model of selfhood (Kondo 1990). There may well be cultural values which are associated with the achievement of certain statuses – for example, skilled artisanship – but these do not determine the composition of selfhood. They are among the qualities from which individuals craft their selves; and, indeed, apprenticeship to these crafts may well be seen as contributing to the enhancement of selfhood as well as to the acquisition of a skilled trade. But she shows that, far from conforming to a cultural matrix, the craftsmen construct selves which are complex, multifaceted, and informed by their perception of what is required in specific situations.

In a lucid exegesis of the elementary structures of Japanese selfhood, Takie Lebra argues that particular value is accorded to a selfhood which is so highly individualised, so impervious to social pressures, that it might be thought of as autonomous and even asocial (Lebra 1992). She identifies three dimensions of the self, of which the least valued (ibid.: 117) is the social or 'interactional'. This is the 'face-sensitive' self, tuned to the responses of others with whom it strives for empathy and sympathy. The highest order of selfhood, she suggests, is the 'boundless self', which amounts really to selflessness. Founded on a Buddhist transcendentalism, this collapses the boundaries between self and other, between subject and object, and is thus neither contingent nor absolute. It seems to me that it may be more appropriate to think of this as a highly idealised state of being, akin to Turner's *communitas*, an ideal which is the object of aspiration but rarely, if ever, of achievement.

Between these high and low orders of selfhood, Lebra locates the 'inner self', *kokoro*, identified with the heart or chest (in contrast to the face and mouth, loci of the interactional self). It is morally superior to the social self precisely because of its resistance to social pressure, its absoluteness:

> It is the inner self that provides a fixed core for self-identity and subjectivity, and forms a potential basis of autonomy from the ever-insatiable demands of the social world.
>
> (Lebra 1992: 112)

There is the strong implication that *kokoro* is the test of personal integrity:

> The inner self is also identified as the residence (shrine) of a god that each person is endowed with.
>
> (Lebra 1992: 112)

It represents the ascendancy of the spirit over matter.

Curiously, Ohnuki-Tierney completely ignores the notion of *kokoro* and the proposition of an inner or autonomous self (nor does she even refer to Lebra). To the contrary, she insists that the Japanese self, both at the levels of the collectivity and the individual,

> is constructed in a dialogic relation to the other – other individuals – in a given social context.
>
> (Ohnuki-Tierney 1990: 207)

in the Japanese conception, the self, individual or collective, is defined always in relation to the other.

(Ohnuki-Tierney 1990: 198)

Far from acknowledging the existence or importance of an asocial dimension of the self, she says that the Japanese

vision of society does not consist of atomized individuals (but) of interdependent individuals.

(Ohnuki-Tierney 1990: 207)

She goes so far as to use the term 'non-self' for 'the self without the other' (ibid.: 208), and it is clear that she does not have the higher-order, transcendental self in mind, but simply an impossible conception. I am bound to say that I distrust her version of the self, not least because she tries to make it do too much work. Rather than an inquiry into the self as such, she is concerned with it as one among a number of tropes which she sees as indicative of the imitative and refractive impulse in Japanese culture, and assimilates it to her more general examination of dualisms and oppositions. Thus, *she* constructs the self as contingent and ephemeral (see also Ohnuki-Tierney 1991), but then imputes her own version to Japanese as such. The three-level hierarchical self which Lebra outlines seems both more substantial and more convincing in its complexity.

These three dimensions of selfhood are embedded in a cultural vocabulary which is shared and transactable among Japanese, although pre- sumably subject to similar divergences of meaning and use as is the English of Rapport's Wanet villagers. But the actual construction of selves is clearly not generalisable: it is in the minds (or, more literally, the chests, stomachs, faces and mouths) of individuals to whom the boundaries of selfhood are not adequately expressed by those of Japan or of any other collectivities to which they may claim membership.

Perhaps the point may be clarified by turning back briefly to the subject of initiation. In dealing with ritualised status passage, we do not commonly seem to have explicitly applied the concept of boundary to divisions between statuses. Why should we not do so? We have the evocative notion of liminality to describe the blurriness of transformation and the acute consciousness of status on either side of it. This seems not unlike the exaggerated concern with social identity which is commonly found in geopolitical borderlands (e.g. Sahlins 1989; Brown 1990; Wilson 1993) to which I shall return shortly. But in ethnographic accounts the difficulties of passing from status to status seem curiously understated, as if such adjustments were as unambiguous, even if more troublesome, than crossing a national frontier: one moment you are in Spain, the next in France. The worst one is usually likely to suffer is a brief spell in no-man's land. So it is in accounts of initiation. One day the initiate is a child; the next, he or she is initiated and, after due process of seclusion, re-emerges into society bearing the new status of adult, or initiated youth, or marriageable girl. Fitz John Porter Poole's graphic account of the complexities and traumas of this transformation is the exception which demonstrates the general rule (Chapter 3, pp. 58–65). The confusion of liminality, the blurriness of being 'betwixt and between', or of being in the social equivalent of no-man's land, is somehow confined temporally by the ritual process and spatially to the initiates' lodge. It is ended by the next ritual phase of re-aggregation.

This hardly seems plausible. Transformations of status, like crossing geopolitical frontiers, require a process of adjustment, of rethinking, which goes beyond the didactic procedures about which we have been told so much. They require a reformulation of self which is more fundamental than admission to items of lore, or being loaded with new rights and obligations. The difficulties which inhere in such self-adjustment may vary according to the nature of the frontiers which are crossed; but our experience of politics and travel should also alert us to the deceptively innocuous character of crossing between supposedly proximate statuses or cultures. The first intimation to us that we are really in a different place may be the look of incomprehension on the faces of our interlocutors, or the pained censure by others of our newly inappropriate behaviour.

Boundaries are zones for reflection: on who one is; on who others are. There is no axiomatic rule which stipulates that the boundaries of selfhood are less significant in this regard than are those of collectivity. The subordination of self to society is achieved by power. Within the boundary zone self-contemplation does not merely refract the presence of the other, as the 'identity relativists' might suggest (see Chapter 1, pp. 9–11), but also expresses the *kokoro*, the inner self, the non-contingent identity. But if we may grant the existence of collective ideas of self-identity, even if as no more than aggregations or lowest common denominator expressions of individuals' thoughts, they may also be considered as having a similarly introspective character to those of the individual.

There is a real challenge to the practice of anthropology here. I have argued that we, and social scientists generally, have invented selves in the image of the generalisation 'culture': that to do otherwise was regarded either as improper or as too difficult. But we have also invented cultures by seeing them as reflexes of a boundary encounter: culture as a more or less self-conscious differentiation from a contiguous group; culture as 'playing the vis-à-vis' (Boon 1982); or, as in Barth's version, as modulating itself to the requirements of contingent social interaction and boundary transaction. If there is an absoluteness in self-identity, so also is there in collective identity. Anne Salmond has argued powerfully against the use of an easy relativism to understand the impact on Maori of their encounter with Europeans. Rather than bouncing their selves off the *pakeha*,

> In Maori epistemologies, the knowing self is constituted in relationship with ancestors and kinsfolk.
>
> (Salmond 1993: 22)

The Maori reference is not to the other (even if it may be occasioned by contact with the other) but to themselves in the genealogical guise of their forebears and descent groups. She insists that the contingency model, the assumption that selfhood is constituted entirely by Lebra's 'interactional' dimension, is a device of occidentalism which denies equality to the other. Her argument expresses for collectivities what mine attempts for individuals. Anthropological practice has created the Other as Object:

> For objects have these negative properties in Western thought – they cannot speak, they cannot think, and they cannot know. 'Objectivity' creates an immediate epistemological privilege for the 'observer' – only he/she can truly know.
>
> (Salmond 1993: 18)

By this means, we provided ourselves with the justification for neglecting 'their own experience of the world' (ibid.), just as we have ignored self-perceptions. We cannot understand cultural boundaries without coming to terms with the discourse they enclose. We cannot do that without sensitivity to the claims and perceptions of those individuals who constitute the discourse.

If we recognise boundaries as matters of consciousness rather than of institutional dictation, we see them as being rather more amorphous and ambiguous than we otherwise have done. It may be this very ambiguity which inclines societies to invest their various boundaries so heavily with symbolism. The contributors to the symposium *Symbolising Boundaries* (Cohen 1986a), all describe such processes of marking in the rather less dramatic circumstances of the British Isles, whether dealing with the imagery of suburban Manchester or with adolescence in rural Northumberland. As a matter of ideology, the boundary may be given dogmatic form. But its internalisation in the consciousness of individuals renders it much less definitely.

This offers us a clue to the helpful discrimination of boundary from border. Border has about it the quality of finity, definity. When it is crossed, one has definitely moved from the Cerdagne to Cerdanya. That is undeniable, for my passport stamp tells me so. What is much less certain is what this crossing-point means to those who live on either side of it. The uncertainty may be glossed by language, currency, by law, lore and by all the iconography of custom and tradition. But, when all this is said and done, it remains a gloss on the much more ambiguous boundaries of consciousness. Borders seem to me to have something in common with the taxonomic absoluteness of anthropological categories; boundaries are more akin to the blurriness and elusiveness of symbols.

Of course it follows that if one does not know quite what it is that has been crossed, then one may also be unaware *that* a boundary has been crossed at all. As an English person resident in Scotland, I feel an intolerant dismay at the insensitivity of many incoming English people to the notion that in Scotland they are actually in a different place. With only a little reflection, the reader will be able to produce numerous instances from personal experience of people who fall over their idiomatic feet because of their cultural boundary errors, and this kind of insensitivity or clumsiness is also readily observable among those crossing unfamiliar status boundaries. Again, the examples are legion and perhaps do not need to be cited to make the elementary proposition that, as objective referents of meaning (rather than of political legitimacy), boundaries are essentially contestable while borders are not.

In an intriguing examination of Canadian fiction writing, Russell Brown has shown how central the border is to Canadian identity. Actually, his claim is more ambitious: 'the border is central to Canada's *self-awareness*' (Brown 1990: 32). There is a difficulty with this claim: countries are not self-aware; people are. If he is saying that the border is significant in individuals' awareness of themselves as being Canadian, that is fine. But if he is saying that in so far as individuals are aware of themselves it is *as* Canadians because the border looms so large, I would have to regard this with some scepticism, and as a failure to appreciate the complexity of self-identity. In a country composed of such heterogeneity, the 'significant others' are almost numberless:

> Canada is not so much a country as a holding tank filled with the disgruntled progeny of defeated peoples. French Canadians

consumed by self-pity; the descendants of Scots who fled the Duke of Cumberland; Irish the famine; and Jews the Black Hundreds. Then there are the peasants from the Ukraine, Poland, Italy and Greece, convenient to grow wheat and dig out the ore and swing the hammers and run the restaurants, but otherwise to be kept in their place. Most of us are still huddled tight to the border, looking into the candy-store window, scared by the Americans on one side and the bush on the other. And now that we are here, prospering, we do our damn best to exclude more ill-bred newcomers, because they remind us of our own mean origins in the draper's shop in Inverness or the *shtetl* or the bog.

(Richler 1991: 367)

Brown points to the ubiquity of oppositions as a theme in Canadian literature, but it does not need a structuralist to point out that there is nothing peculiarly Canadian, nor even 'border-ish', about this. Any anthropologist with experience of peripheral societies, or of societies in which boundaries are heavily invested symbolically, would have made similar observations – but not because of the *border*: the border is a social fact. Whether or not it signifies difference is a matter of social construction, and is more properly thought of as one of *boundary*. If border is fact, boundary is consciousness, and the difference between them is crucial. Brown muddies my waters by talking about border-consciousness: living on the border-line, on the edge, 'Canada's fear of being overwhelmed by American culture and values' (Brown 1990: 44). In Wilson's terms, this would be better described as consciousness of The Border.

I beg indulgence for suggesting a distinction the significance of which I can only assert but not demonstrate. There is a difference between being conscious of what is on either side of a border, and being preoccupied with the boundary as such. The first, again, implies definity: if I go this way, I will be X; if I go that way, Y. The latter seems to me more authentically boundary-conscious: liminal, aware that one is walking a risky line, but not knowing whether one risks falling up or down or what one might fall into. If this sounds unduly cryptic, I would say that it is this kind of uncertainty which drives people to grasp for certainty, and which in turn motivates identity. This may be formulated around a collective stereotype or dogma, such as 'Canada's self-awareness'. Or, it may proceed the other way around, by assimilating such cultural products to self-experience. Writing with respect to the Cerdagne/Cerdanya border, and following Benedict Anderson, Sahlins says that national identity appeared less as a result of state intentions than from the local process of adopting and appropriating the nation without abandoning local interests, a local sense of place, or a local identity.

(Sahlins 1989: 9; see also 269–70)

Historically, anthropology has privileged the collective and dogmatic and neglected the individual and experiential, as a consequence of its general neglect of selfhood and self consciousness. It is a neglect which requires repair if we are really to get to grips with the meanings of boundaries. Sahlins argues here that national identity – the meaningful appropriation of a national boundary to a locality – is accomplished through the medium of local experience. Similarly, Appadurai (1993) maintains that global forms are locally mediated. I agree with both these writers, and have long argued the same point with respect to locality (see, e.g., Cohen 1986b). But if national identity rests on its substantiation by local consciousness, then the same logic suggests that local identity is informed and substantiated through individual consciousnesses. The locality is an aggregate of selves each of whom produces it for themselves. As Rapport shows, what these various productions have in common may well be more a matter of formal appearance than one of meaningful reality. The self has primacy in the creation of locality, in rendering boundaries meaningful, in the interpretation of national identity. It is the obvious point at which to begin.

Chapter 6

The thinking self

THINKING CULTURE

To assert the primacy of the self does not entail the redundancy of categories of collectivity, such as 'culture', 'society', 'ethnic group'. It does require that we cannot merely derive the individual self from these categories, and that we have therefore to regard their relationship as problematic. With the exception of some of the more eccentric post-modernists, there has been no serious aspiration or attempt in anthropology to deny the significance of the impact of culture and society on individuals. Such a position would be subversive of anthropology itself. The argument of this book is not to reduce social aggregates to their individual components. It is to insist, first, that individuals are more than their membership of and participation in collectivities, and, second, that collectivities are themselves the products of their individual members, so that ethnographic attention to individuals' consciousness of their membership is an appropriate way to understand the collectivity, rather than seeing it as constituted by an abstracted, if compelling, logic. Culture is and remains the key concept in anthropological thought. The investigation of self consciousness is another route to it, not an attempt to supplant it.

This may be the significant difference between the ways in which social anthropologists, on the one hand, and sociologists and social psychologists, on the other, approach the matter. Our concern is not with the individual self as such, but with the constitution and content of social relationships. This being so, one is bound to regard sceptically the conceptualisation by some sociologists of the 'existential self' as having 'recognized autonomy' and being 'an independent phenomenon' and 'free-floating' (Lyman 1984: vii). It is predicated on a view of society as being 'absurd' (Lyman and Scott 1970): formless, meaningless, insubstantial, an amorphous mass which is then pressed into their own shapes ('constituted') by individuals in social interaction. With other major sociological theorists such as Berger and Luckmann (1967) and Giddens, anthropologists have insisted that interaction must be seen in its *social* context. Individuals do not come to interaction asocially and without culture. Part of the debate within anthropology and with other social theorists has been about how to balance the individual with social forces in the explanation of behaviour. Part, related to this, has hinged around the issue of where we locate society and culture: in the overwhelming logic of productive relations? In cognitive structures? In integrative institutions and relationships? Or in the interpretative, sensemaking capacities of social members? This book reviews attempts to show how concern with this latter option can inform our understanding of social forces. I return to the concept of culture to suggest again why attention to the self is essential for the understanding of society.

Before 'agency' became a vogue term, Berger and Luckmann argued persuasively for the recognition of people's creativity in structuring their worlds of meaning (Berger and Luckman 1967). They credited to social actors the powers of 'externalisation' – the generation of meanings and their projection into the world. In the process of interaction, meanings may become so objectified as to acquire a compelling authority which returns to dominate them. They internalise these socially sanctioned meanings; but rather than merely reproducing them, they transform them and externalise these new meanings. The 'social construction of reality' is thus accomplished through the endless cycle of 'externalisation' → 'objectivation' → 'internalisation' (Berger 1973).

In the anthropological literature, the culture theory to which this most closely approximates is that of Geertz, expressed in his frequently quoted description of culture as the 'webs of significance' which people spin and in which they are then suspended (Geertz 1975: 5). Geertz's notion of culture is of a kaleidoscope, composed of a finite body of materials which can be rearranged by their user into numerous different shapes and further modulated by being held at different angles to the light. Geertz's model thus acknowledges members' capacity to manipulate cultural materials – symbols, rituals, religion, law, language and meaning – but stops short of conceding their power to create them. He moves away from the modernistic notions of objectively apparent meaning to argue that meaning is the product of interpretation. To this extent, culture might be regarded as being in the mind of the beholder. But it also imposes interpretative constraints on its bearers. As well as providing them with the conceptual and cognitive means by which to interpret ('models for'), it also provides them with models of interpretation.

The influence of the functionalist tradition, and particularly of its Parsonian expression, is evident here. Society protects itself from entropy by contriving to produce shared meanings in its members. Geertz is never shy of generalisation: Balinese villagers think alike; Modjokuto townspeople believe alike; Sefrouians know alike. Individuals know, think and believe in the image of their collective cultures, and anthropology's task is to pick away at their behaviour to reveal 'thickly', and to 'read over their shoulders' (Geertz 1975 [1972]: 452) as they read the deep symbolic texts of their culture. Culture is available to its bearers as 'an ensemble of texts'. As individuals, they can interpret these texts somewhat differently from each other (although in Geertz's ethnographies they seem not to) just as different musicians can make differing readings of the same score. But they are limited in their variability both by the finite number of texts and by the concepts with which their culture equips them to engage competently in the practice of interpretation.

By the rather different standards of ethnomethodology and of the so-called post-modern ethnographers who have followed him, Geertz's position may not seem in retrospect to be very radical. Yet, by shifting the anthropological view of culture from its supposedly objective manifestations in social structures, towards its subjective realisation by members who compose those structures, Geertz paved the way for anthropologists to recognise that culture is not an intractable social force imposed on members, but is continuously recreated by their interpretative prowess. He characterised this transition as being from 'laws-and-causes social physics' to a view of cultures as 'significative systems posing expositive questions' (Geertz 1983: 3). Basically, he depicted culture as being a more imprecise, much hazier idealistic system than the institutional configuration suggested by anthropologists from both sides of the Atlantic. He was seminal in leading anthropologists to regard culture as more a matter of thinking than of doing.

Perhaps not surprisingly, therefore, he was an important genitor of the interest in 'reflexivity', much though he may later have regretted its more extreme expressions and its deterioration into, what became known generically as, 'postmodern anthropology' (Geertz 1988; also, Rabinow 1977). The reflexive turn was clearly of great importance for the kind of argument I am making here. Anthropologists need to think about themselves in order to think about how other people think about themselves. The axiomatic self/other distinction on which the discipline had developed validated a lazy imputation to 'others' of modes of thought which were characterised by definition as being different, one of the many devices and artifices which justified their description as 'other', and thereby legitimated their selection as proper objects of anthropological study (see, e.g., Fabian 1983; McGrane 1989). It is perhaps an indication of its former intellectual insularity that anthropology took so long to recognise what it had been doing. The philosophers had arrived there much earlier. A heated exchange in the pages of *Mind* in 1950 culminated in a statement which was prescient for anthropology:

> Mr Flew (the interlocutor) would, I take it, have no objection to my talking about my being 'conscious of myself'. Nor should he object to the assumption that everyone is 'conscious of himself' in some sense. . . . This may be called the 'introspective point-of-view', and there is a sense, however oblique, in which, whoever the person that is being considered from the introspective point-of-view may be, the point-of-view from which he is being considered *is his own*. But from his *own* point-of-view a person thinks of himself primarily as 'I' or 'myself'. He is only secondarily, or only for certain specific purposes, 'Jones' or 'Flew'.
>
> (Jones 1950: 234)

Jones' point is that my experience of my own self consciousness should sensitise me to the fact that other people also are self conscious, an elementary fact which invalidates my construction of them in terms limited to a consciousness *I* impute to *them* on the basis of the social roles they play or the cultures in which they participate. Quite apart from recalling Mauss' distinction between personhood and selfhood, this is also clearly pertinent to the cultural agency of the individual, for it insists that we focus on the individual as self-motivated rather than as socially- (or 'other') driven.

This issue has never been far from us in this book, surfacing in the discussions of whether identity is absolute or contingent, and of ethnicity as a reflex of boundary transactions. I raise it again now in considering how reflexivity – using our selves to think about others – has affected the ways in which we have recently thought about cultural process.

In his *Other Tribes, Other Scribes* (1982), Boon argued that the self-awareness of all social entities – individuals, societies, ethnic groups – is constituted by their reflexive awareness of others. Without the need to juxtapose themselves to others, they simply would not require the self-awareness which they formulate in terms of 'identity' and 'culture'.

Furthermore, this contingency is not just imperative but is also inevitable: individuals and cultures can be approached only from the perspective of another culture or individual. We are back here to Ayer's problem of 'knowing other minds' (Ayer 1963 [1953]) and to Winch's insistence on the impossibility of an empirical social science (Winch 1958). We cannot have sight or knowledge of another individual/culture/ethnic group which is unmediated by ourselves, or which is not 'culturally embedded' and which thereby entails 'translation' (Boon 1982: 6):

> [We] recognise other languages only from vantages of what they are *not*. Languages cannot be approached as if the observer stood beyond all of them; neither can cultures.
>
> (Boon 1982: 25)

We are always inevitably engaged in contrast and comparison, with the consequence that cultures (and, presumably, identities and personae) exaggerate themselves: they are inherently antithetical and 'comparative' (Boon 1982: 230).[1] Anthropology may have a second-order gaze at societies doing anthropology on each other; at the very least, the anthropologist is bound to have a specific cultural prism through which she or he observes others (ibid.: 47, 168–77). Being unable to see through and past its own categorical and monographic practices, anthropology has 'paradoxically inscribed' strikingly different cultures 'in disarmingly similar books' (ibid.: 14, 23).

Boon argues that just as social entities exaggerate themselves for the purposes of juxtaposition (Boon 1982: 114), so also anthropologists exaggerate them in order to be able to categorise them as 'other'. They then invent analytic systems (such as 'kinship', 'ritual') which they use to show how the system of one society can be compared to the system of another, with the consequence that the differences they have themselves invented can be collapsed by their ingenious theoretical devices and methodological procedures (ibid.: 25ff., 230. See also McGrane 1989: 125). Boon proposes that in order to avoid this academic sleight of hand, anthropologists should engage with other cultures interpretatively – that is, as cultures engage with each other – rather than pandering to the fiction of collecting positivistically and ordering scientifically 'cultural facts':

> This discourse of cultures confesses its own exaggeration and seeks to control and assess it by becoming interpretive, at times even literary, while remaining both systematic and dialectical.
>
> (Boon 1982: 26)

But, as Boon insists, the discourse of cultures is inevitably self-reflexive. Although it is largely beyond the scope of his book, he would logically also have to accept that this must be true of discourse *within* cultures among different individuals and groups. So far as the self consciousness which arises from 'comparison' is concerned, he concedes this explicitly:

> Every discourse, like every culture, inclines toward what it is not: toward an implicit negativity.

> (Boon 1982: 232)

Moreover, since by the very nature of their enquiry anthropologists are inevitably engaged in a similar discourse of cultures, their own stance must be one of self-reflexivity (see ibid.: 42–3). Their interpretative question, 'what would this mean to *me*?', inevitably points them towards the question, 'what would it mean to *them*?' Anthropologists' acknowledgement of their own selves and of their interpretative creativity should therefore lead them to similar acknowledgement of the selves of others, of their cultural creativity, and thereby invalidate the use of those categorical devices by which they have previously rendered others as qualitatively different (inferior) and as generalisable.

Notwithstanding its inevitability, in Boon's thesis individuals and groups put juxtaposition to creative use: they think through it – specifically, they think about themselves through it. We can thus see ego formulating a sense of his or her self by refracting it from a view of the bounded other. The thinking self bounces off the embodied other by crossing a system boundary; and, in Boon's argument, whether the system in question is personal or cultural does not alter the fact of this contingency.

Another version of the thinking self is prominent in the work of James Fernandez, a former associate of Geertz at Princeton, whose work over many years has shown how individuals use tropes to think their way through problematic situations. In so doing, they both borrow and invent cultural figures which become available to others for their own interpretative uses and for modification. Throughout more than thirty years of ethnographic work in various parts of West, Central and Southern Africa and Spain, Fernandez's particular interest has been in metaphor: in the place of metaphor, 'and the dynamic of the tropes' (Fernandez, pers. comm.) in behaviour. The use of metaphor takes the individual not across personal or cultural boundaries (although it could), but across the boundaries of domains of meaning. Metaphor connects a 'pronoun' (person) to a predicate (a form – say, a parrot – or a quality of being – for example, a wise owl) in such a way as to anchor the pronoun, otherwise inchoate, in a condition which is intelligible either through experience or imagery. For example, father says to young, chattering child: 'You are a parrot.' Child asks, 'What are you, Daddy?' 'I am a wise owl.'

The premise for Fernandez's concern is the proposition that individuals struggle continuously against uncertainty, the 'inchoate', 'the dark at the bottom of the stairs', and employ cultural tropes to secure themselves. As they cross into unfamiliar domains of experience, they reach out to seek and grasp a lifeline from one which is familiar (Fernandez 1982a: 28; cf. Wagner 1986: 6).[2] The movement from the insecurity and danger of the unknown to the comforting familiarity and certainty of the known is necessary for people to behave competently, to 'perform' (Fernandez 1986 [1972]: 8). Fernandez argues that effecting this movement is strategic. He repeatedly talks about the use of metaphors both in 'shifting' individuals ('pronomial subjects') (Fernandez 1986 [1974]), and in 'securing' them when linguistic 'shifters' have undermined certainty (Fernandez 1982a: 21–2). It is important to remember that it is not only the self which is thus mobile: the individual may use metaphor to shift, or 'affectively move' (Fernandez 1986 [1974]: 38), another individual, and to fix that person with the associations of some particular image. Metaphor is clearly an instrument for the expression of value, both positive and negative. Neither of the two statements, 'Professor X is God' and 'Professor X thinks he's God', are intended to be taken literally. Both are powerful in persuading an audience to take a particular view of the wretched man.

Here again we can see that competent social behaviour cannot be explained by treating the individual as simply the creature of culture or of society. Culture makes available the metaphoric terms, makes some more or less compelling or appropriate than others, but leaves their manipulation (and even, possibly, their invention) to thinking individuals. Indeed, metaphorisation is thinking:

> However men may analyze their experiences within any domain, they inevitably know and understand them best by referring them to other domains for elucidation. It is in that metaphoric, cross-referencing of domains, perhaps, that culture is integrated, providing us with the sensation of wholeness.
>
> (Fernandez 1986 [1974]: 25)

Metaphor also provides a way of making the private public, of externalising the self by providing terms for the expression of sentiments which may otherwise be inexpressible or unintelligible to others (ibid.: 6, 11), and is presumably, therefore, an essential means of engaging in meaningful social interaction. Although he may not choose to put it this way, Fernandez does attribute to metaphor (and to other tropes) the instrumentality by which thinking individuals create (and 'move' in) their social worlds. For Fernandez, the construction and use of metaphor is the 'elementary form' of social life (ibid.: 58).

Fernandez's central organising notion of the inchoate locates his own work within the abiding concern of social anthropology and sociology with the production and maintenance of social order. For the great modernistic theories, of course, influenced predominantly by Marx and Durkheim, order was inherent in social relations structured by economic and/or politico-jural logics and sustained by the generation of solidarity. In the various post-structuralist paradigms, far from inhering in a particular configuration of structural relations, order was seen as having to be accomplished. Fernandez is not much interested in such abstracted doctrine. Rather, he set himself the task of showing how people keep at bay that particular kind of disorder which he terms the 'inchoate'. It is literally disorderly because, being unknown or unfamiliar, the individual does not know how to perceive order in it, or how to render it orderly. Ordinary mortals require the world to be predictable in order to feel that they can engage with it competently. When we find ourselves in unfamiliar situations we hunt for precedents in our experience which we can use in order to render it comprehensible to ourselves and therefore know how to behave. The unfamiliar phenomenon which resists being made 'choate' in this way is frightening indeed.

This frantic hopping from one domain of experience to another is so ubiquitous, so routine, that we are probably unaware most of the time that we are doing it – unless, perhaps, we are stymied. For example, linguistic translation entails just such a boundary journey, the sheer complexity of which may well not occur to us until we try to go beyond a certain level of competence. My schoolboy French leaves me with the expectation that these languages, and others, will have vocabulary equivalents to my stock of English words. I can prove this to my own satisfaction by being able to make myself understood in the *boulangerie*. Life is not so simple when I want to talk in French (or Spanish, for that matter) about the self and selfhood. The absence of unambiguous equivalents is still further complicated by the need to indulge in various circumlocutions, none of which achieves my intentions precisely.

This kind of failure to join different domains is frustrating, but it leads to nothing worse than me berating myself for my linguistic incompetence (although with respect to other, more exotic languages, it has led some anthropologists to the ludicrous conclusion that the absence from the 'other's' language of such equivalents must mean that *they* lack a concept – of self, God, rationality, whatever – with which *we* are blessed). But in other matters the failure to make predications from one domain to the other has more disturbing and serious consequences. Alone at night in a dark, strange house, any unfamiliar noise can be frightening. As I hear it, I ransack my store of experience for a rational explanation: the central heating system? an unlatched window? a mouse? When finally I have managed to pin it down, I become aware of the rate at which my heart is thumping. Prior to this I am plagued by other possibilities which are terrifying because, not having encountered them before, I do not know how to cope or if I can cope. Suppose it's a ghost? Even a mortal intruder? What would I do?

In Whalsay, Shetland, tropic movement across domains was an effective means of coping with rapid and pervasive social, economic and technological change (see Cohen 1987: 130; 1989b). Terminology originating in small open-boat fishing would be applied to the £2m spanking new purser-trawler, crammed with the latest electronic and mechanical wizardry; or a patient would describe the hi-tech surgery he had just endured in terms of a sheep's ailment with which he would be familiar, as a competent crofter. Fernandez's informants, both in the Asturias and in the West African *Bwiti* cult (Fernandez 1982b), also work tropically to manage change, and the increasing intrusion of the world upon them. But the uncertainties and dangers of the inchoate are not just to do with the unpredictabilities of looming change. Uncertainty is a constant threat, whether consequent on social change, or on the more routine eventualities of having to switch roles, to move milieux, to confront problems to which the solutions are not evident. In a sense, nothing is so certain as the prospect of uncertainty. When dogmatic responses to these troublesome situations are inappropriate, we have to turn to metaphor,

> to find images and symbols to live with, and live by.
>
> (Fernandez 1982a: 38)

While the repertoire of such images may be cultural, and therefore collective, their selection must be individual for the simple reason that if solutions were uniform, uncertainty would not arise. Fernandez's ethnography is striking for being populated by individuals (Fernandez 1982b: 12). This may in part be because he is particularly interested in masters and manipulators of images – poets and preachers – but, although he does not make an explicit argument to this effect, must also in part be because individuals have to dispel for themselves the spectre of the inchoate. They may be provided with doctrine (political and/or religious) and with lore, but they have to do the interpretative and visualising work to assimilate these impersonal images to themselves. The Fernandez *oeuvre* is a sustained demonstration, *par excellence*, of culture as the product of thinking individuals, rather than as a set of behavioural prescriptions mechanically imposed on them.

PUBLIC FORMS, PRIVATE MEANINGS

The inchoate is a private problem, resolved, in Fernandez's view, by predication on a public form. His argument is consistent with symbol theory in anthropology, developed especially from the work of Turner onwards, although with crucial earlier precedents in such different sources as Freud, Peirce, Lévi-Strauss and Audrey Richards. Symbols are cultural (therefore public) forms, the meanings of which are substantially private. Over the last twenty years, it has become a commonplace of symbolic anthropology that the meanings of symbols are not exhausted by their shared or public elements, but are essentially a matter of private interpretation and, as such, may well be inaccessible to others (including, alas, to ethnographers). Metaphor is public in so far as its terms are culturally salient and compelling; but its meaning to the different individuals who are oriented to it may be utterly different.

There is nothing contentious about this proposition. Selfhood rests on the essential privacy of meaning; in what else might it consist? It is a proposition which can be tested by even a cursory inspection of belief systems which subordinate private thought and interpretation to dogma, and which, in so doing, demand 'selflessness' of their adherents. Recollecting the television image of a million choreographed Chinese punching the air with their 'little red books' and chanting the thoughts of Mao in unison sends shivers up the spine of this self-conscious writer. But we do not have to turn to totalitarian extremes to find examples. Consider again Carol Greenhouse's gloss on beliefs and attitudes about the person among middle-class Southern Baptists in Hopewell, Atlanta:

> Jesus eliminates individualism and instead joins the individual to society in a concert of interests.
>
> (Greenhouse 1986: 100)

Further, because the Baptist self is known entirely to God, it 'has no private space but no need for privacy' (ibid.: 98). Even speaking in tongues is rejected as a sign of grace or religiosity, since the meanings of such utterances are not publicly accessible.

However selfless the Hopewell Baptists manage to become, they certainly appear to have abdicated their rights to personal discretion in favour of a regime which is so regulated by doctrine as to be mindless. Individuals are their family roles, the family being the interface between 'the world of humans and God's heaven' (Greenhouse 1986: 48). The self, such as it is, finds its natural expression in the family role. Whatever relationships are contingent on role are 'expressed as performances of duty' (ibid.: 53) rather than of personal choice, since individuals do not believe that they have any control over them (ibid.: 49). This denial of self, rather like the Japanese Buddhist transcendental selflessness described by Lebra (see p. 126 above), is spoken of as a liberation, conjuring the paradox that individuals can only realise their selves in their selflessness, the promise of their faith. The discretionary self becomes a doctrinaire automaton:

> because Jesus is presumed to have everyone's interest in mind in his plan, untoward events should not be questioned. . . . Second, since Jesus has everyone in mind, pressing one's own interests in the form of a claim or expression of anger is superfluous.
>
> (Greenhouse 1986: 109)

Hopewell Baptists regard themselves as superior by dint of having been saved, and having liberated themselves from materialism and secular hierarchy. Greenhouse strongly suggests that there is a darker history to their commitment, in the form of a reaction against intense local conflict in the now distant past, complemented by the enduring legacy of the Civil War (ibid.: 192). One can understand the feeling of an overwhelming need to create harmony and prevent a recurrence of internecine conflict. However, the solution of apparently repressing self and submitting oneself to the scrutiny of the Church seems somewhat incongruous for a congregation of middle-class achievers. The turn to totalising religions is common enough among people living on the margins or who feel themselves excluded from the mainstream of society. It may not be unprecedented among other, more affluent groups which, like the Hopewellians, also elaborate a discourse of community as the integration of their mature individual members (e.g. Eriksen 1993).

The claim to selflessness is logically consistent with the apparent denial of privacy. Even individual prayer seems to be regarded as a public communication – if God can be considered public. This is remarkable, since there is neither litany nor prayer book, but the individual's prayer is supposed to be spontaneous. People may pray together face-to-face or over the telephone. The prayer should be an expression of gratitude, rather than a petition (regarded as a 'conceit' [Greenhouse 1986: 88]). The intention would seem to be to effect personal sublimation by externalisation.

But the aspiration to selflessness is surely as hopeless as it is eccentric. The selflessness of the Hopewell Baptists is provided by the ideological forms of the Church and congregation. For example, the doctrine that individuals *are* their family roles begs the question of what it is that provides the continuity between the various roles which any individual thereby plays. One person is the incumbent of the roles wife, daughter, mother and sister, each of which must surely be informed by her occupation and experience of all the others. The obligations of role may be a convenient legitimation for the way in which a group organises itself – people relating to others who occupy similar roles (Greenhouse 1986: 53) – or in which an individual behaves, and may serve as an explanation to the individual of her 'isolation' within relationships over which she has no control (ibid.: 49). But this is not to say that they convince the incumbent that she is nothing other than the roles she plays, nor that she is the same as anyone else who has to acknowledge similar family obligations. There is nothing selfless about the justification I offer for my behaviour, 'I was being a father'. I may wish to draw attention to the obligations and responsibilities which father-hood places on me, but I do not thereby suggest that I am nothing other than father, or that I am like every other father. I say, 'what else could I do?' not 'who else could I be?' I could perform exactly the same behaviour using the mutually exclusive justifications of (a) absence of personal discretion, and (b) exercise of personal discretion. My choice between them is an assimila-tion of my self to the 'public' rhetorical terms which seem most pertinent.

In Hopewell, selflessness is a public term and a posture put to the service of the highly individualised self. There may be nothing tropic about Hopewell Baptist dogma; but, like metaphor, it offers a lifeline for the uncertain self to grasp, one which is especially attractive because of its inherent certainties, and because it collapses the self into a public persona. The emblematic language of faith, like the concepts of 'grace' and 'commitment' among Stockholm Pietists (Stromberg 1986, see pp. 18–19), provides labels for the less ordered contents of the individual's consciousness, combining to form a mask with which the wearer announces to the world, 'here is another potential sinner saved for Christ, an otherwise self-indulgent miscreant serving as a Christian mother/sister/daughter/wife.' What goes on *behind* the mask is another matter.

We saw a comparable dissonance between 'role-play' and self-consciousness in the context of constructions of gender in rural Greece (Chapter 4, pp. 80–90). The discussion led to the suggestion that public muting of self-expression does not necessarily diminish reflexivity, indeed may well enhance it. After all, Christianity offers me another means of expressing myself to myself rather than just to my social associates, a vocabulary for *self*-expression as well as for public discourse. Non-religious ideologies may have a similar competence. In describing the imagery and values imputed to the various *aliyot* (waves of immigration) to Israel between the late nineteenth and late twentieth centuries, Robert Paine (n.d.) has shown how the 'pioneer' immigrants (the second and third *aliyot*, 1904–23) associated the remaking of their selves with the making of the nation. As socialists, they reacted against the status discriminations, religiosity and folk culture of the *shtetl*. The doctrinal instruments of their personal reorientations were their commitment to physical labour, and to a return to the land, to nature, as their primary means of subsistence, and the supremacy of group over personal identity. The self was to be subordinated to communalism, and the remade self was expressed in the adoption of Hebraicised names which stressed fortitude, 'signalling Zionist rejection of city life' and rejecting names commonly used in the Diaspora.

Paine describes this self-reconstruction as an attempted 're-birth', arguing that the rejection of the past left the pioneers and the *sabra* children with only the murkiest (most inchoate) of pasts and uncertain futures, a

> shocking contrast to Jewish youth's socialization and the social reproduction of generations in that previous world of Orthodoxy and *shtetl*.
>
> (Paine n.d.: 20)

Its motivating logic was

> to eliminate the contradiction between the individual and society . . . through the fusion of personal identity with social identity,
>
> (Paine n.d.: 7)

precisely the kinds of intended transformation which we saw Fitz John Porter Poole attribute to the Bimin-Kuskusmin *ais am* (Chapter 3, pp. 62–5), and which Greenhouse finds in the 'selfless' dogmas of the Hopewell Southern Baptists.

Paine observes that the audacity of such attempted personal reconstruction was reflected in the numbers of people for whom it proved too demanding, that it succumbed to the urban and bourgeois inclinations of later immigrants, and that it was prejudiced by its elitist origins and its imposition by the leadership and ideology of the kibbutz movement. We are back here to the frailties of totalising regimes which we encountered in the earlier discussion of Goffman. Although possibly changed, even damaged in some way, the self breaks through, not because of its mystical resilience, but because the self can be suppressed only in a loss of identity tantamount to the *un*consciousness of self which we usually regard as a condition of insanity.

Religious, nationalist or political doctrine may give people ways in which to think about themselves, forms within which to locate themselves. But there is a vital distinction to be made between these *forms* of thought and expression, and their content. As an immigrant, I might become Amos, rather than my former Avraham; I might turn myself from small trader into a jack of all agricultural trades; I may shed my previous social isolation to become an assiduous and solidary kibbutznik. My self consciousness may change with the accumulation of these new experiences, but it is not discarded to be replaced with a selfless consciousness of 'I' as an organisational member. However compelling its structural and theoretical logic may be, the organisation does not produce *me* (see Burns 1992: 155): *it* is reproduced through *me*. Thus doctrinaire religious sects and political groups fragment into disputatious factions; the most ideologically committed of movements and their leaderships dissolve into contentious differences of personal interpretation and aspiration. This is not to say that solidarity always gives way to selfishness, society to individualism. It is to suggest that the ambition to invent selfless social groupings is foolish. For all its institutional power, its capacity to generate and impose social forms, society is constituted by self consciousness and substantiated by the meanings which conscious selves impute to those received forms.

I do not suggest that the mass society is an illusion, only that its substance is more complex than its appearance. In his classic essay, 'Post-liberal democracy', Macpherson argued brilliantly that the theories of the market, of demand-and-supply economics and of consumer-led choice were mere rhetorics which masked the essential transformation in capitalist economies between the eras of liberal free trade and of monopoly and state-regulated capital. The rhetoric 'still asserts the ultimate moral worth of the individual' (Macpherson 1964: 491). However, individuals, defined as choice-makers in the market, are managed and manipulated. The choices which they make are those which the producers permit them to make at the prices which the producers themselves dictate: 'the market system . . . creates the wants which it satisfies' (ibid.: 496). As 'the market' becomes concentrated in fewer and larger corporate hands, 'the tendency of the system to create the wants which it satisfies will become stronger' (ibid.).

We assume that the power of producers in this contrived mass market has grown at the cost of the individual. Our freedoms of choice have been severely curtailed and channelled by the economics of fashion. There is no point in my searching the High Street for flared trousers if tapered trousers are 'in'; and, although I felt perfectly well-served by long-playing records and recorded cassettes, it seems now that in order to exercise such choice as I am allowed I must buy my recorded music on compact discs.

I accept all this. If Macpherson was persuasive in 1964 (and it is worth noting that Hans Speier [1969] had made a very similar argument more than thirty years earlier in respect of Germany), he is much more so thirty years later after decades of the tiddly-wink economics with which the British Conservative Government and successive Republican administrations have amused themselves and belaboured us. However, the mass consumption of similar objects, the apparently slavish following of fashion, does not necessarily mean the loss of selfhood or of individuality. It may mean nothing more than a great many bodies tediously clothed in similar uniforms, ingesting similar foods and having the same music drilled into their inner ears through the earphones of similar personal stereos. But there is no more reason to suppose that two people listening to the same rock song are hearing the 'same thing' than are two people listening to the Jupiter symphony. We do not expect Mozart's music to *mean* the same to its various listeners, because we define art as interpretable. We accept that artists provide us with forms, substantiate them in ways which may or may not be apparent to us, and leave us – players, audience, readers, viewers – to exercise our own interpretative skills and inclinations. The form is in the public domain; we make its meaning privately, and it remains private until and unless we choose to disclose it.

Of course, mass-ness is not just manifest in apparent uniformity. Social scientists have long been interested in 'mass movements', in the crowd and the mob, and in collective behaviour which appears to subordinate individuality. The latter has particularly engaged anthropologists in studies of ecstatic phenomena and spiritual experience in which self consciousness seems to be transcended by either a temporary condition of possession or other loss of conscious control, or by the intense communion of minds and souls which Victor Turner rendered as 'communitas'.

The explanation of mass movements has been couched within the entire spectrum of social theory from a variety of disciplines. A paradigm case, to which I have referred extensively elsewhere, was Tilly's study of the Vendée counter-revolution (Tilly 1963, 1964). Tilly's problem was to explain why, alone among the different regions of France, the counter-revolution emerged in the Vendée. He was unable to find a compelling explanation in objective sociological and historical factors, and came to the conclusion that the motives of followers should not be confused with – indeed, may be significantly different from – the terms in which they are articulated by their leaders. The mere existence of a plausible structure for the expression of a grievance or for the mobilisation of a mass following might be sufficient to persuade people *with very different kinds of motivation* to gather behind its banner. In other words, the explanation of *collective* behaviour is to be sought among its *individual* participants.[3]

It is beyond my disciplinary competence to say whether this kind of argument might reasonably be applied to crowd behaviour, but it seems to me intuitively persuasive. The crowd clearly does have a transformative effect on the individual. At a soccer match, spectators unthinkingly rise out of their seats, roaring with pleasure or groaning in dismay at their team's triumph or ignominy. The experience of marching in a demonstration, placard held aloft, chanting slogans in unison, may well strengthen one's commitment both to the cause itself and to comrades, an experience which activists refer to as 'consciousness-raising'. While both occasions may reveal the participating individual's loss of self-control, there seems no case for suggesting that there is a loss of self. Notwithstanding the apparently regimented behaviour of the participants, there is so much of crucial importance which cannot be generalised. What motivates individuals to attend? What do the teams/causes mean to them? How do they interpret the symbols which represent the key elements in the event? What does the event mean? Again, it would seem very suspect indeed to assume that in these fundamental matters, individuals were alike.

Wherever one looks, we see people confronted by forms which they render meaningful to themselves in ways which are intuitively, logically or ideologically compelling, while powerful agencies try to steer them towards, even to impose, exclusive interpretations. If individuals resist these attempted interpretative hegemonies, they do not necessarily do so consciously, but because the constitution of the self in unique personal experience makes such mediation inevitable. Rushdie's *Satanic Verses* clearly resonates quite differently among fundamentalist Shia Moslems than among British liberals. For the former, the very translation of Mohammed to the pages of a satirical novel was sacrilegious, regardless of what was said about him. I understand this view, but my own reading of the novel was different: I saw it less as a satire on Islam or organised religion in general, and much more as a biting and bitter attack on the racism which is endemic in Britain, and on the moral vacuity and crass *poujadism* of Thatcherism. But beyond these gross differences, it is surely undeniably the case that the Islamic militants in Bradford and Manchester who firebombed shops which stocked the offending book were not motivated identically to the Ayatollas and the Iranian crowds who demonstrated their support for the *fatwah*. By the same token, my reading of the book must have differed significantly from those of others among Rushdie's more sympathetic readers, since each of us would have become inclined in non-generalisable ways towards the political views which we thought we could identify in the book. To say that we are all 'left wing', 'anti-racist', 'opposed to censorship' is to say virtually nothing. It is the ways in which we have *individually* experienced *generalised* phenomena, such as discrimination, religious dogma and political hypocrisy, which informed our reading of the book and of the reactions to it. Artists, like politicians, advertisers, preachers and other would-be managers of meaning, can only try to lead us towards the meanings they wish to communicate, but which they cannot impose on us. Our interpretations may be variations on cultural, political or cosmo-logical themes; but we can only make sense of the themes through the media of our variations on them.

THINKING THROUGH CULTURE

Theme and variations are strikingly present in Marilyn Strathern's 'cultural account' of the ideas behind English kinship. Her evocation of these ideas and images is necessarily elusive and difficult, sometimes impressionistic. A clinically precise text of 'English kinship' would have been a misrepresentation of a very indeterminate and hetero-geneous phenomenon, a matter which anthropologists would do well to remember in offering us versions of other peoples' kinship systems. Kinship exists in a discourse of relationships, and its meanings to those who participate in it must again be seen as significantly variable, even though its forms may be stated in the generalised terms of kinship analysis (nucleated, bilateral, cognatic or whatever).

In her study of the Essex village of Elmdon, Strathern showed that, rather than just being a strategic basis for social interaction, kinship in

Britain, as elsewhere, provides models for the conceptualisation of social life and of social relationships (Strathern 1981). These models are subject to change over time and with fashion, and have the character of interpretative resources rather than of dogmatic prescriptions. Elmdon had long experienced considerable population mobility. Its 'indigenous' families were ageing and attenuated by the outmigration of their younger members. The village had become repopulated by outsiders, among whom middle-class commuters were especially prominent. There remained at 'the core' (as their members saw it) of the village a cluster of long-established, interrelated working-class families. They had intermarried with each other over generations, and referred to themselves as 'real Elmdoners'.

Elsewhere, such putative authenticity refers to the possession of distinctively local skills, knowledge or other traits. But in Elmdon it seems to have designated only a genealogical core on which 'real' Elmdoners then predicated models of village and class (arguably, I would suggest, of their very Englishness). Their children had been geographically and, in some cases, socially mobile. Their local space had been occupied and transformed by incomers who also appropriated to themselves control of local institutions. One can imagine that they had a sense of themselves as a kind of anachronistic, even displaced, residue. Yet, their view of themselves and their families as 'real', authentic Elmdon seems to counterbalance any sense they may have had of their marginality. To be 'real' Elmdon is to be *of* the village, rather than merely *in* it; it is to be 'really' English in the way that only the yeomanry or working class represent the essence of the nation. Here, then, kinship was revealed as a symbolic resource of the greatest importance, as something to 'think with' rather than just to 'act out'.

In a series of articles which followed the publication of *Kinship at the Core*, Strathern began to explore some of the ideas and images which her Elmdon study revealed as implicated in English kinship, an exploration which was given further point by the development of new reproductive technologies. She saw technological intervention in reproduction as calling into question popular notions of 'nature' and 'culture'. In her book, *After Nature: English Kinship in the Late Twentieth Century* (1992), she showed how an edifice of ideas fundamental to English culture was built on this discrimination, and might be subverted or otherwise transformed by both technology and the changing nature of family values and obligations.

She identified a series of 'facts' of English kinship – although, far from depicting these as constituting simple texts which are reproduced in family relationships, displayed the character of cultural complexity by showing that they are stated both as theses and antitheses and with shades between. For example, 'the first fact of English kinship' is 'the individuality of persons'. Yet, the individual is produced by 'a relationship':

> Individuality would thus be both a fact of and 'after' kinship.
>
> (Strathern 1992: 15)

Relationships which themselves have the character of organic wholeness (such as 'parents' engaged in reproduction) are the product of diversity, the 'second fact of modern kinship' (ibid.: 22; also 76). These do not suggest troublesome contradictions: rather, they demonstrate how elementary models of thought and their complexities can be depicted as predicated on kinship itself and are thus vulnerable to changes in the ideology and practice of kinship. Their vulnerability arises from the fact that change calls into question convention and the taken-for-granted assumption: it makes the implicit explicit. In being thus held up to the light for inspection, its frailty becomes evident:

> what was once taken for granted becomes an object of promotion, and less the cultural certainty it was.
>
> (Strathern 1992: 35)

Technology threatens to undermine our assumptions about the reproduction of diversity. In blurring the distinction between nature and culture, it has subverted nature as a model for thinking.

The implications of this go far beyond our popular notions of kinship. Drawing on representations of English stereotypes in nineteenth- and twentieth-century art, literature and advertising, Strathern argued that the idea of kinship was implicated in a conceptualisation of class which could be plotted on a nature–culture axis. The genteel middle class was represented as self-consciously cultured, not least in its 'cultivation' of 'natural' values, a discrimination made evident then and later by the bourgeois appropriation (and, therefore, control) of nature in domestic and landscape architecture. Inherent in this middle-class genre was the cultural value of privacy –

> The English imagined that the 'real' nature of something lay within, if only one could see
>
> (Strathern 1992: 130)

– and of the implicit: 'one looked inside the genteel person and found morality' (ibid.). But, when the implicit had to be made explicit it was transformed, and degraded:

> Morality made public became respectability. . . . once something was brought outside and made an object of knowledge, it stayed there. . . . there now seem only surfaces. There are no more depths.
>
> (Strathern 1992: 130)

This bleak conclusion is itself a comment on the discourse of Thatcherism which was instructive in using idioms of kinship ('family values') to reinvent a rhetorical (and, as I shall argue in the next chapter, bogus) individualism in which the state abdicated its moral responsibilities for social welfare, imposing it instead on individuals regardless of their circumstances. 'There is no such thing as society,' said the then prime minister, there are only individuals – a sentiment which, as Strathern pithily observed, subverted the very basis of her government's claim to legitimacy (ibid.: 168).

Strathern's position was that society is misconceived as an entity *apart* from (or over and above) individuals. Rather, society *is* its relationships, among individuals, insitutions, between individuals and institutions, so that it would be perfectly proper to talk of the 'relationship between society and the individual' without conceiving of the individual as somehow separable from society itself (Strathern 1992: 189). She writes as an anthropologist steeped in Melanesian ethnography and experience, and, therefore, as one who has engaged at length in documenting and describing the use of the discourse of exchange to create and maintain complex relationships. At crucial points in her text, she brings her Melanesian expertise to bear on England. By implication, she shows that the contrast evident in the assumptions we make about our own society and others is instructive about our practice as anthropologists. We recognise the aesthetic and complexity in the engineering of relationships in New Guinea, whereas we have been at best myopic, at worst blind, in failing to recognise them at home, seeing relationships instead as reflexes of institutionalised arrangements, and perhaps not surprisingly, since conventionality and orthodoxy have been so much part of the dominant ideology:

> Westerners took on as their own cultural project the ever-receding goal of inventing convention [and of] conventionalising inventions.
>
> (Strathern 1992: 190)

Anthropologists and other social commentators have thus fallen prey to the compulsion to make 'evident to themselves the principles upon which they constructed society and culture' (ibid.) by confusing principles (for example, those of class, generation, even gender) with their modification/qualification/subversion in practice and process (cf. the earlier discussion of Tory Island kinship, pp. 110–14).

Her point surely is that we inherit the cultural materials with which to construct our relationships and our understandings of them. But far from their design being prescriptive, we have continuously to employ these same materials to render intelligible what we and others have made. In other words, we create difference, but interpret what we have made by using a finite set of notions. Inevitably, therefore, we contrive variations on a theme. The key cultural notions and their associated 'facts', which Strathern identifies, appear singly, in combination and in endlessly differing combinations, permitting us, as thinking and creative selves, to speak the same cultural language while saying very different things.

I would push Strathern's intricate and ingenious argument a step further. At the heart of this variability-within-culture is her concept of the 'merographic' individual who seems to belong in different ways to different domains of social being, whose 'appearance' differs depending on one's angle of vision (kaleidoscopes again) and whose aspects are distinguishable because they pertain to different domains. I am simultaneously an individual, and yet part of relationships; unique, but conventional; the product of my genetic endowment, but also of society (see Strathern, in press).

In this last-cited work, Strathern declares that she is 'wary of "the self" as an object of enquiry' for the familiar and well-rehearsed reason that other people's selves are accessible only to them. She speaks here with the anthropologist's cautious methodological rigour. Perhaps it is this wariness which inhibits her from exploring the self as the agent of his or her own 'merography'. For Strathern, the shifting and multi-faceted individual is the product of 'perspectival depth' (Strathern 1992: 150) – that is to say, is in the eye of the beholder (or not, as the case may be). I have been trying to argue here that the 'beholden' has some discretion in this as well. We take some responsibility for how we are viewed, or how we wish to be viewed; we try to impress ourselves (our selves) on others, subject, of course, to the same limitations of control over other people's meanings to which I referred above. But how can my many guises be understood if I am not also acknowledged as their author or, at least, as having some responsibility for their selection?

I do not suppose that I will be seen by others as I see myself (in any guise), and no doubt a guise, even a self, will be imputed to me of which I believe myself to be innocent. But where am 'I' in all this, if I am not the one who composes the variations on the cultural themes; and why would I (speaking as member, rather than just as observing anthropologist) do it if not to navigate a social path for my self? I concur entirely with Strathern (*inter alia*, 1987b), among others, that however indistinct may be the cultural line between anthropologist and anthropologised, its reality cannot be denied. But that is why we need all the help we can contrive in order to minimise the extent to which it obfuscates our view. To understand the thinking selves who we observe we have to invoke our personal experience as thinking selves, in as controlled a manner as our discipline will allow. This need not entail an experience of the kind so agonisingly endured and movingly recounted by Hastrup (1992b), of seeing herself objectified in a dramatic performance, but simply requires that we admit personal reflection explicitly into our anthropological work. The anthropologist is part of the merographic me, indissoluble from the self who struggles constantly to make competent interpretations of what is going on around me in order to behave competently in society. The compulsion to interpret certainly does not stop short of recognising/constructing other people's selves (Strathern, in press), an activity which is necessarily founded on my own reflexivity as well as on whatever anthropological expertise I may possess.

So, we have culture, manifest in dominant theme and innumerable interpretative variations. We have its putative facts, their declensions and negativities, which are made questionable by being made explicit. We have individuals, apparent in as many poses as there are perspectives on them. The individual makes sufficient sense out of this 'inchoateness' to be able to behave competently within it. But how? By thinking about and ordering it through the medium of self consciousness and experience, and then using that self consciousness as the premise for imagining the experience of others.

Culture requires us to think, gives us forms – metaphors, dogmas, names, 'facts' – to think with, but does not tell us *what* to think: that is the self's work.

Strathern's cultural account ingeniously predicates the merographic individual on kinship, and, in so doing, substantiates and develops the identification of the individual as the elementary form (and icon) of English society (see, *inter alia*, Macfarlane 1978). However, she offers the account explicitly as an analyst who also participates in the culture and its kinship forms which she discloses. She makes no claim regarding the general distribution of her own view, nor about its place in the popular consciousness. It is an account of middle-class Englishness, the degradation of which in the late twentieth century gives her book a polemical character as a trenchant critique of the banal and debased individualism which informed Thatcherite and post-Thatcher Conservatism.

The further step which I would take, of which she is properly wary, is to suggest that this view of the individual may indeed form part of the individual's self-consciousness. As an approximation to her idea of the merographic individual, I venture the more familiar image of the crystalline structure of multiple surfaces, all contained within an organic unity on which the integrity of their individual planes depends.

In Whalsay, Shetland, this view of the individual modelled the self-image of the community as well (see Cohen 1987, esp. Ch. 3). There was a constant tension between the notion of Whalsay people as essentially alike, and yet as enriching the community with their differences from each other. I have suggested elsewhere (ibid. and 1978) that this apparent contradiction was resolved by allocating identities to persons which drew on publicly acceptable and valued expressions of 'Whalsayness': it constructed individuality within strict limits. But I also drew attention to the more private expressions of selfhood which lay beneath this public discourse, and which expressed people's frustration with the difficulty of reconciling their own self-identity with the public versions of themselves.

Their difficulties went beyond the sheer intractability of the labels imposed on them, but lay also in the disciplines of restraint and egalitarianism which characterised public conduct and which severely inhibited personal assertiveness or quarrelsomeness. This personal constraint was also a source of the community's resilience. By defining the distinctive personal qualities which could be acknowledged, the qualities themselves were celebrated, rather than just the individuals to whom they were attributed. This rationing and distribution of distinctive identities was also apparent in the imputation of stereotypical character to kinship groups. Yet, as with the individuals, the private discourse was about difference and variety rather than similarity or uniformity.

My view was that people accepted the distinctions between public and private spheres of discourse as a necessary condition of community life. They were not fooled by it. In public, individuality was tailored to the terms permitted by the community; the pursuit of selfhood was regarded as a private matter. There was evident here an acknowledgement of the disciplines required to sustain a community which occupies difficult ecological, social and economic niches. It was also a conscious strategy, as was the management of kinship. Like other segmentary social forms, kinship is a basis of social division as well as of solidarity. In a community such as Whalsay in which local endogamy had prevailed over such a long period, it would have been ineffective if strictly applied since most members of the community were interrelated in numerous ways. As a consequence, kinship in Whalsay, as in Tory Island, was more a matter of practice than of genealogical fact, and was underpinned in this respect by crofting tenure and collaborative labour, and by crew membership and the co-ownership of fishing boats.

People mapped kinship on to the range of their close social associates (Cohen 1982), designating them 'wir folk' (occasionally, 'folk we ken') as opposed to 'yon folk'. Whalsay thus developed 'practical' kinship to complement its practical individuality. But I would insist that this social praxis was deliberate and self-conscious, rather than the product of a cultural or structural *deus ex machina*, that it suggests individuals navigating paths for themselves through the thickets of social life. Referring to our earlier analogy, they might be seen in this respect as rotating and revolving their crystals to present their inextricably connected planes in different circumstances. They act on their own readings of the circumstances, rather than as a reflex.

Whalsay is most definitely not English. However, as a society to compare with whatever England Strathern had in mind it suggests to me that this kind of self consciousness and self-direction was understated in her account of English culture and individuality: indeed, that an account of individuality without self consciousness may be a rather incomplete story.

CULTURING THOUGHT: NATION(-STATE) AND SELF

Anthropologists are not alone in neglecting selfhood and underestimating consciousness. Politicians do it all the time in supposing that they can invent people's consciousness for them. They claim to know what people think, and spend a good deal of time and effort in trying to put words into our minds, if not our mouths. The attempt to manipulate meanings is the essence of politics, and I have already touched on some instances of it earlier. In concluding this chapter, I wish to dwell briefly on one expression of it which continues to attract the attention of anthropologists. The manufacture of national identity might reasonably be regarded as the attempt to diminish people's consciousness of their individuality, and to superimpose over this a consciousness of both their similarity to their co-nationals and their difference from others. Much has been written about the contrivance and symbolisation of national identity, from the 'invention of tradition' (Hobsbawm and Ranger 1983) to 'political religion' (Apter 1963). We are also acquiring a substantial comparative literature which decodes the contrived symbolism of national festivals. I turn to it now to focus on attempts to subordinate individuals to the collective representations (and putative conscious-ness) of the nation through its manufactured 'cultural' forms.

The rhetoric of nationalism attempts to create a homology between the individual and the nation. From the top downwards, the individual is represented as the nation writ small; from the bottom up, the nation is the individual writ large. In his study of Quebec nationalism, Handler sees this homology as an instance of, what C.B. Macpherson termed, 'possessive individualism' (Handler 1988). The nation and nationhood are seen as 'patrimonial property' (ibid.: 153), the product of the indivi-dual's creativity (ibid.: 6):

> choice is the creative manifestation of self, the imposition of self on to the external world. Property is what results from choices – products that exist in the external world yet remain linked through proprietorship to the self that created them.
>
> (Handler 1988: 51)

Individuals 'own' the nation; the nation conducts itself as a collective individual. This relationship between individual and nation has to be engineered and actively maintained, with the nation depicted as the realisation of individuals' aspirations for their selves, and individuals' aspirations tailored to what the nation is able to deliver. It is a relation-ship which is strongly reminiscent of Macpherson's post-liberal demo-cratic market (1964, and see pp. 146–7 above).

Handler's rich account does not impute cunning and design to the province's leaders in the contrivance of Quebec cultural nationalism. Indeed, he does not suggest that any deliberate attempt to formulate personal and collective identity in Quebec has ever succeeded. Rather, he seems to see leaders reacting to events which they read through the compelling ideology of Quebec nationhood. Over time, different, even contradictory elements of Quebecois life achieve iconic significance: the French language; Quebecois French (*joual*, otherwise regarded as degraded French); the Catholic Church; the ascendancy of secular Quebeckers over the Church; folklife, and its reconstruction; the land-scape, and built impositions upon it.

There are two striking features of these changing representations of Quebec culture. The first is that in their very inconsistency they recall the desperate attempts made in Canada itself to find its national soul and a convincing symbolic means of portraying it. But, secondly, unlike the larger and even more intractable issue of Canadian identity, Quebec-ness is represented by (because supposedly experienced through) items which characterise everyday life. In this regard, the vocabulary of

Quebec nationalism is more like that of ethnicity, particularly of an ethnicity which is felt to be under severe threat and in which, therefore, even the most mundane items can be regarded as eloquent testimony to the integrity of the ethnic group and its distinctive culture.

The impulse to Canadian identity derived from the need to find a convincing means of discrimination from the United States, but, arguably was not sufficiently convincing to overcome the more compelling ties and distinctions of province, region, language and ethnic origin. Quebecois identity, on the other hand, had an immediacy. The English Canadians were not on the other side of a national or provincial frontier, but were in their very midst and, to the Quebecois militants, were adulterating their culture. Their own space, the space within which they experienced themselves, was being appropriated. Not surprisingly, therefore, the representation of Quebec identity is more intimate than that of Canada's, and somehow suggests loss, or threatened loss. Although Scottish nationalism can draw on much greater historical depth, its representation is not dissimilar. The iconic intimacy of collective identity, its proximity to the circumstances of everyday life, make Handler's association of selfhood and nationalism plausible and persuasive. By emphasising diversity among Quebecois and continuous change in the discourse of cultural nationalism, he shows the sheer difficulty of accommodating a convincing collective identity to the plurality of interests which it must represent.

Although the same theme of the logical continuity between individual and nation features prominently in it, a rather different approach is evident in Kapferer's account of the marking of Australian identity in the annual Anzac Day celebrations (Kapferer 1988). He describes a hegemonic representation of Australian-ness and of the relationship between the individual and the state which has appropriated 'the nation' to itself:

> Nationalism makes culture into an object and a thing of worship. Culture is made the servant of power.
>
> (Kapferer 1988: 209)

The objectification of culture – Kapferer sees it as being sacralised, even fetishised – must entail its alienation from the individual on whom it is then imposed. Turned into an instrument of nationalism, it becomes 'totalitarian in form', collapsing 'diverse realities' into its own uniformity (ibid.: 4).

Kapferer characterises the self-concept of Australian society as egalitarian and as constituted by self-determining individuals who can be thought of as preceding it. Their coalescence into groups has therefore to be regarded as wilful, as the product of 'an elective affinity' which is consistent with nature and which finds its highest expression in the nation (Kapferer 1988: 17). In this respect, and unlike the state (the power of which feeds on the individual's capacity for self-determination), the nation again appears as an extension of the individual.

This distinction, indeed tension, between state and nation is clearly fundamental to Kapferer's argument. The nation is an expression of individuality; the state is its denial. He finds them to be celebrated on separate occasions, the state on Australia Day, the nation on Anzac Day. The latter commemorates the defeat by Turkey of Australian and New Zealand forces in Gallipoli during 1915, and its tradition

> expounds the doctrine of the Australian male egalitarian virtue of mateship.
>
> (Kapferer 1988: 123)

This notion of mateship implies that relationships among leaders and followers, even in the fighting forces, rest on voluntarism rather than hierarchy and, therefore, responds to, rather than impugns, their individuality. It is contrasted to the regimented and hierarchical discipline of the British, against whom Gallipoli-bound Australian troops rioted in Cairo on Good Friday, 1915, and to whom they were subordinated in the wider context of the Allied forces. Kapferer argues that the Anzac campaign was regarded as having transformed the disorderly, fractious, even chaotic, nascent nation of Australia into a coherent and solidary entity. It is significant that this transformation took place in the cradle of Western civilisation (which they sought to defend against the infidel), rather than at home:

> The Anzacs symbolize in their youth the rebirth of the very soul of Western civilization and their embodiment of its fundamental ideals.
>
> (Kapferer 1988: 127)

The campaign took place a mere fourteen years following the achievement of independence from Britain, and the values which were seen to arise from it were thus portrayed as being impressed on the nation.

Kapferer focuses on the sacralisation of the nation, the process through which nationalism becomes tantamount to a political religion. Those very characteristics through which the nation could be perceived as an extension of the individual are transformed by state power, objectified and, having been turned into venerable objects, are alienated from individuals who then require ideological direction in order to reorientate themselves to them.

National rites, such as Anzac Day, are developed, embellished, choreographed, to provide texts, complete with interpretative instructions, through which individuals are induced to identify with the nation which they have themselves created. Nationalism is here converted into 'state nationalism', a historical transformation which has been described by Michael Keating as typical of nationalistic traditions originating in western Europe where the state 'preceded the nation' (Keating 1993). Kapferer maintains that the device by which the state attempts to recruit the rite to its own service is only partly successful, if at all, for it remains 'a nationalist rite of the people' (Kapferer 1988: 147).

This thesis provides the formula by which Kapferer decodes Anzac Day ceremonies in different Australian cities. For example, in Sydney, following the Dawn Service, a march is formed which at one point passes an empty chair which belonged to Billy Hughes, Prime Minister in 1915. The marchers salute the chair and the soldier's hat which reposes on it, in an act which recognises the people's 'collective identity in the idealized person of Hughes' (Kapferer 1988: 153). Since he was the head of the government, it might reasonably be supposed that there is acknowledgement here of the state. But Kapferer insists otherwise:

> The Anzac rites represent little real identity with the state. It is rather an identity with the nation. . . .
>
> (Kapferer 1988: 153)

The justification of the distinction seems tenuous: the marchers progress behind the state governor who

> reflects the collective unity of the people in the nation,
>
> (Kapferer 1988: 153)

encompassing the state. Other discriminations between state and nation seem more reliable. For example, the march is disciplined by civilian marshals – that is to say, by representatives of 'the people' – rather than by the police who are agents of the state (ibid.: 155). But the argument becomes a little suspect again with the significance which Kapferer imputes to the consumption of alcohol throughout the Anzac Day rite. He insists that drinking is invested with ideological importance as 'a sign of personal autonomy', and suggests that the drinker's personal power is augmented by the potency of the alcohol (ibid.: 156). Anzac Day drinking

> is an expression of individual power, of autonomy, of individual control. It is . . . reinvigorating and regenerative. The heavy

consumption of alcohol on Anzac Day, virtually a cultural and national duty, is literally reempowering.

(Kapferer 1988: 157)

It ritually signs the participant's rebirth.

My scepticism may result from the frailty of my anthropological imagination. However, having done fieldwork over many years in a society in which heavy drinking is the normal culmination of significant festive social events, I need to be persuaded further that it signifies anything other than the rather prosaic fact that it is regarded as the proper and normal way of marking such occasions. It was not always so, and my older informants suggested that the mode of drinking which prevails now on such occasions – drinking whisky to become drunk – is a modern tendency. Nevertheless, drink and drunkenness is a prominent feature of yarns about earlier times (see Cohen 1987: 196–8). When I began fieldwork in Whalsay in the early 1970s, I became convinced that one of the attractions of drinking was simply that it provided a licence to depart from the normal restraints which governed interpersonal interaction: taken on these special occasions, it was a legitimate excuse to behave in ways which would normally be disapproved. I would not expect my friends in Whalsay to take my suggestion seriously, and would be more than a little surprised to find Anzac Day drinkers who would seriously entertain Kapferer's view that they drink to celebrate their individuality, personal autonomy, their commitment to the nation and their opposition to the state.

Of itself, this does not invalidate his argument about Australia, or mine about Whalsay. However, it does behove both of us to show that there is empirical substance to our contentions, and that what we witness is something more than the mere enjoyment of drink and sociability, even of inebriation, and the practice of customary behaviour: if it is Anzac Day, or the Whalsay Regatta, it must be time to drink. I doubt whether either of us have done so, although I suspect that his task would be even more difficult than mine, given the level of generality at which he pitches his interpretation.

But there are aspects of Kapferer's analysis which are less demanding of our credulity. He sees drinking as an expression of 'mateship', and, as already noted above, mateship is seen as the quintessence of the nation's characteristic egalitarianism. The Anzacs' march signifies a body of individuals moving, literally and figuratively, in unison, and is thus emblematic of the nation itself. Finally, his continual emphasis on the 'naturalness' of individuals acting in solidarity with each other is challenging. It recalls the Enlightenment origins of white Australian settlement, provides a formula through which society can be rendered interpretatively as 'natural' rather than contrived by the imposition of state power, and thus allows a contrast to be drawn between independent Australia as a nation of autonomous individuals, and its origins as an instrument of British penal policy. Of most relevance to my argument in this book is that it resolves the contradiction between individual and society by locating the impulse to sociality within the individual and thus *makes society an embodiment of individuality*. In this respect, the nation stands as a 'natural' form of society, unlike the state. As in Handler's book, the logical continuity of individual and nation is a constant reprise in Kapferer's account.[4]

The trouble with nationalism is that power, vested in the state or elsewhere, tends to turn this into a self-fulfilling principle. Consistent with my argument throughout this book, I have reservations about Kapferer's readiness to generalise beliefs and behaviour to Australians, and, incidentally, to the Sinhalese to whom he contrasts Australians. My qualms are egocentric, or self-informed: I think that if I was Sinhalese or Australian, I would not recognise myself in the highly generalised formulations which he offers. I cannot think of anything similarly generalised which I would be confident in formulating now about one thousand Whalsay islanders, nor about my three sons. Perhaps I err in the opposite extreme by focusing on the *ir*regularities among people.

I have more sympathy with the view that nationalism attempts to force individuals into a matrix of ideology and practice, with the consequence that the 'nation as individual writ large' becomes axiomatic. In what he strikingly calls 'the arithmetic of nationalism', Kapferer does show that as Australia has become more heterogeneous ethnically and culturally through immigration, so there has grown pressure to establish a cultural orthodoxy:

> Nations must multiply likeness, not difference, otherwise national identity is weakened.
>
> (Kapferer 1988: 191)

It is precisely this interventionist mathematics that I would see as lying behind the Anzac Day ceremonies in the provision of formulaic texts and interpretations. The foisting of uniform national ideas of the person on to the individual is what I see as the attempt to 'culture thought'. He insists that even if traditions are 'invented', their elements must have some cultural authenticity (ibid.: 211). I agree, but this is only to make the obvious point that if they are to draw individuals into their net, political managers must select symbols which have a cultural resonance. They must then put them together with sufficient ingenuity that they appear to respond to the needs of disparate individuals so that they can recognise themselves in such collective entities as the nation.

During the 1980s, there began to appear analyses of state rituals in the communist countries, which focused on attempts by their respective regimes to replicate the ritual life of displaced religious and cultural traditions (*inter alia*, Binns 1979/1980; Humphrey 1983; Lane 1981; and see Warner 1984: 265, 278ff.). Most found that these state ceremonies suffered the fate of imposed ritual anywhere: that however well contrived their forms, they could not control the meanings read into them by their audiences. Participants could subvert the intentions of the authors of these rites by supplying their own texts for them. Henriksen graphically presented the case of the Naskapi congregation dutifully answering the call to communion in their Catholic missionary's church, and, while chewing on the wafer, communing with the Caribou Spirit as they were used to doing while eating caribou bone marrow in their own *mokoshan* rite (Henriksen 1973; and see Cohen 1985: 46-8). The presently burgeoning studies being conducted within the newly independent states of east and central Europe will doubtless bring forth many more rich examples of the use of symbolic devices in the recreation of national identity.

I close this chapter by referring to one further example of contrived nationalist rites. It combines the features of internal diversity which Handler emphasises in his study of Quebec, with an analytical approach which closely resembles Kapferer's. It is Handelman's account of Remembrance and Independence Days in Israel (1990). These two commemorations are held on successive days, and, although marked by starkly contrasted symbolism and behaviour, may be seen as contingent texts. Remembrance Day should not be confused with commemoration of the Holocaust which has its own Day beforehand. Rather, it is a memorial to those Israelis who died in the War of Independence and in subsequent wars and armed conflicts. The adjacency of the two days thus has an implicit message: independence was won and can only be maintained at a cost; conversely, the loss of life makes it imperative to sustain independence. Each valorises and validates the other. As Handelman says, 'they make meaning together' (Handelman 1990: 194).

First, an understatement: the Jewish population of Israel are so heterogeneous in provenance, history, language, religious and secular traditions and political orientation that the creation of a national (as opposed to religious) identity is clearly politically imperative and extremely difficult.

The difficulty is exacerbated by the extent and intensity of antagonisms among the population. In the past, observers have drawn attention to the divisions between Jews of European and of Maghrebian and Middle Eastern origins, between *askenazim* and *sephardim*. The divisions have become more complex with the huge increase in immigration from the former Soviet Union, with unemployment and underemployment, with the tensions over settlement policy in the occupied territories, with confrontation between secularism and religiosity, with the huge expansion of the Hasidic communities and the growth in numbers and political influence of the right-wing, religious settlers. This list of complicating factors merely skims the surface and does not even take into account the fact that Israel is an occupying and expansionist power which has incorporated a large Arab population within its own boundaries, and has intruded massively and destructively upon neighbouring Arab countries. The occupation and the military aggression have themselves produced further tensions and divisions within the Jewish population.

We must assume that the complexities of the context are taken for granted in the ceremonial texts and in the imperative to create symbolic devices which are capable of engendering solidarity. If we multiply the significantly different constituent groups by the individuals who compose them, we have some measure of the task which has to be accomplished by the political management of nationhood. I would suggest that this explains what are superficially scanty texts. The rites themselves are sparse and brief. However, as Handelman describes them they are clearly 'thick' (in Geertzian terms), capable of being endlessly substantiated through personal experience and interpretation: they allow participants and onlookers to tell themselves a story.

Independence Day, *Yom Ha'atzma'ut*, is focused on the grave of Theodor Herzl, the founder of modern Zionism, on the summit of Mount Herzl in Jerusalem. This overlooks the military cemetery and the graves of other notable national figures, and Yad Vashem, the Holocaust memorial, a location which thus encompasses the modern history of Judaism and overlooks its biblical past. It follows on immediately from Remembrance Day, *Yom Hazikaron*, which is opened ceremonially in front of the Western Wall, a sacred location which has featured increasingly in state occasions since its capture in 1967. The ceremonial spaces for both Days are themselves thick with associations which speak to

> the profundity of feeling that they evoke. The Wall . . . is a powerful synthesiser of sentiment and symbol, of the present making the past.
> (Handelman 1990: 201–2)

Remembrance Day is opened at night, with the ceremonial space in semi-darkness. The ceremony is of mourning, led by the state President, and emphasising the familihood of the nation of which he is the father figure. National flag at half-mast, the evocative sound of the military bugle, the kindling of a memorial flame (an element borrowed from Jewish domestic mourning), brief speeches from the President and the Chief-of-Staff, and prayer: it is over within fifteen minutes.

> The spareness and simplicity of the program, and of its enactment, are striking. So too are the stillness and darkness, the vacant spaces, the constrained and restricted movement. These aspects reflect and reinforce one another, and are echoed in rhetoric to evoke a focused cast of mind, mood and sentiment. The ceremony is composed all of a piece, its unity of symbolism not to be broached. The occasion is characterized by a high degree of symbolic synthesis of person, position, performance, and place, from which variation and individualism are quite effaced.
>
> (Handelman 1990: 205)

I wonder. No doubt the intention may be to preempt variation, but those who watch the ceremony filter it through their own experiences and perceptions. To suppose that these are really uniform, even significantly uniform, is to deny individuality and to assume that the meanings which people attribute to the rites are as simple as their enactment; it is to confuse form and substance. If they all interpreted the text in the same way, there would be no need to contrive sentiments of solidarity in nationhood for they would already exist.

Handelman reads off the symbolic components of the ceremony in minute detail, from its timing in the sequence of the Holocaust, Remembrance and Independence Days, to its spatial configuration, the flags and flames, incantations and speeches. The ceremony is a theatrical production under the direction of the Defence Ministry which is clearly intended to unite its audience in commitment to the state – and, indeed, to a view of the state as the embodiment of the nation in its guise as extended, bereaved family (Handelman 1990: 211).

The transition between the two days is ceremonially marked at Herzl's tomb where the state shows its civilian face. Although the military remains much in evidence, their presence reiterates the ideological view of them as a citizen army. At the end of the memorial prayer, the plaza is flooded with light as the state flag is run to the masthead – the enlightening state! The iconic display – of flags, of Herzl's tomb, of beacons lit by distinctively dressed representatives of

different groups – speaks to the moral unity of the nation engendered by
the state:

> The ceremony that opens Independence Day demands unquestioned
> allegiance to the integrity of the nation-state
>
> (Handelman 1990: 217)

and then depicts selectively its multifaceted character. The symbolism
plays on the theme of the twelve tribes of Israel, and, thus, on the composition of the nation itself. The historical diversity of the Jewish people is
presented as precedent for the heterogeneity of the modern state:

> [T]he state is shown as composed elementally of autonomous indivi-
> duals, each of whom stands for more than his or her self, and each of
> whom in their own way is dedicated to . . . the greater good of the state.
>
> (Handelman 1990: 221)

Selective individuality is expressed to give point to the coalescence of
individuals in the state.

Handelman's ethnography suggests very neat authorship in the composition of the ceremonies. But though he pays meticulous attention to the
nuances of the text, he gives us only authorial intentions; we do not know,
have no way of knowing, how efficacious they are in communicating with
the public. We have no reason to assume that they are any more successful
in subordinating individuality and homogenising participants' interpretations than are any other rituals, including those which are constituted
by symbolism of possibly more immediate relevance.

However ingeniously designed the show may be, it is still viewed
from the unique vantage of the self. The state may well overestimate its
capacity to culture thought and subordinate, even eliminate, the self.
The conclusion to this chapter returns to an earlier statement: 'society:
individual:: form: meaning'. Society may well be greater than the sum
of its parts, the excess including the means by which to compel the
actions of its members. But as an intelligible entity, it cannot be conceptualised apart from the individuals who compose it, alone and in their
relationships. So far as they are concerned, it is what *they* perceive it to
be, and their actions are motivated by their perceptions of it. Theories of
society which ignore those perceptions would therefore seem to be
partial at best, vacuous at worst. Similarly, cultural forms, such as
language, ritual and other symbolic constructions, are made meaningful
and substantial by people's interpretations of them. They are given life
by being made meaningful. We may well regard these symbols as being
compelling: the flag, the tomb, the soldier's slouch hat, the mateship and

the booze. But the power they exercise lies in providing us with the means by which to think. The assumption that under normal circumstances they can make us think in specifiable ways is mistaken. It privileges culture over thinking selves, instead of seeing it as the product of thinking selves.

Chapter 7

Individualism, individuality, selfhood

THE INDULGENT SELF?

At the outset of this book, I insisted that a concern with selfhood should be clearly distinguished from an infatuation with individualism. Individualism is a dogmatic posture which privileges the individual over society. By contrast, anthropological attention to the self recognises the need to address individuals' perceptions of society: first, to establish the elementary point that they differ and, therefore, are misunderstood if regarded as produced by superordinate social forces; second, because they are the premises for individuals' behaviour. I have used extensively a third cognate word, individuality, to suggest a property of selfhood: the perception of an individual's distinctiveness. Individuality is an ideologically neutral concept and is therefore quite different from individualism. It may not be synonymous with selfhood, for it does not necessarily imply the consciousness of self which I take to be the defining characteristic of selfhood. However, it is difficult to conceive of a self-consciousness which does not also entail a sense of individuality.

I do not labour these distinctions for their own sake, but because they seem all too frequently to be blurred in both lay and anthropological discourse. It is crucial to establish the point that the incorporation of self consciousness into social analysis does not concede the political contention either that individualism is a defensible proposition, or the contract-theoretical position that the individual should be regarded as somehow prior to society. To argue, as I have done above, that the *self* has primacy is different: it is to offer the view that the behaviour of individuals is initiated by their perceptions or consciousness of themselves and of their relationship to society. It is most certainly *not* to suggest that the behaviour of individuals is motivated by their inherent drive or desire for self-gratification.

In a recent book, *The Human Career* (1990), Goldschmidt aspires to make the self the focus of social analysis, but in a way which eschews much interest either in self consciousness or in individuality, which he confuses with individualism and which he treats as the pursuit of self-interest. He postulates the self as driven throughout the 'career' of its life-course by the need for self-gratification. He argues that selfhood is not determined by social structure – so far, so good – but that it has its origins in neurophysiological drives to self-gratification. Cultures universally transform these drives into the aspiration for prestige.

Goldschmidt sees cultural and biological evolution as having co-occurred until humans developed the capacity for symbolisation and language, and then culture took over. It had to find ways of transforming into communicable and acceptable social behaviour the putative fact that the neural development of the infant demands a strong emotional and tactile relationship which, in due course, inclines the maturing individual to become 'affect-hungry' (Goldschmidt 1990: 32) and to seek other forms of self-gratification. He thus presents the individual as being self-driven ('motivated') rather than society-driven, but in a single direction. Defined and redefined through social interaction, the sense of self is built on the universal need for affect (ibid.: 106).

Goldschmidt draws on a wide range of ethnographies to come to the unsurprising conclusion that societies differ in the ways in which they tackle a common imperative, the restraint of the self-gratifying individual. He finds that ritual is a ubiquitous means of restraint, a device for 'ordering' sentiments (Goldschmidt 1990: 174) and for creating an emotional climate, a view not very far removed from Durkheim's.

Though Goldschmidt avoids some of the ideological excesses and sillier statements of the sociobiologists, many social anthropologists would instinctively be sceptical about his attempt to marry biological and cultural evolution. Whatever its merits may be, his thesis is fundamentally flawed by giving 'self' the restricted connotation of egoism or self-indulgence. The neo-Hobbesian conception of the individual as self-serving is posited axiomatically, and ignores the more interesting and open-minded (if problematic) question of the individual's self-awareness.

An account of the historical evolution of this broader view of the self is to be found in a study by the Chinese-American geographer, Yi-Fu Tuan (1982). Drawing on a formidable range of sources, but treating culture and 'cultures' with a certain lack of discrimination, Tuan argues that the peculiar concern of 'Western culture' with the self arises from the tendencies in its developing civilisation (note the singular) to differentiate and segment holistic forms and the strict observance of these segmentary boundaries. To illustrate his argument, he sketches the development of cuisine and table manners, of domestic architecture and of the theatre, maintaining that in each of these contexts the holistic, undifferentiated and universalistic styles of the ancient and medieval worlds were gradually broken down as they moved into the modern era. They then emerged in the forms, respectively, of highly specialised place settings to serve the distinctive needs of the now discrete courses and their characteristic foods; of domestic space, now organised around the complementary values of functional specificity and privacy; and of the theatre's retreat from the global arena to the proscenium arch – from performance in the midst of an audience, to a stark separation of the performer from the spectator. Replicating this process at the micro level, the self emerged as a segmented and introspective aspect of the person.

Tuan's argument is built on the false assumption that in 'pre-modern' societies, the self is irreducible; later, in modernity, it becomes divisible and separated into discrete components. Once again we find ourselves back in the midst of old-fashioned role theory of a kind which has been animating debate among social psychologists for decades. Prominent among the participants in this debate was Ralph Turner who, in an article published in 1987, argued conclusively for a position he has been advocating for thirty years, namely that the individual's capacity to manage roles is based on a fundamental sense of his or her un-differentiated, irreducible organic self (Turner 1987: 121; and cf. 1962) which, despite Tuan's grand generalisations, is not necessarily qualified either by modernity or by non-Western provenance.[1]

We should applaud Turner's perseverance. Tuan contends that societies such as the Dinka, Tswana and Wintu do not discriminate between the self and the collectivity. These cases are well-rehearsed in the literature and are unconvincing. The argument confuses cross-cultural theories of personal agency with cross-cultural theories of causality. It thereby conflates two different questions: who acts? And what causes acts to occur? The tribal ideology may say that if I commit an action, then the entire patrilineal descent group to which I belong is implicated in my action, even, perhaps, that it acts through me. But this is not the same as saying that my action was mindless, or that I had no control over what I did, that I was the unconscious agent of the collective will. As Campbell has demonstrated in his study of Wayãpí, the comparison of different cultures' theories of causality is not simply a matter of tabulating for different societies their attributions of cause and effect. It has first to take account of the cultural specificity of the very concept of 'cause' and its linguistic expression (Campbell 1989: 91). Tuan confuses awareness of self with theories of causation, echoing a similar mistake made earlier by anthropologists such as Lienhardt and Zahan.

If Ralph Turner has been correct all along in insisting that roles are accretions of the self, rather than its divisions (or 'partitions' as Tuan would have it), then there is no basis for discriminating *a priori* between concepts of the self in pre-modern and modern, non-industrial and industrialised, 'Western' and non-Western societies. Rather than having to prove the existence and saliency of selfhood in other cultures, we might reasonably assume it – unless anthropologists can marshal sufficiently weighty ethnographic evidence of their informants' experience to suggest otherwise. It is a mark of our own intellectual naïveté that we have sceptically required anthropologists to *prove* the existence and saliency of selfhood in other cultures. If part of our problem lay in our methodological inhibitions about studying people's awareness of themselves, then we compounded it by our clumsy confusions of selfhood with individualism and egocentricity, and of group membership with the group's determination of the individual's behaviour.

CONSERVATISM AND ENGLISH INDIVIDUALISM: A POLEMIC

In late-twentieth-century Britain, this gauche naïveté became elevated into political dogma which informed the policy of successive Conservative governments, and which, ironically, made individualism and individuality mutually exclusive stances.[2] 'The individual' was central to the rhetoric of Thatcherism, which abounded in such notions as individual responsibility, individual initiative, individual freedoms, and even led to the denial of the very existence of 'society' in favour of its individual components. The individual was projected as the object of government action, to which was opposed the ultimate in Thatcherite demonology, the collectivist state.

This opposition was paradoxical, since the state is the political and legal instrument of government policy. While the rhetoric abhorred the state, the government also vastly augmented its power. Under the premiership of Margaret Thatcher, the state began routinely to intervene in areas of public policy (such as local government, curriculum and educational philosophy, broadcasting practice, moral conduct and religious life) in which it had previously trodden lightly other than in times of exceptional national crisis.

The paradox is instructive because it parallels and explains another. The personally responsible, free individual, so highly vaunted by the rhetoric, stood on the wreckage of the self-conscious, self-directing idiosyncratic individual who resisted conformity, rejected the social categories which provided the bases of marketing and planning strategies, the individual to whom were assimilated the classifying and homogenising devices of the mass society, rather than the other way around. This autonomous individual was the victim of the privilege accorded by Thatcher governments to economic power: sacrificed to economies of sale; despised not only for economic weakness, but also for a refusal to conform to a regimented, and therefore bogus, individualism. The integrity of such individuals was contemptuously impugned (for example, as being 'wet') for they were manifestly 'not one of us'. The individual who figured so prominently in Thatcherite rhetoric was the creature of an authoritarian view of the self, to whom may be opposed the autonomous, self-directing, 'authorial' self.

'Individualism' has long been the hackneyed term used by writers to characterise English society. Lukes (1973) showed cogently that the word has been given discrepant meanings in different philosophical traditions (see Taylor 1989). Applied to England, it may refer to liberation from ideological, dogmatic or other coercive orthodoxies (Morris 1987), or to the obligation on men to forge their own economic destinies without the support which elsewhere may be drawn from the convention of partible inheritance (Macfarlane 1978). As we saw in the last chapter, it has been used metonymically to describe the value of domestic privacy (Strathern 1992) and, jurisprudentially, to refer to a doctrine of legalistic egalitarianism. It has been deployed to emphasise the ego-centred nature of bilateral kinship and cognatic descent systems, which are supposedly typical of Britain (see Fox 1965), and to refer to a spurious freedom of conscience, which has been simultaneously promulgated as a principle and denigrated as a practice by Conservative opinion, with no apparent embarrassment at the contradiction.

Individuality can be juxtaposed to all of these various constructions of individualism. Conservative dogma recognised individuality only as a class-specific value, reserved to those who either by birth or by achievement (however defined) had the right to 'be themselves'. The opposites of this rather limited notion of meritocratic or eccentric individuality are well represented in English life by the anonymity and denial of individuality in the council housing estate (dwellings of identical design, even down to front doors painted in the same colours), the package tour, the union 'mass meeting', the instructively named 'public' bar of the pub, the grim concrete and crush barriers of the football terrace. The British tabloid-journalistic compulsion to stereotyping clouds the perception of, and certainly denigrates, other people's claims to individuality.

This discrimination has been founded on a deeply rooted class chauvinism, perhaps more apparent in England than in Scotland, which reserved intellect, sensitivity and self-awareness to the superior orders and denied them to the plebeian others. It would be replicated later in the colonising *self* and colonised *other* of British imperialism (and, later, of British social anthropology). In pre-Victorian literature, in drama, historiography and political theory, individuals somehow seemed to belong to the upper and middle classes; the rest formed an un-differentiated mass from which only the most exceptional became singularly recognisable. It required the insight and skill of writers such as Dickens and Tressell to make working-class self consciousness and personal distinctiveness intelligible and acceptable.

It is for historians to locate the origins of such anti-individuality, but its renaissance in Thatcher's 'enterprise culture' was striking. The puta-tive freedom which it accorded to the individual was redolent with the peculiar scent of nineteenth-century utilitarian liberalism in which one was free to eat or to starve. In Thatcherite Britain (a condition which unhappily has survived beyond her own prime ministership), one became 'free' to choose between private and public health care, school-ing and housing, freedoms which took little account of the financial circumstances of the individual who was the supposed beneficiary of such enlightened policy. The reform of the social benefits system left young people 'free' to choose between an inadequate and exploitative youth training placement, and a home in a cardboard box, on a park bench or in a shop doorway.

It must be said that the speciousness of this freedom is not wholly attributable to the politics of Thatcherism. In his authoritative study, *Freedom, the Individual and the Law*, Robertson (1989) showed that the legalistic protection of individual rights in England hovers between the rudimentary and the non-existent. My concern here is not so much with freedoms under the law or enshrined in political and economic policy, as with the most fundamental of personal freedoms, the right to authorial identity, to selfhood as manifested in individuality. In the dogmas of the so-called New Right, the individual is typed, labelled, limited by the discourses of economic individual*ism* and of generalisation, and gener-ally denied any *self*-perception which does not accord with this ortho-doxy. It is difficult to see how the doctrinaire advocacy of the profit-motive can be reconciled with a view of the self-directing individual. Of course, an individual may be both self-aware and profit-seeking. But the assumptions in Conservative economic policy about the motivating efficacy of profit-maximisation (as, for example, in the privatisation and contracting-out schemes) suggests a naïve belief in stimulus–response theory, in which the stimulus of profit and fear of failure induce the response of competitiveness. In this view, selfhood gives way to the compulsion to maximise profit, the autonomy of the individual undermined by the irresistible impulse to self-gratification. There does not seem much to choose between Thatcher and Goldschmidt.

Yet, the discourse *was* about the individual and personal freedom. How can such a contradiction be explained, assuming that it was not just the consequence of artifice or stupidity? I suggest that the answer lies in a kind of credulousness which defined individuals in terms of the apparent simplicity of their actions, and thus simply failed to acknowledge their complexity and variability. In the Thatcher canon, there were at least three theoretical constructions which would seem to point to this confusion. The first was variously expressed as 'human nature', 'the British people', and Judaeo-Christians (see Raban 1989). It attributed self-seeking as a species-trait to individuals, and then justified it so long as it was exercised within a particular cultural code. The second construed behaviour in terms of a stipulated conscious motive, thereby defining as unnecessary the investigation and interrogation of motives: they could be taken for granted. For example, members of Mrs Thatcher's governments were forever wrapping even the most unpopular of their policies in the constitutional mantle of 'the mandate', a doctrine which they exploited to attribute highly specific policy intentions to electors' voting behaviour in the absence of much reliable evidence. They were invoking a Hobbesian notion: that people *consciously* contract with each other to satisfy their individual interests to the optimal extent. But their putative consciousness may rest on nothing more substantial than the imagination of the Prime Minister's speech writer. Individuals' intentions (and their dogmatic constitution in Conservative theory) were assumed to be informed by an Oakeshottian suspicion of collectivity and organisation. Generally speaking, individuals-as-atoms present much less of a problem to Conservative doctrine than individuals-in-composite bodies.

The third Thatcherite construction which clearly persists in the Conservative Party (I write this in October 1993 as the Party's annual conference is in session) is that of 'robust', 'resolute' leadership. This encodes the attitude that too much thinking is bad for people: they really want to be told what to do. They are confused and debilitated by too great a range of choices. They like most of all to hear the leader's celebrated judgement, 'There is no alternative!' (a judgement subsequently satirised by her acronymic nickname of Tina).

It would be absurd to lay all the blame for the subversion of the self at the door of Thatcherism. It has been a long time with us, and not just in British and Western political and philosophical traditions. As I have argued throughout this book, social science, including anthropology itself, has been complicit in it. But Thatcherism was remarkable for its explicitness, not least in claiming the moral high ground for a doctrinaire position which the preceding British liberal consensus regarded as amoral, if not immoral. It would be consistent with Nikolas Rose's view to see it as symptomatic of the times. In his persuasive study, *Governing the Soul* (1990), Rose argued that the celebration of the self in the late twentieth century masked the extent to which selfhood was shaped by the dominant political and economic institutions of contemporary society. The vested interests of corporate power masqueraded as the interests of the self. The loss of real personal autonomy was hidden by the indulgence of subjectivity. As indicated by the rash of personal therapies, self-ness was fetishised in an apparent obsession with personal identity,

> this tyranny of intimacy in which narcissism is mobilized in social relations and the self is defined in terms of how it feels rather than what it does.
>
> (Rose 1990: 216)

He cites the argument made by Christopher Lasch (1980) that personal autonomy has been devastated by the intrusion of bureaucracy and professionalisation upon all areas of personal life and discretion, a matter to which we will shortly return.

The undoubted loss of personal rights should not be confused with the loss of selfhood: these are two different matters. The intrusive state and its agents and other institutions have certainly curtailed personal discretion in very many respects. But to suggest that they have succeeded in reducing the degree to which individuals are self-aware and self-conscious is quite different. They may well be conscious of different things and of different aspects of their selves, but that is not to concur with a presumption about the zero-sum relationship between selfhood and institutional power. Rose's argument is subtly different. He contends that selfhood is manipulated, 'shaped', that the very terms in which we experience ourselves 'are socially organised and managed in minute particulars' (Rose 1990: 1), and, following Foucault, that our mentalities are transformed into 'governmentalities' (ibid.: 5).

This argument does not admit a null hypothesis, and I can only respond that it underestimates the resilience of the self, neglecting the extent to which individuals are reflexively aware of the attempts made by others to shape their selves. Later in this chapter, I will turn briefly to some depictions of such reflexivity. Perhaps the only line of 'self-defence' is to urge Rose (like the Thatcherites to whom he is so clearly opposed) to recognise that there is a vital difference between what people *think* and what they appear to do. Difficult of access though it may be to us, selfhood is to be found in the former rather than in the latter.

There is an instructive contradiction in both lay and legal discourse in Britain with regard to the self and society. The individual is held to be personally responsible, but that responsibility is expressed in terms of obligations to a group or to society as a whole rather than to oneself. In defending this view, I cannot claim the authority of systematic research, but only the intuitive sense of an observant member. Individuals who exhibit 'cowardice in the face of the enemy', or are judged to have 'let the side down', are regarded in both cases as having failed others, and only secondarily to have failed themselves. To marry out of one's religion, or class, or ethnic group, may be depicted as an act of social betrayal rather than of the free, autonomous self (see MacFarlane 1986). Indeed, to plead the right to self-direction may be dismissed as self-indulgence. The self is supposed to recognise the moral obligation of its subordination to society.

The 'responsible' individual on whose shoulders rested the whole weight of Thatcherism was required to exercise that responsibility in very particular ways, or to refrain from practising it in ways which did not conform to the principles of acquisitive Conservatism. Charity was fine; welfare was not. Community activity (whatever this may mean) was laudable; trade union involvement was regrettable, to say the least. Speculating in the national currency was perfectly acceptable; studying philosophy, or being a social worker, or writing music was to be parasitic on those who created the country's wealth.[3] All ideologies make arbitrary discriminations. But in this peculiar case of an ideology in which the individual is such a prominent icon, the integrity of individuality and of the authorial self is continually tested for its conformity to a very specific, narrow and bleak version of personal responsibility. Individuals were strapped into an ideological straitjacket in which they were idealised players in the market game: everyone plays the *same* game, everyone wants the same things, everyone thus manifestly shares the same values, responds to the same stimuli, *is* the same. Individuality?

THE MASSIFICATION OF INDIVIDUALS, AND THE RIGHT TO IDENTITY

Britain has hardly been alone in having stumbled into a political regime which both enunciates, and appears to believe in, the doctrine of market forces, a doctrine which, as Macpherson (1964) so cogently argued, has been out of date since at least the end of the nineteenth century (see p. 146 above).

The market forces to which we are now subject are heavily managed, and, as Nikolas Rose showed, a crucial element of the management strategy is the manipulation of demand. The pernicious combination of economic and political market management has left us in the invidious condition of being persuaded to experience and express *our* selves by wearing designers' labels, drinking *their* instant coffee (and investing its advertisements with the status of soap opera), driving *their* cars. In consuming their products, we may lose our outward individuality, but we should distrust the suggestion that we thereby also lose our selves. Advertising specialists were quick to associate mass production and mass marketing with the 'massification' of the individual. In order to entice me to consume *their* products as an expression of *my* identity, they try to create an entire persona for me: I am Sony-person, Guinness-man, perhaps both together. If I resist and opt not to conform, I am liable to be treated merely as having swopped one stereotype for another, labelled 'alternative', which will almost certainly soon be colonised by the mainstream market. In this manipulative strategy, style is supposed to displace individuality.

But in all this, I suspect they are more credulous than we are gullible. The techniques of marketing may become more sophisticated (as its jargon grows more obscure), but its objectives are probably not much different than they have been since the market became style-led. However, it is precisely in order to resist the seductive explanation of behaviour in terms of styles, genres, categories and stereotypes that we have to be alert to the self-consciousness which qualifies them. Wherever we look in the world, people are fighting back in a struggle for identities which they can regard as more sensitive to themselves, rejecting self-denying generalisation and subordination to collective categories. People's attachment to collectivities is mediated by their *personal* experience. We know that about ourselves; we have to try to incorporate that knowledge into our understanding of others.

It may well be precisely because of their responsiveness to personal experience that during the last twenty-five years people have been reasserting gender, nationality, ethnicity, sexuality, locality, religious persuasion as means of reappropriating their identities or of creating them anew. Social scientists and others perhaps made the easy assumption that the attraction of these collective categories lay in the ease with which individuals could locate themselves in them. I suggest that we may be nearer the mark if we invert the relationship: people read collectivities through their experience as individuals. They may use collective forms to assert their identities, but we should not mistake these for *uni*formities of identity. These forms are motivated by individuals in their idiosyncratic ways. After all, it is a self-aware, self conscious individual who steps on to the commuter train in the morning and evening. If the best we can do descriptively for this person is to categorise him or her as 'a commuter', we should not be doing any better than the Conservative dogmatists for whom 'free' individuals are cloned by the market.

The issue of personal identity might be brought properly into focus by invoking the metaphor of 'personal rights' (Cohen 1993b). Anthropologists have conventionally concentrated on *rites* of identity through which they have regarded individuals as being led into approved social constructions of the person. But the discussion of initiation in Chapter 3 of this book suggests that we have neglected the often fraught and agonising clash between a person's sense of self and the identity imposed on her or him, a conflict which is essentially about who has the *right* to define an individual's identity.

The notion of a 'right' to identity may seem to stretch implausibly the category of 'rights'. In anthropology, as in other pertinent disciplines, 'rights' appears to imply either an issue of legal concern, or the integrity of person or group in relation to the state or to some other legally constituted body. Identity does not fit obviously into these frames of reference. In their comprehensive survey of anthropological literature, Downing and Kushner (1988) divided human rights into nearly seventy classes, but they did not include a class for 'identity'. It is arguably the case that by failing to take due account of self consciousness, we validate the neglect of identity as a human right. Given the legalistic connotation which we conventionally apply to 'rights', this neglect may suggest that we do not see identity as being subject to abuse. If the state explicitly interfered with, curtailed, or in other ways threatened a person's identity – say, by torture, in a penal regime, even through the peculiar disciplines of the armed forces – this surely *would* be seen as abuse of rights. To revert to a topic we touched on earlier, if a 'total institution' really did exist, it would probably command the attention of civil liberties activists. The conclusion must be that it is only in the breach that identity is regarded as an issue of rights. This must surely be unsatisfactory.

The 'right to identity' is a sensitive, subtle and complex matter, which may explain why novelists have dealt with it more satisfactorily than social scientists. But its neglect also leads us to conduct flawed social science. Anthropologists may well argue that their subject is concerned with social relations rather than with the individual. But the ways in which we have rendered social relationships have understated, even ignored, the sense and definitions of themselves that individuals take into their relationships, and we have therefore rendered them inadequately.

Moreover, in treating individuals as incidental to their social relationships (which is what is entailed in the neglect of self consciousness and self-definition), we make ourselves complicit in the processes of homogenisation through which dogmatic individualism triumphs over individuality. The demand to attend to an individual's right to identity also makes it incumbent on us to take account of individuals' sense of their difference from others. The proof of our failure to do this and of the consequences of this failure is evident in the shortcomings of public policy and planning, from public housing (Hulme; Broadwater Farm; Nanterre; the Bronx 'Projects') to development aid (examples too numerous to mention), which can be attributed to our readiness to be satisfied by overgeneralised analyses, theories and prescriptions. If public discourse and policy are ever to be rescued from such grotesque simplifications (with their grotesque consequences), the primacy of difference has to be placed firmly on the agenda. Politicians and practitioners may continue to dismiss difference as eccentric, or to subvert it by collapsing it into such gross categories as ethnicity, religion or class. Anthropologists should insist that difference is a matter of consciousness, of *self* consciousness, not of official licence and recognition. The alternative is to sanction blindness to personal identity, a wilful blindness which, taken to now familiar extremes, can lead to the barbaric trampling of collective identities.

Functionalist social science gave us the word 'actor' to use for individual. It went with 'role'. But roles are inventions, the performance of fictions, which are supposed to mask the actors who play them, to conceal them from us as persons with other identities. We have developed a social science which, consistent with these metaphors, depicts the individual as a performing self. We cannot see the actors, because in anthropology we say that they are methodologically out of reach. The dogmatic advocates of individualism do not see them because they do not wish to. So we settle for the script, which we invent ourselves through our ingenious use of categories. In the new entrepreneurial revolution, we invented the selfish self, and have continued to ignore the self conscious self. Yet, if we dare to reflect on the resilience of our own self consciousness, even on that of the unfortunate victims of prolonged imprisonment which is calculated to destroy their selves, we must recognise the strength of the authorial self. If we do, we find that Thatcherism was wrong about individualism, and that social scientists have been wrong in treating personal and collective identity as the products of social relativities.

We must make deliberate efforts to acknowledge the subtleties, inflections and varieties of individual consciousness which are concealed by the categorical masks which we have invented so adeptly. Otherwise, we will continue to deny to people the right to be themselves, deny their right to their own identities.

NOVELISTS AND THE REFLEXIVE SELF

Man and writer were the same person.
But that is a writer's greatest discovery. It took time –
and how much writing! – to arrive at that synthesis.

(Naipaul 1987: 102)

Throughout this book, we have encountered illustrations of the ways in which societies attempt to occupy or to colonise the individual's consciousness. Writers on initiation, religious belief and practice, political rhetoric and organisational regimes see societies as impressing themselves so firmly on members' minds that they identify themselves substantially with the society or group in question. Culture theorists and authors such as Strathern, Fernandez and the interpreters of ritual and ceremony explore the ways in which culture is so insinuated into cognitive processes that it presses people into matrices of perception. To all of these, I seem to have been saying, 'Yes, but. . .' When all of this has been done to the self, is there nothing left with which she or he can bite back?

I do not suggest that anthropology conventionally sees people as automata who are motivated by structural or cultural forces beyond their control. Such a view is not unprecedented, but may reasonably be regarded as untypical, even eccentric. However, I would certainly not be inclined to moderate my contention that we have been inclined to exaggerate the vulnerability of the self to these social forces, and have thereby underestimated its resilience and consistency. I commented earlier on the cases of kidnap hostages and concentration camp victims. But by pointing to such extreme instances, we also divert attention away from the quotidian struggle, or conflict, or tension between self and society, in which the self *routinely* resists and eventually triumphs, perhaps does not succumb at all. These are not heroic battles, but are mundane. Yet somehow we seem to have failed to notice them or to give them due attention, and end up by default privileging society over the individual in our analyses. This may be because of the now-familiar difficulties which attend the study of the self – or because our disciplines require us to portray *social* mechanisms, and fail to recognise that in thus neglecting the self consciousness which informs these mechanisms, 'portrayal' inevitably becomes invention.

The irony is that in deliberately inventive writing, in fiction, we find the self portrayed far more convincingly, precisely because the tensions between it and intrusive others are depicted explicitly and are given full measure. Novelists seem much more reluctant than anthropologists to concede that the self succumbs to these pressures, however powerful they may be. This is not the place, and I am not the writer, to make a comprehensive survey of the self in the modern English language novel. But I illustrate my contention from three novels which, though very different in theme and style, all seem to me to treat the self with exquisite ethnographic skill.

Tom Wolfe's *The Bonfire of the Vanities* (1988) is an avowedly documentary (or 'realistic') novel (Wolfe 1988: xiv) of its time and place, New York in the late 1980s during the age of 'self-seeking speculation', as Crapanzano has described it (Crapanzano 1992: 4). The plot is simple: an affluent Wall Street bond dealer is party to a road accident in which a black youth from the Bronx is fatally injured. With a dreadful inevitability, the petty ambitions of a few otherwise un-connected people, and a fundamentally flawed legal system, combine to ensure the utter ruin of the implicated, but legally innocent, man. There are many stories being told here: about the grotesque inequalities in the world's most affluent society; that the privileged cannot be innocent in such an unjust, even corrupt society; that apparent wealth may rest on the very insecure bases of loans and debt; that those who stand as the advocates of the oppressed are just as likely to be corrupt or corruptible as their oppressors; that the distinctions to be made between guilt and innocence are tenuous indeed; that it is in the nature of society that *nothing* is simple – or, at least, that apparent simplicity conceals the reality of complexity; that appearance is illusion. Wolfe exploits the licence of fiction to show how unconnected events and people converge on the central character. The aspect of his writing to which I draw attention here is the subtlety with which he displays selfhood and its relation to its encompassing society.

The anti-hero, Sherman McCoy (a member of the New York social, professional and moneyed elite), has collected his beautiful young mistress (married to a *nouveau-riche* Jew) from the airport. Driving back to Manhattan, they get lost in the Bronx. McCoy stops the car to move a wheel which is lying in the road. Seeing two black youths approaching, he believes he has been ambushed. He throws the wheel at them, and screams at his mistress to drive off as he just manages to get into the passenger seat. As she pulls away, he is aware that the car may have hit one of the youths as it slewed. Against McCoy's better judgement, but deferring to the woman who had been driving, they do not report the incident. It transpires that the boy has indeed been hit, collapses into a coma and dies a year later without ever regaining consciousness.

The incident is exploited for their own very different political purposes by a black populist preacher-racketeer and by the Bronx District Attorney who is seeking re-election. It is also grist to the mills of the sexual and career ambitions of the Assistant District Attorney, an alcoholic English journalist and his paper's proprietor, two other New York lawyers, and an assortment of media folk and glitterati.

The net inexorably closes in on McCoy, abandoned by his socially ambitious wife, his daughter (who, besides the victim himself, is about the only innocent in the book), his employer (a prestigious investment house), his neighbours and peers, and, eventually, by his lawyer whose bills he can no longer pay. His downfall, from extreme wealth to bankruptcy and to his fate as 'a career defendant' (Wolfe 1988: 728), is accompanied by, what he experiences as, the degradation of his self.

The social bases of his self-assurance – his family and educational background, his career, his wealth, the social milieu in which he moves – are quickly revealed to him as shallow. Even as he moves among his peers, he silently satirises them for their pretensions, their noise, their preoccupations. As he is engaged in conversation with others, we hear him communing with his self.

The same is true also of his alter-ego, Kramer, the Assistant DA who pursues him partly in order to impress the young woman he wants to seduce. Kramer sees himself as a failure in the game of material and professional success, and is oppressed by his own relative penury. A Jew from a *petit bourgeois* background, he has none of McCoy's advantages, is frightened of his environment, whereas McCoy has grown used to

seeing himself as a 'Master of the Universe', a man who can manufacture riches from virtually nothing. Kramer is a body builder, and his
self-defences seem to be located only in his exaggerated muscles.
Before McCoy's saga has ended, Kramer too is brought down, in a
characteristically tawdry way, by his pettily corrupt attempt to secure by
blackmail the rent-controlled apartment used by McCoy and his
mistress which he wants for his own sexual adventures. But before then
we are aware of him constantly talking to his self as he struggles to make
himself inconspicuous among his colleagues by using degraded language and being one of the (Irish or Italian) boys. His downfall comes
when his self fails in this monitoring function, and he allows himself to
be dazzled and fooled by his illusory professional and sexual success.

McCoy experiences his degradation as the alienation of his self,
literally, his loss of self-control: he feels himself to have been invaded
by society-at-large, his consciousness becomes an open house for all
would-be colonisers,

> an amusement park to which everybody, *todo el mundo, tout le
> monde*, comes scampering, skipping and screaming, nerves a-tingle,
> loins aflame, ready for anything, all you've got, laughs, tears, moans,
> giddy thrills, gasps, horrors, whatever, the gorier the merrier.
>
> (Wolfe 1988: 546)

He watches himself in the cells beneath the courtroom, at the fashionable dinner party, sees other people occupying the space of his self in
order to nurture their own career ambitions. He becomes a spectator as
they tug the strings attached to his puppet-like person.

We are not told what happens to Kramer following his disgrace. Nor do
we know McCoy's eventual fate as he comes to trial for manslaughter.
However, it is made abundantly clear that he has triumphed in reclaiming
control of his self. He has abandoned whatever former pretensions he may
have had, reverting to his pre-Wall Street scepticism about 'the system'. In
taking control of his own legal defence, he also undertakes his self-defence.
While career, wealth, status and social attachments crumble into the dust,
his self seems to rise, phoenix-like, from the rubble of his career.

Wolfe makes selfhood an explicit theme of his novel. As he watches
his own personal disaster unfold, McCoy comes to a kind of intuitive
realisation that he had previously been mistaken about what and where
his self was. I think that the metaphors of invasion and appropriation
suggest that he had confused his persona (a social construction) with his
self. He tells his uncomprehending lawyer that he feels as if the person
known to other people has died:

'I can't explain the feeling. All I can tell you is that I'm already dead, or the Sherman McCoy of the McCoy family and Yale and Park Avenue and Wall Street is dead. ... Your *self* ... *is other people*, all the people you're tied to, and it's only a thread.'

(Wolfe 1988: 587)

That is to say, the McCoy who is anyway appropriated by others through his social relationships – as husband and father, as colleague, as customer – has become discardable, both by others and by himself. This is the aspect of McCoy which anthropologists would know, following Mauss, as 'the person', social property, but not self-conscious.

On the other hand, there is his authentic self which he discovers only when his persona is trampled into the ground:

They had closed in for the kill, and they hurt him and humiliated him, but they could not reach his inviolable self, Sherman McCoy, inside the brass crucible of his mind.

(Wolfe 1988: 547)

It is this discovery which provides McCoy with his lifeline, as he despairingly contemplates suicide. The notion of the irreducibility of the self is well rehearsed in Anglo-American scholarship, and is clearly implicated in my own argument. Perhaps the metaphysical (even slightly mystical) connotations of the idea explain why rationalist anthropologists have been wary of it. But scholarly caution does not excuse the failure to address a problem, whose neglect has had profound consequences for the ways in which we understand and describe social behaviour. Hywel Lewis was eloquent on the matter:

[If I am asked] What is this 'I' that has these thoughts and this pain, how is it in turn to be described over and above describing the thoughts or the pain ... I am wholly nonplussed. There is nothing I can begin to say in reply, not because it is exceptionally difficult to give a correct description, but just because there is no description that can be offered. My distinctness, my being me, is quite unmistakable to me, there can be nothing of which I am more certain, but it is also unique and ultimate, not unique like a rare vase or painting where we can indicate the properties that make it unique, but unique in a final sense of just being itself.

(Lewis 1982: 55)

It may be this notion of the essentialism of the self which scholars have mistaken for a Western preoccupation with the self as such. I am not convinced that there is anything peculiarly Western about either, although the contention that there is may be an expression of an occidental self-image as well as an anthropological mistake.

In his Introduction to the novel, Wolfe takes a stance which social scientists would recognise as 'deterministic': people are fated by the contemporary configurations of power. But as the story unfolds, it becomes clear that, while individuals may not be in control of events, they are extremely resourceful in clinging on to their selves, protecting the deep parts of themselves which society cannot reach. When they do so, the events in which they get caught up become oddly incidental; like McCoy, they become spectators at their own social funerals.

Note again the testimony of hostages. Chained to a radiator or clamped in leg irons, they compose novels in their heads, mentally translate Shakespeare into Pharsee, rehearse arithmetic calculations . . . and survive. Wolfe, I think, has seen this, and uses his novel brilliantly to bring it out. Anthropologists, by contrast, are either dazzled by the events and blinded to what goes on beneath them, or feel compelled to restrict themselves to the events. Whichever is the case, their accounts cannot be other than partial or, worse, misleading.

In the end, then, McCoy survives by digging in to his irreducible self, which is revealed to his readers throughout the book as we are told what he is thinking. Another, but very different tale of the resilience of self is told by Paul Bailey in *Gabriel's Lament* (1987). Despite the stylistic and substantive differences between these two books, similar themes occur: the confusion, and then discrimination of appearance and reality; the distinction between persona and self; the rescue of the self from self-destruction; and the use of an alter ego.

Gabriel Harvey is born to a man already in his late fifties, and a woman thirty years younger. The family live in the pinched circumstances of working-class London in the immediate aftermath of the Second World War. Among various other jobs, his father had been a servant to a minor aristocrat, and his mother, Amy, worked in 'her secret place', which, like much else, is only revealed at the end of the book to have been the kitchens of Buckingham Palace. They both appear to dote on their gifted, undersized young son, the garrulous father bestowing benevolent worldly wisdom on him, while Amy is fussily affectionate and proud of his precociousness.

All is to change when Gabriel is twelve, and his elderly father suddenly inherits a sizeable sum of money from his aristocratic erstwhile master. The money goes instantly to his head, and he removes his family to a large suburban villa in south London. There he lavishes luxuries of all kinds on his increasingly unhappy wife, while his attitude to his son becomes hectoring, where it had previously been affectionate. He abruptly stops using his son's name, addressing him only as 'Young man', thereby depriving him of identity and somehow making him insubstantial. He will not refer to his son's mind, but only to his 'skull', acknowledging the vessel, but not the content.

After a few months during which he was dimly aware of her unhappiness and of the tension between his parents, Gabriel's mother leaves home. Gabriel is told that she has gone on holiday, and for the next twenty-seven years firmly believes that she is still alive. This belief and his increasing love for her, or for her memory, become the bedrock of his sense of security. Traumatised by Amy's disappearance and by his father's increasingly tyrannical behaviour, he becomes a chronic bed-wetter ('Piss-a-bed', as his father calls him) and fails at school. Sustained only by his belief in his mother and his love of music, he finally resolves to rescue himself by leaving home.

He spends the best part of the next twenty years living in bed-sitters, working first as a postal sorter, and then for years as a 'skivvy' in a run-down home for elderly women. During all this time, his father courts him while continuing to belittle him, but Gabriel resists, visiting him only occasionally and at the behest of his much-loved aunt, his father's despised Swedenborgian sister. In his solitude, he conjures up his mother's presence and calms himself by donning a Moygashel dress, similar to one she had worn, and reciting, mantra-like, the reference number of a Heddle Nash record of which his mother had been particularly fond.

Eventually, Gabriel publishes his book (dedicated 'with undying love' to his 'mummy') on itinerant preachers, which becomes the basis for a successful Hollywood film. His success coincides with his father's increasing infirmity. As Gabriel accrues at least the material bases of personal security, his father has first one, then the other leg amputated, and thereby loses the physical foundations of his aggressive and chauvinistic masculinity. The old man, obsessed by his own career of promiscuous 'rogering' and dazzled by his only lately acquired purchasing power, is contrasted to his asexual, ascetic son who, despite his frailty and reserve, is going to survive his tormentor.

During his father's last illness, and after his death, Gabriel discovers much about his parents of which he had previously been ignorant. He meets his homosexual half-brother, thirty years his elder, of whom he had secretly known, but whose existence had never been admitted to him by his father. He then also finds that he has a half-sister, who hates the old man implacably for having deserted her and her mother, one of his three wives. Gabriel had not known that he had been married to anyone other than Amy. As he learns how much of his taken-for-granted world had been based on illusion, his hold on his mind, his self-control, grows increasingly tenuous. His mother invades his consciousness ever more insistently until he can barely distinguish imagination from reality.

Finally, during a visit to the United States to lecture on his book, and with the support of a considerable quantity of whisky, he opens the packet of letters, left to him by the old man, which had been written by his mother when she left home. These reveal the terrible truth: that within three weeks of leaving the husband who had destroyed her contentment, during which time she had slept with casual acquaintances, she had committed suicide. His father had felt that he had to protect Gabriel from this knowledge, and his subsequent behaviour to him, even though obviously mistaken and damaging, might now be seen at least as well intentioned rather than gratuitously malign.

Now utterly deprived of the constant reference points of his self (his mother's continuing loving presence, and his father's contemptible insensitivity), Gabriel manically performs a series of impersonations, in effect adopting other people's selves. But, perhaps alerted by his own experience of the differences between appearance and reality, we have a sense that he is aware of these as performances of the persona, rather than of the hidden self. Everything has now been stripped away, leaving his own irreducible 'I'. Its capacity to sustain him is put to the test. He goes to the hotel bedroom in which his mother took the poison which killed her, intending to kill himself. Time has obliterated any of the features of the room which Amy had described in her last letter. He is reminded of a recent conversation about the historical transformation of landscape which, like the altered bedroom, reminds him of the contrast between the superficial appearance and the concealed reality. It is enough; he decides to live. He will use whatever devices he needs to survive. First, he may again cross-dress in private – because he knows now the distance between privacy and appearance. Second, having exorcised the ghosts of his father's malignity and his mother's purity, he becomes a little more his father's son: 'Father, I have taken to rogering' (Bailey 1987: 330). Even the discovery that he had been born out of wedlock makes no impression on him. Discovering that his self resides within him, rather than resting on real or imaginary relationships, and is within *his* control, he has found the means by which to survive.

Where Wolfe is explicit in the depiction of McCoy's self, Bailey works through implication. Wolfe tells us what McCoy (and everybody else) is thinking; Bailey tells us what they are *saying*, and we have to fend for ourselves to interpret their thoughts. Appropriately, it is only as Gabriel grows through adolescence that hints are given of a distinction between what he says – since the verbal is so prominent a feature of this novel – and what he thinks. As he grows older, the narrative balance between the spoken and the thought shifts towards the latter.

Different though they are in so many respects, these two novels both test the reader's instinctive antagonism to their aggressive, egocentric characters. We know there is more to them than is revealed socially, and are therefore enabled to begin to identify with them. We may even come to question our sympathy with their victims. Of course, the novelist plays with the reader. But what is so striking to this anthropological reader is that in order to make sense of these characters, he has to use his own self, in effect, to do some fieldwork on his self. Without my own introspection, they are mere ciphers. But that is also how I begin to do fieldwork among others, others whom my own self-experience and introspection tell me cannot and must not be treated as mere ciphers of a collective social and cultural condition.

If anthropologists believe that there is more to be understood than a structural configuration of social institutions, they have to look for self consciousness, because the institutions cannot be understood without the selves which create and populate them. But in order to start looking for those selves, we have no option but to use our own, not as the models for them (as in medical diagnostic 'countertransference' [Kleinman 1980; Stein 1985]), but as paradigms which, as our understanding of them deepens, can be discarded and replaced by what we perceive of *their* self consciousness. They remain paradigms only in our assumptions that they *do* have self consciousness.

As a final illustration of this use of the self, I offer a third novel, V.S. Naipaul's *The Enigma of Arrival* (1987). I do not claim any authority for my literary judgement, but simply state my personal view that, for the sharpness of its observation and the beauty of its prose, this is self conscious writing at its best. Moreover, in the ways in which he elicits, locates and interrelates his characters, and in which he makes explicit the process and craft of observation, Naipaul has written a strikingly *anthropological* book. There is no plot to the novel. In this respect, it is like life, and could be said to be about life in general and *a* life in particular, that of the narrator. This character is never named, but appears only as 'I'.[4] It is thus written explicitly from the perspective of self, and, indeed, is largely about self: about how one's initial attempts to understand people and situations are predicated on self-experience and reflect the apparent circumstances of one's own life. Like Bailey and Wolfe, Naipaul continuously draws attention to the illusory nature of perceived reality, and shows, in ways which are meat and drink to ethnographers, how time, repeated observation and reflection qualify and revise these perceptions.

The narrator recounts his emigration to England from his native Trinidad at the age of eighteen. He is destined for Oxford, and thereafter for a career as a writer. The journey and his initial arrival in London sharpen his awareness of the fragility and naïveté of his knowledge of the outside world, gathered only from books, but unable to strike a chord in his personal experience. He senses that his intuitive interpretations of what he sees are fundamentally flawed. He writes assiduously and, soon after leaving Oxford, he finds his *métier* as a writer: drawing on the world he knows best, rather than one to which he still feels alien. He is sufficiently successful to feel that he has liberated himself from England, and writes a book to a commission in which he explores Trinidadian history, his own Asian diaspora roots.

He is shocked and dismayed when the publisher rejects his book as 'unsuitable'. Perhaps this reaction exacerbates his sense of his own foreignness, his 'unsuitability'. In any event, it precipitates a personal crisis from which he recovers in a Wiltshire valley, where he rents a cottage on the remnants of a once-grand estate. He is to stay there for twelve years. Again, his arrival in the countryside replicates the earlier experience of his arrival in London: he does not know what he is seeing, is aware that his own experience is inadequate and inappropriate to make sense of it. Over time, his eye becomes better tutored. He learns that appearance is, if not illusion, at best a superficial gloss on complex realities. Nothing is as it seems. People, buildings, landscape, even animals have a reality which may be markedly different to their appearance.[5] He finds this distinction has an especially poignant dimension in the countryside, where it marks the difference between people's assumptions about their privacy, and the reality of remorseless scrutiny. I think there is a message here about a discrimination between self-knowledge and public perceptions of the self.[6] Personal crises follow from the individual's failure to recognise the difference. His valley has its share of personal crises – as, of course, does he.

Experience also rapidly shatters his illusion of bucolic permanency. He becomes aware of the ubiquity of change. Gardens are grassed over, fences moved, buildings erected and then abandoned, terraced cottages are knocked together to form large houses. At first, he regards change as tantamount to decay. He experiences the regeneration of the land as

winter turns to spring, but associates it with the death of a neighbour
(Naipaul 1987: 46). This theme of decay and death recurs throughout the
narrative. There is a certain fatalism here, as if change speaks of crisis,
and necessarily means a loss of authenticity. It encourages atavistic
sentiments in him:

> I dreaded change both here and on the droveway; and that was why,
> meeting distress half-way, I cultivated old, possibly ancestral ways of
> feeling, the ways of glory dead, and held on to the idea of a world in
> flux: the drum of creation in the god's right hand, the flame of
> destruction in his left.
>
> (Naipaul 1987: 53)

But later he comes to realise that the implied idealisation of the past was
itself both naïve, and symptomatic of his failure to come to terms with
himself (ibid.: 190). Indeed, it was a damaging ideal, and he reconciles
himself instead to a view of change merely as 'flux' (ibid.: 250). Amidst
the rubble of the past, he finds a niche for himself. After all, there would
have been no place for him on the manor's property in its hey-day, nor
in Oxford, nor as a successful author in the world of English letters, nor,
earlier, even in Hindu exile in the Caribbean. In the end, he is exhausted
by change, and seems to resign himself to the incapacity of individuals
to manage the cycles in which they are caught up and for which they
were initially responsible. The world will be regenerated by succeeding
generations, each in their own self-images, until they too are succeeded.

What seems to come through here is the parallelism between his
self-awareness and the sense he makes of the world. His introspection
and his construction of the world are perfectly congruent. His eventual
life-threatening and life-transforming illness coincides with yet further
profound crises in the economy of the valley and in the life of the manor
house of which his cottage is part, precipitating his decision to move and
to begin yet another cycle, both in the house which he reconstructs and
in his own life. For Naipaul's 'I' (the narrator), the self is the premise
and the paradigm:

> the only way we have of understanding another man's condition is
> through ourselves, our experiences and emotions.
>
> (Naipaul 1987: 220)

The self constructs the world from experience so that, just as we noted
earlier with respect to the interpretation of symbolism, two people look
at the same object and see different things, participate in the 'same'
event, and experience it quite differently: yet again, then, the argument

for the imperative need to inform our understanding of the world by self consciousness.

Naipaul's limpid prose makes crisply and movingly the argument around which this rather less accomplished author has stumbled and blundered throughout the present book: that the self, located in time and space and subject to the superordinate forces of society and culture, constitutes his or her world as meaningful, and behaves accordingly. That is why an adequate understanding of society cannot be based on an analysis of its institutions which sees them as somehow apart from self consciousness.

It may be that Naipaul's sensitivity to the self derives from his sense of his own outsiderhood, from England, from India where his forebears originated, and from Trinidad where they settled. Even the accounts of his occasional return visits to his family are written from the outside looking in. Elsewhere, I have similarly speculated on the implications for my anthropology of my own marginality (Cohen 1992a). But far from making his (or my) views of the self exceptional or eccentric, it simply underlines the point: our interpretations of what we witness around us proceed from our own experience, our consciousness, of ourselves, even though we may not be conscious of its peculiarity to ourselves. Anthropologists have to qualify their self-experience by subjecting it to the disciplines of comparison and of theoretical and methodological rigour. But they subvert their own enterprise if they permit their science to obscure the primacy of the self.

NON-CONCLUSION

There is no proper conclusion to this book, in the sense of a summation. It simply ends, and I have chosen to end with this discussion of three authors' novels because, in focusing on selfhood, there is a completeness to the characters they portray, and, therefore, a plausibility, a substantiality with which we can identify ourselves, which is too often lacking in anthropological description.

I began the book with the contention that by neglecting self-consciousness, we inevitably perpetrate fictions in our descriptions of other people, a practice all the more damaging because of the authenticity which we claim for our accounts, and the methodological rigour which we see as validating our research. I then tried to show both how different our ethnographies look if we read them as populated by self conscious individuals, and how many of our studies can be seen to be based on self consciousness, reluctant though their authors may be to concede this. Finally, I have argued that paying attention to the individual and to self consciousness does not privilege the individual over society, but that it is a necessary condition of the sensitive understanding of social relations. I turned to explicit fiction in order to suggest the paradox that it may offer accounts which are more authentic than our documentary studies, precisely because, to be convincing, it has to present the reader with the self conscious individual.

I am uncomfortably aware that the tone of this book has about it a certain missionary zeal, and the reason is in the subject matter of this final chapter. As I remarked in Chapter 1, I regard social anthropology as the fundamental discipline in the humane study of society. This is not just the idle claim that 'we do it better' than other scholars. Rather, it is a plea that we *must* do it better in order not to allow a licence by default to those dull political dogmatists to whom I referred earlier in this chapter to invent selves for us in the image of their own self-interestedness.

For the anthropologist to give others back their selfhood is to contribute modestly to the decolonisation of the human subject. Beyond the strict confines of the academic debate – and anthropologists are increasingly to be found outside the academy, struggling in the policy trenches – it also signals the bankruptcy of the cheap political ideology which values individualism rather than individuality, and which justifies itself by parroting a fictitious, and anthropologically offensive 'human nature' in which the self is selfish and society is an irritating encumbrance. The rehabilitation of the self in social science does not offer the self as an alternative to society: it proposes a view of society as composed of and by self conscious individuals.

Notes

PREFACE AND ACKNOWLEDGEMENTS

1 I have deliberately used the hyphen to distinguish between self consciousness – consciousness of the self (the real subject matter of this book) – and
self-consciousness – the colloquial sense of heightened sensitivity to the self.
The apparent inconsistency is not due to poor proofreading!

1 THE NEGLECTED SELF: ANTHROPOLOGICAL TRADITIONS

1 Philosophy and psychology would probably claim a more explicit concern with
the self than would these other disciplines. I have not attempted to address their
literatures here, other than occasionally in passing, simply because I have found
them unhelpful in enlightening an anthropological perspective on the topic.
Philosophers have tended to concentrate on issues connected with the definition
of the self and of identity, and on the historical development of the concepts in
different intellectual traditions. Further, Morris' recent book (1992) is a comprehensive survey and exposition of philosophical positions, written from an anthropological perspective. While I do refer to the work of some influential social
psychologists, I do not dwell on it. Much of it has focused on aspects of the
implication of the self in social relationships, tending to a position of which I am
highly critical in this book, but in relation to its manifestation in anthropological
and sociological studies.
2 See the further discussion of Southern Baptists by Greenhouse (1986) in
Chapter 6 below.

2 THE CREATIVE SELF

1 Lock has argued that self-awareness is necessarily anchored in time and
space (1981: 24).
2 This is an image I owe to Robert Paine, from a book-length critique of
Goffman which he wrote more than twenty years ago, but unfortunately did
not complete.

3 This commitment to balance and harmony may also help us to understand the Mbuti's rather attenuated mystical system which seems so different from those of other central and east African peoples, and, most strikingly, from the religious beliefs and practices of their near neighbours in the villages. Turnbull repeatedly characterises the Mbuti as 'happy'; as having a highly developed and easily triggered sense of humour and fun; of relishing, rather than taking for granted, the abundance of their surroundings. Given this condition of plenty, he suggests that they have little need of a developed sense of malign or evil forces, or of spirits to be propitiated. They recognise a need to protect their forest from incursion by villagers and other outsiders; but that is protection from the mundane and the secular rather than from the sacred or mystical. Even when dealing with these potential social enemies and rivals, they do not invoke mystical aid, but engage with frank pragmatism in a relationship of patronage, *kpara*, in which they beguile the villagers (who are dependent on them) into the belief that the Mbuti are somehow dependent on them. Their patrons' gullibility seems to have furnished them with much amusement.

4 In *Never in Anger*, Briggs consistently uses the word *ihuma*. In more recent publications, she renders the syndrome as *isuma* (e.g. 1987).

5 To whom in an earlier publication I regrettably managed, by dint of careless proofreading (an 'e.g.' instead of a 'cf.'), to attribute the completely contrary view.

3 INITIATING THE SELF INTO SOCIETY

1 The bias among the cognatic Bimin-Kuskusmin is patrilineal. See Poole 1982: 106–7.

2 The *ais am* certainly fulfils this condition by identifying each cohort of initiates with one of the four *ais am* ancestors.

3 I return to this matter in Chapter 7.

4 A topic which was pursued contemporaneously in sociology with some similarities by Berger and Luckmann, and, later, by Giddens.

5 The following section is drawn from Cohen 1993b.

6 See, for example, Bamberger (1974: 364) on the Kayapó; Ramos (1974: 172) on the Sanumá.

7 See, for example, Sabar (1974) on Kurdistani Jews, and Collier and Bricker (1970) on Zinacantan Indians.

8 Part of our error lay, and still lies, in the inadequacy of the category 'name'. We apply this category to terms which are used to perform such disparate tasks: to signify respect; to address and/or refer to someone; to denigrate, greet or associate a person with his or her forebears. See Zabeeh 1968: 65.

4 SOCIAL TRANSFORMATIONS OF THE SELF

1 In a way which recalls the identification of an individual Tallensi man with his lineage through the medium of his own destiny ancestor. See Fortes 1959, 1970.

2   This section owes much to protracted discussions among Nigel Rapport (University of St Andrews), Ed Young (Manchester Business School) and myself.

3   Apart from the highly speculative and abstract *How Institutions Think* (Douglas 1987), the literature still lacks an *anthropological* appraisal of the concept of culture in the context of organisations.

4   I accept that the denigration of old age may be more common in industrialised than in non-industrialised societies (see Holy 1990).

5   Myerhoff's study was also the subject of an Oscar-winning documentary film.

5   THE PRIMACY OF THE SELF?

1   For example, the principle: our political leaders are superior to us in terms of power, and must therefore also appear to be morally superior. The practice: they are merely flesh and blood. They are caught *in flagrante delicto* (or with their trousers down), or lying to the legislature. They are revealed as being no better than us. The resolution: they must resign in order to reassert the principle which is continually being transgressed in practice.

2   Likewise, degrees of kinship were reckoned by reference to an ancestor, rather than to ego. First cousins were thus referred to in Tory (with impeccable logic) as 'grandchildren only'. Their children were *da ua*, second grandchildren; their children as *fionn ua* (fair grandchildren) – the ostensible logic lapses here – and their children (fourth cousins) as *dubh ua* (dark grandchildren). Beyond fifth grandchildship, the relation was described simply as 'far out'.

3   Parts of the following section are drawn from Cohen 1993c.

4   He excludes from his taxonomy the term 'march', referring to the outer limits of a given territory, as being 'archaic'. However, in a possibly modernised form, 'margin', it has been heavily used, perhaps indiscriminately, by anthropologists.

5   In her recent study of the annual Beltane festival in a Scottish Borders community, the geographer Susan Smith (1993) conflates all three terms by making them expressive of 'space' (a word to which human geographers seem to resort much as anthropologists do to 'culture'). While there may be no intrinsic value in discriminating the three words, there surely is something to be gained from distinguishing the material from the ideal.

6   THE THINKING SELF

1   Boon studiously avoids using the word 'relative', unlike, say, McGrane:

> Culture, by definition, by anthropological definition, is *cultures*; and cultures, by anthropological definition, are *relative*.
>
> (McGrane 1989: 117)

To be fair, Boon's point is not that they are merely relative to each other, but that they are self-*consciously* so.

2   Wagner argues that by engaging different domains of experience, metaphor 'introduces relativity *within* coordinate systems' – i.e. cultures – as well as between them (Wagner 1986: 5).

3   An intriguing study of contrary attitudes to the Albanian civil war between
    two neighbouring villages reached a similar conclusion (Bequiraj 1966).
4   For example:

> The nation is individual, a person, and the individuality of this nation is
> fashioned according to the character of that ideal individual present at its
> beginning,
>
> (Kapferer 1988: 165)

and, 'Australian egalitarian nationalism equates individual, people, and nation'
(ibid.: 185).

7 INDIVIDUALISM, INDIVIDUALITY, SELFHOOD

1   See pp. 11, 29 above.
2   This and the following sections draw heavily on Cohen 1992b.
3   In 1993, the British Government published a White Paper which explicitly
    adopted 'wealth creation' as the test of acceptable scientific research and
    scholarship, a standard which was quickly and supinely adopted by the
    Economic and Social Research Council.
4   It may be interesting for literary scholars to speculate about the extent to
    which the narrator is Naipaul himself. My point is that whether or not the
    book is about his life is irrelevant: it is 'about' his self consciousness, in the
    sense that his self consciousness is the *sine qua non* of his ability to write
    about people in the way that he does. This proposition would appear to be so
    uncontentious for novelists and literary scholars that they may well object
    that it is hardly worth repeating. That is a measure of the difference between
    the explicit fiction of the novelist, and the implicit or 'staged' fiction
    (Rabinow 1986; also Crapanzano 1992) of the ethnographer.
5   Naipaul makes the point with a characteristically light hand. A famous race
    horse is put out to grass in a field near the narrator's cottage. He admires his
    still-lithe body, his glossy coat. It is only on close inspection that he
    discovers that the horse has the sight of only one eye, the other having been
    removed.
6   On the liner carrying him to England for the first time, he becomes aware that
    other people compress his identity simply into his colour:

> I was ashamed that, with all my aspirations, and all that I had put into this
> adventure, this was all that people saw in me so far from the way I thought
> of myself, so far from what I wanted for myself.
>
> (Naipaul 1987: 116)

References

Alford, R.A. (1987) *Naming and Identity: a Cross-Cultural Study of Personal Naming Practices*, New Haven: HRAF Press.

Allaire, Y. and Firsimotu, M.E. (1984) 'Theories of organizational culture', *Organizational Studies*, 5 (3): 193–226.

Anderson, M. (1982) 'Political problems of frontier regions', *West European Politics*, 5 (4): 1–17.

Anderson, M. (n.d.) *Frontiers* (University of Edinburgh, typescript).

Antoun, R. (1968) 'On the significance of names in an Arab village', *Ethnology*, 7: 158–70.

Appadurai, A. (1993) 'The production of locality', paper presented to the *ASA Fourth Decennial Conference*, Oxford.

Apter, D. (1963) 'Political religion in the new nations', pp. 57–104 in C. Geertz, ed., *Old Societies and New States: the Quest for Modernity in Asia and Africa*, New York: Free Press of Glencoe.

Atkinson, J.M. (1984) *Our Masters' Voices: the Language and Body Language of Politics*, London: Methuen.

Aubert, V. (1965) 'A total institution: the ship', *The Hidden Society*, Totowa, N.J.: Bedminster Press.

Ayer, A.J. (1963 [1953]) 'One's knowledge of other minds', pp. 191–214 in *Philosophical Essays*, London: Macmillan.

Bailey, F.G. (1971) 'Gifts and poison', pp. 1–25 in F.G. Bailey, ed., *Gifts and Poison: the Politics of Reputation*, Oxford: Blackwell.

Bailey, F.G. (1977) *Morality and Expediency: the Folklore of Academic Politics*, Oxford: Blackwell.

Bailey, F.G. (1981) 'Dimensions of rhetoric in conditions of uncertainty', pp. 25–38 in R.P.B. Paine, ed., *Politically Speaking: Cross-Cultural Studies of Rhetoric*, Philadelphia: ISHI.

Bailey, F.G. (1983) *The Tactical Uses of Passion: an Essay on Power, Reason and Reality*, Ithaca: Cornell University Press.

Bailey, P. (1987) *Gabriel's Lament*, Harmondsworth: Penguin.

Bamberger, J. (1974) 'Naming and the transmission of status in a central Brazilian society', *Ethnology*, 13: 363–78.

Barth, F. (1966) *Models of Social Organisation*, Royal Anthropological Institute occasional paper 23.

Barth, F. (1969) 'Introduction', pp. 9–38 in F. Barth, ed., *Ethnic Groups and Boundaries: the Social Organisation of Culture Difference*, London: George Allen & Unwin.

Bate, P. (1984) 'The impact of organizational culture on approaches to organizational problem solving', *Organization Studies*, 5 (1): 43–66.

Bequiraj, M. (1966) *Peasantry in Revolution*, Ithaca: Center for International Studies, Cornell University.

Bérenger-Féraud, L. (1971) *Réminiscences populaires de la Provence: Légendes de la Provence, 1885–1888*, Nyons: Chantemerle.

Berger, P. (1973) *The Social Reality of Religion*, Harmondsworth: Penguin.

Berger, P. and Luckmann, T. (1967) *The Social Construction of Reality: a Treatise in the Sociology of Knowledge*, Harmondsworth: Penguin.

Binns, C.P. (1979/1980) 'The changing face of power: revolution and accommodation in the development of the Soviet ceremonial system', *Man* (n.s.), 14 (4) and 15 (1): 585–606 and 170–187.

Bloch, M. (1975) 'Introduction', pp. 1–28 in M. Bloch, ed., *Political Language and Oratory in Traditional Society*, London: Academic Press.

Bloch, M. (1986) *From Blessing to Violence: History and Ideology in the Circumcision Ritual of the Merina of Madagascar*, Cambridge: Cambridge University Press.

Bloch, M. (1987) 'The political implications of religious experience', pp. 23–50 in G. Aijmer, ed., *Symbolic Textures: Studies in Cultural Meaning*, Göteborg: Acta Universitatis Gothoburgensis.

Bloch, M. (1992) *Prey into Hunter: the Politics of Religious Experience*, Cambridge: Cambridge University Press.

Blythe, R. (1979) *The View in Winter: Reflections on Old Age*, London: Allen Lane.

Boon, J.A. (1982) *Other Tribes, Other Scribes: Symbolic Anthropology in the Comparative Study of Cultures, Histories, Religions and Texts*, Cambridge: Cambridge University Press.

Bourdieu, P. (1977) *Outline of a Theory of Practice*, Cambridge: Cambridge University Press.

Brewer, J.D. (1981) 'Bimanese personal names: meaning and use', *Ethnology*, 20: 203–15.

Briggs, J. (1970) *Never in Anger: Portrait of an Eskimo Family*, Cambridge, Mass.: Harvard University Press.

Briggs, J. (1982) 'Living dangerously: the contradictory foundations of value in Canadian Inuit society', pp. 109–31 in E. Leacock and R. Lee, eds, *Politics and History in Band Societies*, Cambridge: Cambridge University Press.

Briggs, J. (1987) 'In search of emotional meaning', *Ethos*, 15 (1): 8–15.

Brown, R. (1990) *Borderlines and Borderlands in English Canada: the Written Line*, Borderlands Monograph Series, 4, University of Maine.

Burns, T. (1992) *Erving Goffman*, London: Routledge.

Campbell, A.T. (1989) *To Square with Genesis: Causal Statements and Shamanic Ideas in Wayãpí*, Edinburgh: Edinburgh University Press.

Campbell, J.K. (1964) *Honour, Family and Patronage: a Study of Institutions and Moral Values in a Greek Mountain Community*, Oxford: Oxford University Press.

Campbell, J.K. (1992) 'Fieldwork among the Sarakatsani, 1954–55', pp. 148–66 in J. de Piña-Cabral and J.K. Campbell, eds, *Europe Observed*, Basingstoke: Macmillan.

Carrithers, M., Collins, S. and Lukes, S. (eds) (1985) *The Category of the Person: Anthropology, Philosophy, History*, Cambridge: Cambridge University Press.

Coakley, J. (1982) 'National territories and cultural frontiers: conflicts of principle in the formation of states in Europe', *West European Politics*, 5 (4): 34–49.

Cohen, Abner (1980) 'Drama and politics in the development of a London carnival', *Man* (n.s.), 15: 65–87.

Cohen, Abner (1992) *Masquerade Politics: Explorations in the Structure of Urban Cultural Movements*, Oxford: Berg.

Cohen, A.P. (1978) '"The same – but different!" the allocation of identity in Whalsay, Shetland', *Sociological Review*, 26 (3): 449–69.

Cohen, A.P. (1982) 'A sense of time, a sense of place: the meaning of close social association in Whalsay, Shetland', pp. 21–49 in A.P. Cohen, ed., *Belonging: Identity and Social Organisation in British Rural Cultures*, Manchester: Manchester University Press.

Cohen, A.P. (1985) *The Symbolic Construction of Community*, London: Tavistock.

Cohen, A.P. (1986a) (ed.) *Symbolising Boundaries: Identity and Diversity in British Cultures*, Manchester: Manchester University Press.

Cohen, A.P. (1986b) 'Of symbols and boundaries, or, does Ertie's greatcoat hold the key?', pp. 1–19 in A.P. Cohen, ed., *Symbolising Boundaries: Identity and Diversity in British Cultures*, Manchester: Manchester University Press.

Cohen, A.P. (1987) *Whalsay: Symbol, Segment and Boundary in a Shetland Island Community*, Manchester: Manchester University Press.

Cohen, A.P. (1989a) 'La tradition britannique, et la question de l'autre', pp. 35–51 in M. Segalen, ed., *L'autre et le semblable: régards sur l'ethnologie des sociétés contemporaines*, Paris: Presses du CNRS. Published in English as 'Self and other in the tradition of British anthropology', *Anthropological Journal on European Cultures*, 1 (1): 35–63, 1990.

Cohen, A.P. (1989b) '"Hablando Walsa": mnemotecnias históricas de una comunidad isleña de Shetland', pp. 131–54 in J.A. Fernandez de Rota y Monter, ed., *Lengua y Cultura: Aproximación desde una Semántica Antropológica*, La Coruña: Edicios do Castro.

Cohen, A.P. (1992a) 'Self-conscious anthropology', pp. 221–41 in J. Okely and H. Callaway, eds, *Anthropology and Autobiography*, London: Routledge.

Cohen, A.P. (1992b) 'The personal right to identity: a polemic on the self in the enterprise culture', pp. 179–93 in P. Heelas and P. Morris, eds, *The Values of the Enterprise Culture: the Moral Debate*, London: Routledge.

Cohen, A.P. (1992c) 'Post-fieldwork fieldwork', *Journal of Anthropological Research*, 48: 339–54.

Cohen, A.P. (1993a) 'The future of the self: anthropology and the city', pp. 201–21 in A.P. Cohen and K. Fukui, eds, *Humanising the City? Social Contexts of Urban Life at the Turn of the Millennium*, Edinburgh: Edinburgh University Press.

Cohen, A.P. (1993b) 'Rites of identity, rights of the self', *Edinburgh Review*, 89: 56–74.

Cohen, A.P. (1993c) 'Culture as identity: an anthropologist's view', *New Literary History*, 24 (1): 195–209.

Collier, G.A. and Bricker, V.R. (1970) 'Nicknames and social structure in Zinacantan', *American Anthropologist*, 72: 289–302.

Combs-Schilling, M.E. (1985) 'Family and friend in a Moroccan boom town: the segmentary debate reconsidered', *American Ethnologist*, 12 (4): 659–75.

Cowan, J. (1990) *Dance and the Body Politic in Northern Greece*, Princeton, N.J.: Princeton University Press.

Crapanzano, V. (1992) *Hermes' Dilemma and Hamlet's Desire: on the Epistemology of Interpretation*, Cambridge, Mass.: Harvard University Press.

Dahl, R.A. (1961) *Who Governs? Democracy and Power in an American City*, New Haven: Yale University Press.

Dandridge, T.C. (1976) *Symbols at Work: the Types and Functions of Symbols in Selected Organizations*, unpublished Ph.D dissertation, University of California, Los Angeles.

Deal, T. and Kennedy, A. (1982) *Corporate Cultures: the Rites and Rituals of Corporate Life*, Harmondsworth: Penguin.

Dorian, N.C. (1970) 'A substitute name system in the Scottish Highlands', *American Anthropologist*, 72: 303–19.

Douglas, M. (1987) *How Institutions Think*, London: Routledge.

Downing, T.E. and Kushner, G. (1988) *Human Rights and Anthropology*, Cambridge, Mass.: Cultural Survival Inc.

Du Boulay, J. (1974) *Portrait of a Greek Mountain Village*, Oxford: Clarendon Press.

Dumont, L. (1980) *Homo Hierarchicus: the Caste System and its Implications*, Chicago: University of Chicago Press, 2nd edn.

Dumont, L. (1986) *Essays on Individualism: Modern Ideology in Anthropological Perspective*, Chicago: University of Chicago Press.

Eidheim, H. (1969) 'When ethnic identity is a social stigma', pp. 39–57 in F. Barth, ed., *Ethnic Groups and Boundaries: the Social Organisation of Culture Difference*, London: Allen & Unwin.

Epstein, A.L. (1978) *Ethos and Identity: Three Studies in Ethnicity*, London: Tavistock.

Erchak, G.M. (1992) *The Anthropology of Self and Behavior*, New Brunswick, N.J.: Rutgers University Press.

Eriksen, E. von Hirsch (1993) *Reproducing Moral Agents: the Concept of Human Nature in an Orthodox Jewish Community*, Unpublished Ph.D thesis, University of Durham.

Evans-Pritchard, E. E. (1964) 'Nuer modes of address', pp. 221–7 in D. Hymes, ed., *Language in Culture and Society: a Reader in Linguistics and Anthropology*, London: Harper & Row.

Fabian, J. (1983) *Time and the Other: How Anthropology makes its Object*, New York: Columbia University Press.

Favret-Saada, J. (1980) *Deadly Words: Witchcraft in the Bocage*, Cambridge: Cambridge University Press.

Feldman, M.S. and March, J.G. (1981) 'Information in organizations as signal and symbol', *Administrative Science Quarterly*, 26 (2): 171–86.

Fernandez, J.W. (1982a) 'The dark at the bottom of the stairs: the inchoate in symbolic inquiry and some strategies for coping with it', pp. 13–43 in J.

Maquet, ed., *On Symbols in Anthropology: Essays in Honor of Harry Hoijer*, Malibu: Undena Publications.

Fernandez, J.W. (1982b) *Bwiti: an Ethnography of the Religious Imagination in Africa*, Princeton, N.J.: Princeton University Press.

Fernandez, J.W. (1986 [1972]) 'Persuasions and performances: of the beast in every body and the metaphors of everyman', pp. 3–27 in *Persuasions and Performances: the Play of Tropes in Culture*, Bloomington: Indiana University Press.

Fernandez, J.W. (1986 [1974]) 'The mission of metaphor in expressive culture', pp. 28–70 in *Persuasions and Performances: the Play of Tropes in Culture*, Bloomington: Indiana University Press.

Finkelstein, J. (1991) *The Fashioned Self*, Cambridge: Polity Press.

Fortes, M. (1959) *Oedipus and Job in West African Religion*, Cambridge: Cambridge University Press.

Fortes, M. (1970) 'Pietas in ancestor worship', pp. 164–200 in *Time and Social Structure, and Other Essays*, London: The Athlone Press.

Fortes, M. (1973) 'The concept of the person among the Tallensi', pp. 283–319 in G. Dieterlen, ed., *La notion de la personne en Afrique noir*, Paris: Editions du CNRS.

Fortes, M. (1983) 'Problems of identity and person', pp. 389–401 in A. Jacobsen-Widding, ed., *Identity, Personal and Socio-cultural: a Symposium*, Uppsala: Acta Universitatis Uppsaliensis.

Fox, R. (1965) 'Prolegomenon to the study of British kinship', pp. 128–43 in J.R. Gould, ed., *Penguin Survey of the Social Sciences*, Harmondsworth: Penguin.

Fox, R. (1978) *The Tory Islanders: a People of the Celtic Fringe*, Cambridge: Cambridge University Press.

Fox, R. (1982) 'Principles and pragmatics on Tory Island', pp. 50–71 in A.P. Cohen, ed., *Belonging: Identity and Social Organisation in British Rural Cultures*, Manchester: Manchester University Press.

Friedman, J. (1987) 'Comment on Keesing, "Anthropology as Interpretive Quest"', *Current Anthropology*, 28 (2): 17–71.

Galaty, J.G. (1981) 'Models and metaphors: on the semiotic explanation of segmentary systems', pp. 63–92 in L. Holy and M. Stuchlik, eds, *The Structure of Folk Models*, London: Academic Press.

Gearing, F.O. (1970) *The Face of the Fox*, Chicago: Aldine.

Geertz, C. (1975) 'Thick description: toward an interpretive theory of culture', pp. 3–30 in *The Interpretation of Cultures*, London: Hutchinson.

Geertz, C. (1975 [1972]) 'Deep play: notes on the Balinese cockfight', pp. 412–53 in *The Interpretation of Cultures*, London: Hutchinson.

Geertz, C. (1983) 'Introduction', pp. 3–16 in *Local Knowledge: Further Essays in Interpretive Anthropology*, New York: Basic Books.

Geertz, C. (1983 [1974]) '"From the native's point of view": on the nature of anthropological understanding', pp. 55–70 in *Local Knowledge: Further Essays in Interpretive Anthropology*, New York: Basic Books.

Geertz, C. (1988) *Works and Lives: the Anthropologist as Author*, Oxford: Polity Press.

Gergen, K.J. (1977) 'The social construction of self-knowledge', pp. 139–69 in T. Mischel, ed., *The Self: Psychological and Philosophical Issues*, Oxford: Blackwell.

Giddens, A. (1984) *The Constitution of Society: Outline of the Theory of Structuration*, Cambridge: Polity.

Giddens, A. (1991) *Modernity and Self-identity: Self and Society in the Late Modern Age*, Cambridge: Polity.

Gluckman, M. (1962) 'Les rites de passage', pp. 1–52 in M. Gluckman, ed., *Essays on the Ritual of Social Relations*, Manchester: Manchester University Press.

Gluckman, M. and Devons, E. (1964) *Closed Systems and Open Minds: the Limits of Naivety in Social Anthropology*, Edinburgh: Oliver & Boyd.

Goffman, E. (1964) *Asylums*, Harmondsworth: Penguin.

Goldschmidt, W. (1986) *The Sebei: a Study in Adaptation*, New York: Holt, Rinehart & Winston.

Goldschmidt, W. (1990) *The Human Career: the Self in the Symbolic World*, Oxford: Blackwell.

Goodenough, W. (1965) 'Personal names and modes of address in two Oceanic societies', pp. 265–76 in M.E. Spiro, ed., *Context and Meaning in Cultural Anthropology*, New York: Free Press.

Greenhouse, C. (1986) *Praying for Justice: Faith, Order and Community in an American Town*, Ithaca: Cornell University Press.

Greger, S. (1988) *Village on the Plateau: Magoulas, a Mountain Village in Crete*, Studley: K.A.F. Brewin Books.

Guemple, D.L. (1965) 'Saunik name sharing as a factor governing Eskimo kinship terms', *Ethnology*, 4: 323–35.

Handelman, D. (1990) *Models and Mirrors: Towards an Anthropology of Public Events*, Cambridge: Cambridge University Press.

Handler, R. (1988) *Nationalism and the Politics of Culture in Quebec*, London: University of Wisconsin Press.

Harré, R. (1987) 'The social construction of selves', pp. 41–52 in K. Yardley and T. Hohness, eds, *Self and Identity: Pyschosocial Perspectives*, Chichester: John Wiley & Sons Ltd.

Hastrup, K. (1985) *Culture and History in Medieval Iceland: an Anthropological Analysis of Structure and Change*, Oxford: Clarendon.

Hastrup, K. (1992a) 'Writing ethnography: state of the art', pp. 116–33 in J. Okely and H. Callaway, eds, *Anthropology and Autobiography*, London: Routledge.

Hastrup, K. (1992b) 'Out of anthropology: the anthropologist as an object of dramatic representation', *Cultural Anthropology*, 7 (3): 327–45.

Hazan, H. (1980) *The Limbo People: a Study of the Constitution of the Time Universe among the Aged*, London: Routledge & Kegan Paul.

Hazan, H. (1990) 'Dimensions of change: three studies of the construction of aging', pp. 183–93 in P. Spencer, ed., *Anthropology and the Riddle of the Sphinx*, London: Routledge.

Heelas, P. (1981a) 'Introduction: indigenous psychologies', pp. 3–18 in P. Heelas and A. Lock, eds, *Indigenous Psychologies: the Anthropology of the Self*, London: Academic Press.

Heelas, P. (1981b) 'The model applied: anthropology and indigenous psychologies', pp. 39–63 in P. Heelas and A. Lock, eds, *Indigenous Psychologies: the Anthropology of the Self*, London: Academic Press.

Henriksen, G. (1973) *Hunters in the Barrens: the Naskapi on the Edge of the White Man's World*, St John's: ISER.

Herzfeld, M. (1985) *The Poetics of Manhood: Contest and Identity in a Cretan Mountain Village*, Princeton, N.J.: Princeton University Press.

Hobsbawm, E. and Ranger, T. (1983) (eds) *The Invention of Tradition*, Cambridge: Cambridge University Press.

Hockey, J. (1989) 'Residential care and the maintenance of social identity: negotiating the transition to institutional life', pp. 201–17 in M. Jefferys, ed., *Growing Old in the Twentieth Century*, London: Routledge.

Holy, L. (1979) 'The segmentary lineage structure and its existential status' and 'Nuer politics', pp. 1–48 in L. Holy, ed., *Segmentary Lineage Systems Reconsidered*, Belfast: Queen's University of Belfast.

Holy, L. (1989) *Kinship, Honour and Solidarity: Cousin Marriage in the Middle East*, Manchester: Manchester University Press.

Holy, L. (1990) 'Strategies for old age among the Berti of the Sudan', pp. 167–82 in P. Spencer, ed., *Anthropology and the Riddle of the Sphinx*, London: Routledge.

Howe, L.E.A. (1990) *Being Unemployed in Northern Ireland: an Ethnographic Study*, Cambridge: Cambridge University Press.

Hsu, F.L.K. (1985) 'The self in cross-cultural perspective', pp. 24–55 in A. Marsella, G. DeVos and F.L.K. Hsu, eds, *Culture and Self: Asian and Western Perspectives*, London: Tavistock.

Humphrey, C. (1983) *Karl Marx Collective: Economy, Society and Religion in a Siberian Collective Farm*, Cambridge: Cambridge University Press.

Jacquemet, M. (1992) 'Namechasers', *American Ethnologist*, 19 (4): 733–48.

James, A. (1986) 'Learning to belong: the boundaries of adolescence', pp. 155–70 in A.P. Cohen, ed., *Symbolising Boundaries: Identity and Diversity in British Cultures*, Manchester: Manchester University Press.

James, A. (1993) *Childhood Identities: Self and Social Relationships in the Experience of the Child*, Edinburgh: Edinburgh University Press.

James, W. (1979) *'Kwanim Pa: the Making of the Uduk People*, Oxford: Clarendon Press.

James, W. (1988) *The Listening Ebony: Moral Knowledge, Religion and Power among the Uduk of Sudan*, Oxford: Clarendon Press.

Jell-Bahlsen, S. (1988) 'Names and naming: instances from the Oru-Igbo', *Dialectical Anthropology*, 13 (2): 199–207.

Jerrome, D. (1989) 'Virtue and vicissitude: the role of old people's clubs', pp. 151–65 in M. Jefferys, ed., *Growing Old in the Twentieth Century*, London: Routledge.

Jerrome, D. (1992) *Good Company: an Anthropological Study of Old People in Groups*, Edinburgh: Edinburgh University Press.

Jones, J.R. (1950) '"Selves": a reply to Mr Flew', *Mind*, LIX: 233–6.

Kanter, R.M. (1983) *The Change Masters: Corporate Entrepreneurs at Work*, London: Allen & Unwin.

Kapferer, B. (1983) *A Celebration of Demons*, Bloomington: Indiana University Press.

Kapferer, B. (1988) *Legends of People, Myths of State: Violence, Intolerance and Political Culture in Sri Lanka and Australia*, Washington: Smithsonian Institution Press.

Keating, M. (1993) 'Two faces under one flag', *The Times Higher Education Supplement*, 24 September.

Keith, J. (1980) 'Old age and community creation', pp. 170–97 in C.L. Fry, ed., *Aging in Culture and Society*, New York: J.F. Bergin Inc.

Khuri, F.I. (1970) 'Parallel cousin marriage reconsidered', *Man* (n.s.), 5: 597–618.

Kleinman, A. (1980) *Patients and Healers in the Context of Culture*, Berkeley: University of California Press.

Kondo, D. (1990) *Crafting Selves: Power, Gender and Discourses of Identity in a Japanese Workplace*, Chicago: University of Chicago Press.

Kondo, D. (1992) 'Multiple selves: the aesthetics and politics of artisanal identities', pp. 40–66 in N. Rosenberger, ed., *Japanese Sense of Self*, Cambridge: Cambridge University Press.

Lane, C. (1981) *The Rites of Rulers: Ritual in Industrialised Society – the Soviet Case*, Cambridge: Cambridge University Press.

Lasch, C. (1980) *The Culture of Narcissism*, London: Abacus Press.

Lauterbach, J.R. (1970) 'The naming of children in Jewish folklore, ritual and practice', pp. 30–74 in B. J. Bamberger, ed., *Studies in Jewish Law, Custom and Folklore*, New York: KTAV Publishing House Inc.

Leach, E.R. (1954) *Political Systems of Highland Burma: a Study of Kachin Social Structure*, London: G. Bell & Son.

Leach, E.R. (1967a) *A Runaway World?*, London: Oxford University Press.

Leach, E.R. (1967b) 'Introduction', pp. vii–xix in E.R. Leach, ed., *The Structural Study of Myth and Totemism*, London: Tavistock.

Lebra, T. (1992) 'Self in Japanese culture', pp. 105–20 in N. Rosenberger, ed., *Japanese Sense of Self*, Cambridge: Cambridge University Press.

Lee, D. (1976) *Valuing the Self: What we can Learn from Other Cultures*, Prospect Heights, Ill.: Waveland Press Inc.

Lee, R. and Lawrence, P. (1985) *Organizational Behaviour: Politics at Work*, London: Hutchinson.

Léon, M. (1976) 'Of names and first names in a small rural community: linguistic and sociological approaches', *Semiotica*, 17 (3): 211–31.

Lévi-Strauss, C. (1966) *The Savage Mind*, London: Weidenfeld & Nicolson.

Lewis, H.D. (1982) *The Elusive Self*, London: Macmillan.

Lienhardt, R.G. (1985) 'Self: public, private. Some African representations', pp. 141–55 in M. Carrithers, *et al.*, eds, *The Category of the Person: Anthropology, Philosophy, History*, Cambridge: Cambridge University Press.

Lock, A. (1981) 'Universals in human conception', pp. 19–36 in P. Heelas and A. Lock, eds, *Indigenous Psychologies: the Anthropology of the Self*, London: Academic Press.

Lopes da Silva, A. (1989) 'Social practice and ontology in Akwe-Xavante naming and myth', *Ethnology*, 28 (4): 331–41.

Lukes, S. (1973) *Individualism*, Oxford: Blackwell.

Lyman, S.M. (1984) 'Foreword', pp. vii–xii in J.A. Kotarba and A. Fontana, eds, *The Existential Self in Society*, Chicago: University of Chicago Press.

Lyman, S.M. and Scott, M.B. (1970) *A Sociology of the Absurd*, New York: Meredith Corporation.

Macfarlane, A. (1978) *The Origins of English Individualism*, Oxford: Blackwell.

MacFarlane, G. (1986) '"It's not as simple as that": the expression of the Catholic and Protestant boundary in Northern Irish rural communities', pp. 88–104 in A.P. Cohen, ed., *Symbolising Boundaries: Identity and Diversity in British Cultures*, Manchester: Manchester University Press.

McGrane, B. (1989) *Beyond Anthropology: Society and the Other*, New York: Columbia University Press.

Macpherson, C.B. (1964) 'Post-liberal democracy', *Canadian Journal of Economics and Political Science*, 30 (4): 485–98.

Manning, F.G. (1974) 'Nicknames and numberplates in the British West Indies', *Journal of American Folklore*, 87 (2): 123–32.

Mauss, M. (1938) 'Une catégorie de l'esprit humain: la notion de personne, celle de "moi"', *J. Roy. Anth. Inst.* 68.

Maxwell, A.R. (1984) 'Kandayan personal names and naming', pp. 25–39 in E. Tooker, ed., *Naming Systems: the 1980 Proceedings of the American Ethnological Society*, Washington, AES.

Maybury-Lewis, D. (1984) 'Name, person and ideology in Central Brazil', pp. 1–10 in E. Tooker, ed., *Naming Systems: the 1980 Proceedings of the American Ethnological Society*, Washington, AES.

Mbiti, John (1970) *African Religions and Philosophy*, New York: Doubleday.

Mead, G.H. (1934) *Mind, Self and Society: from the Standpoint of a Social Behaviorist*, Chicago: University of Chicago Press.

Mewett, P.G. (1982) 'Exiles, nicknames, social identities and the production of local consciousness in a Lewis crofting community', pp. 222–46 in A.P. Cohen, ed., *Belonging: Identity and Social Organisation in British Rural Cultures*, Manchester: Manchester University Press.

Michaud, E. (1986) *Old Age: Attitudes to Aging and the Elderly in an English Village*, unpublished Ph.D thesis, University of Manchester.

Mines, M. (1988) 'Conceptualizing the person: hierarchical society and individual autonomy in India', *American Anthropologist*, 90 (3): 568–79.

Morgan, G. (1986) *Images of Organization*, London: Sage.

Morris, B. (1992) *Western Conceptions of the Individual*, Oxford: Berg.

Morris, C. (1987) *The Discovery of the Individual, 1050–1200*, Toronto: University of Toronto Press.

Myerhoff, B.G. (1974) *Peyote Hunt: the Sacred Journey of the Huichol Indians*, Ithaca: Cornell University Press.

Myerhoff, B.G. (1978) *Number our Days*, New York: Simon & Schuster.

Myerhoff, B.G. (1984) 'Rites and signs of ripening: the intertwining of ritual, time and growing older', pp. 305–30 in D.I. Kertzer and J. Keith, eds, *Age and Anthropological Theory*, Ithaca: Cornell University Press.

Naipaul, V.S. (1987) *The Enigma of Arrival: a Novel*, Harmondsworth: Penguin.

Needham, R. (1954) 'The system of teknonyms and death-names among the Penan', *South-western Journal of Anthropology*, 10: 416–31.

Needham, R. (1965) 'Death-names and solidarity in Penan society', *Bijdragen etc*, 121: 58–76.

Needham, R. (1981) 'Inner states as universals', pp. 171–88 in *Circumstantial Deliveries*, Berkeley: University of California Press.

Ohnuki-Tierney, E. (1990) 'The ambivalent self of the contemporary Japanese', *Cultural Anthropology*, 5 (2): 197–216.

Ohnuki-Tierney, E. (1991) 'Embedding and transforming polytrope: the monkey as self in Japanese culture', pp. 159–89 in J.W. Fernandez, ed., *Beyond Metaphor: the Play of Tropes in Anthropology*, Stanford: Stanford University Press.

Okely, J.M. (1990) 'Clubs for le troisième âge: communitas or conflict?', pp. 194–212 in P. Spencer, ed., *Anthropology and the Riddle of the Sphinx*, London: Routledge.

Okely, J. and Callaway, H. (1992) (eds) *Anthropology and Autobiography*, London: Routledge.

Paine, R.P.B. (1970) 'Informal communication and information management', *Canadian Review of Sociology and Anthropology*, 7 (3): 172–88.

Paine, R.P.B. (1974) *Second Thoughts about Barth's 'Models'*, Royal Anthropological Institute occasional paper, 32.

Paine, R.P.B. (1976) 'Two modes of exchange and mediation', pp. 63–86 in B. Kapferer, ed., *Transaction and Meaning: Directions in the Anthropology of Exchange and Symbolic Behaviour*, Philadelphia: ISHI.

Paine, R.P.B. (1981a) 'When saying is doing', pp. 9–23 in R.P.B. Paine, ed., *Politically Speaking: Cross-Cultural Studies of Rhetoric*, Philadelphia: ISHI.

Paine, R.P.B. (1981b) *Ayatollahs and Turkey Trots: Political Rhetoric in the New Newfoundland*, St John's: Breakwater Books.

Paine, R.P.B. (1984) 'Norwegians and Saami: nation-state and Fourth World', pp. 211–48 in G. Gold, ed., *Minorities and Mother-country Imagery*, St John's: ISER.

Paine, R.P.B. (n.d.) 'Israel: the making of self in the "pioneering" of the nation', typescript. Publication forthcoming in *Ethnos* special issue, *Defining the National* (U. Hannerz and O. Lofgren, eds).

Park, R.E. (1925) 'The city: suggestions for the investigation of human behavior in the urban environment', in R.E. Park, R.W. Burgess and R.D. McKenzie, *The City*, Chicago: University of Chicago Press.

Parkin, D.J. (1984) 'Political language', *Annual Review of Anthropology*, 13: 345–65.

Peters, E.L. (1967) 'Some structural aspects of the feud among the camel-herding Bedouin of Cyrenaica', *Africa*, 37 (3): 261–82.

Peters, E.L. (1972) 'Aspects of the control of moral ambiguities: a comparative analysis of two culturally disparate modes of social control', pp. 109–61 in M. Gluckman, ed., *The Allocation of Responsibility*, Manchester: Manchester University Press.

Peters, E.L. (1976) 'Aspects of affinity in a Lebanese Maronite village', pp. 27–79 in J.G. Peristiany, ed., *Mediterranean Family Structures*, Cambridge: Cambridge University Press.

Pettigrew, A. (1979) 'On studying organizational cultures', *Administrative Science Quarterly*, 24: 570–81.

Pitt-Rivers, J. (1972) *The People of the Sierra*, Chicago: University of Chicago Press.

Pondy, L.R., Frost, P.J., Morgan, G. and Dandridge, T.C. (1983) (eds) *Organizational Symbolism*, Greenwich, Conn.: J.A.I. Press.

Poole, F.J.P. (1982) 'The ritual forging of identity: aspects of person and self in Bimin-Kuskusmin male initiation', pp. 99–154 in G.H. Herdt, ed., *Rituals of Manhood: Male Initiation in Papua-New Guinea*, Berkeley: University of California Press.

Prescott, J.R.V. (1987) *Political Frontiers and Boundaries*, London: Allen & Unwin.

Raban, J. (1989) *God, Man and Mrs Thatcher*, London: Chatto & Windus.

Rabinow, P. (1977) *Reflections on Fieldwork in Morocco*, Berkeley: University of California Press.

Rabinow, P. (1986) 'Representations are social facts: modernity and postmodernity in anthropology', pp. 234–61 in J. Clifford and G. Marcus, eds, *Writing Culture: the Poetics and Politics of Ethnography*, Berkeley: University of California Press.

Rabinow, P. and Sullivan, W. (1979) *Interpretive Social Science: a Reader*, Berkeley: University of California Press.

Radcliffe-Brown, A.R. (1957) *A Natural Science of Society*, Glencoe, Ill.: Free Press.

Ramos, A.R. (1974) 'How the Sanumá acquire their names', *Ethnology*, 13 (2): 171–85.

Rapport, N.J. (1993) *Diverse Worldviews in an English Village*, Edinburgh: Edinburgh University Press.

Richards, A.I. (1956) *Chisungu: a Girl's Initiation Ceremony in Northern Rhodesia*, London: Faber.

Richler, M. (1991) *Solomon Gursky was Here*, London: Vintage.

Rivière, P.G. (1984) *Individual and Society in Guiana: A Comparative Study of Amerindian Social Organisation*, Cambridge: Cambridge University Press.

Robertson, G. (1989) *Freedom, the Individual and the Law*, Harmondsworth: Penguin.

Rorty, R. (1989) 'The contingency of language', pp. 3–22 in *Contingency, Irony and Solidarity*, Cambridge: Cambridge University Press.

Rorty, R. (1991) 'On ethnocentrism: a reply to Clifford Geertz', pp. 203–22 in *Objectivity, Relativism and Truth*, Cambridge: Cambridge University Press.

Rosaldo, R. (1984) 'Ilongot naming: the play of associations', pp. 11–24 in E. Tooker, ed., *Naming Systems: the 1980 Proceedings of the American Ethnological Society*, Washington, AES.

Rose, N. (1990) *Governing the Soul: the Shaping of the Private Self*, London: Routledge.

Rosen, L. (1984) *Bargaining for Reality: the Construction of Social Relations in a Muslim Community*, Chicago: University of Chicago Press.

Rossi, A.S. (1965) 'Naming children in middle-class families', *American Sociological Review*, 30: 499–513.

Sabar, Y. (1974) 'First names, nicknames and family names among the Jews of Kurdistan', *Jewish Quarterly Review*, 65 (1): 43–53.

Sahlins, P. (1989) *Boundaries: the Making of France and Spain in the Pyrenees*, Berkeley: University of California Press.

Said, E. (1978) *Orientalism: Western Conceptions of the Orient*, London: Routledge & Kegan Paul.

Salaman, G. (1986) *Working*, London: Tavistock.

Salmond, A. (1993) 'Borderlands: Maori–European exchanges with the past', paper presented to the *ASA Fourth Decennial Conference*, Oxford.

Sangren, P.S. (1988) 'Rhetoric and the authority of ethnography: "postmodernism" and the social reproduction of texts', *Current Anthropology*, 29 (3): 405–35.

Schein, E.H. (1986) *Organization Culture and Leadership*, London: Jossey-Bass.

Schwartz, T. (1975) 'Cultural totemism: ethnic identity primitive and modern', pp. 106–31 in G. DeVos and L. Romanucci-Ross, eds, *Ethnic Identity: Cultural Continuities and Change*, Palo Alto: Mayfield.

Sébillot, P. (1886) *Coutumes Populaires de la Haute Bretagne*, Paris: Maisonneuve.

Segalen, M. (1980) 'Le nom caché', *L'Homme*, 20 (4): 63–76.

Segalen, M. (1983) *Love and Power in the Peasant Family: Rural France in the Nineteenth Century*, Oxford: Blackwell.

Smircich, L. (1983) 'Concepts of culture and organizational analysis', *Administrative Science Quarterly*, 28 (3): 339–58.

Smith, S.J. (1993) 'Bounding the Borders: claiming space and making place in rural Scotland', *Transactions of the Institute of British Geographers* (N.S.), 18: 291–308.

Speier, H. (1969) 'The worker turning bourgeois', pp. 53–67 in H. Speier, ed., *Social Order and the Risks of War*, Cambridge, Mass.: MIT Press.

Stein, H.F. (1985) *Psychodynamics of Medical Practice: Unconscious Factors in Patient Care*, Berkeley: University of California Press.

Strathern, M. (1981) *Kinship at the Core: an Anthropology of Elmdon, a Village in North-west Essex in the 1960s*, Cambridge: Cambridge University Press.

Strathern, M. (1987a) 'Introduction', pp. 1–32 in M. Strathern, ed., *Dealing with Inequality: Analysing Gender Relations in Melanesia and Beyond*, Cambridge: Cambridge University Press.

Strathern, M. (1987b) 'Out of context: the persuasive fictions of anthropology', *Current Anthropology*, 28: 251–81.

Strathern, M. (1988) *The Gender of the Gift: Problems with Women and Problems with Society in Melanesia*, Berkeley: University of California Press.

Strathern, M. (1992) *After Nature: English Kinship in the Late Twentieth Century*, Cambridge: Cambridge University Press.

Strathern, M. (in press) 'Nostalgia and the new genetics', in D. Battaglia, ed., *The Rhetoric of Self-making: Approaches from Anthropology*, Berkeley: University of California Press.

Stromberg, P.G. (1986) *Symbols of Community: the Cultural System of a Swedish Church*, Tucson: University of Arizona Press.

Taylor, C. (1989) *Sources of the Self: the Making of the Modern Identity*, Cambridge: Cambridge University Press.

Thin, N. (1991) *High Spirits and Heteroglossia: Forest Festivals of the Nilgiri Irulas*, Unpublished Ph.D. thesis, University of Edinburgh.

Thompson, E.P. (1991) *Customs in Common*, London: Merlin Press.

Tilly, C. (1963) 'The analysis of a counter-revolution', *History and Theory*, 3.

Tilly, C. (1964) *The Vendée*, Cambridge, Mass.: Harvard University Press.

Tsunoyama, S. (1993) 'The age of the city: an introductory essay', pp. 19–35 in A.P. Cohen and K. Fukui, eds, *Humanising the City? Social Contexts of Urban Life at the Turn of the Millennium*, Edinburgh: Edinburgh University Press.

Tuan, Y.-F. (1982) *Segmented Worlds and Self: Group Life and Individual Consciousness*, Minneapolis: University of Minnesota Press.

Turnbull, C.M. (1965) *Wayward Servants: the Two Worlds of the African Pygmies*, London: Eyre & Spottiswoode.

Turnbull, C.M. (1983) *The Mbuti Pygmies: Change and Adaptation*, New York: Holt, Rinehart & Winston.

Turnbull, C. (1990) 'Liminality: a synthesis of subjective and objective experience', pp. 50–81 in R. Schechner and W. Appel, eds, *By Means of Performance: Intercultural Studies of Theatre and Ritual*, Cambridge: Cambridge University Press.

Turner, B.A. (1986) 'Sociological aspects of organizational symbolism', *Organization Studies*, 7 (2): 101–15.

Turner, R.H. (1962) 'Role-taking: process versus conformity', pp. 20–40 in A.M. Rose, ed., *Human Behaviour and Social Processes*, London: Routledge & Kegan Paul.

Turner, R.H. (1976) 'The real self: from institution to impulse', *American Journal of Sociology*, 81 (5): 989–1016.

Turner, R.H. (1987) 'Articulating self and social structure', pp. 19–32 in K. Yardley and T. Hohness, eds, *Self and Society: Psychosocial Perspectives*, Chichester: John Wiley & Sons.

Turner, V.W. (1967) *The Forest of Symbols: Aspects of Ndembu Ritual*, Ithaca: Cornell University Press.

Vitebski, P. (1993) *Dialogues with the Dead: a Discussion of Mortality among the Sora of Eastern India*, Cambridge: Cambridge University Press.

Wadel, C. (1973) *Now, Whose Fault is That? The Struggle for Self-esteem in the Face of Chronic Unemployment*, St John's: ISER.

Wadel, C. (1979) 'The hidden work of everyday life', pp. 365–84 in S. Wallman, ed., *Social Anthropology of Work*, London: Academic Press.

Wagner, R. (1986) *Symbols that Stand for Themselves*, Chicago: University of Chicago Press.

Warner, W.W. (1984) *Distant Water: the Fate of the North Atlantic Fishermen*, Harmondsworth: Penguin.

Weiner, A. (1983) 'From words to objects to magic: hard words and the boundaries of social interaction', *Man* (n.s.), 18: 690–709.

Werbner, R.P. (1977) 'The argument in and about oratory', *African Studies*, 36: 141–4.

White, G.M. and Kirkpatrick, J. (1985) 'Exploring ethnopsychologies', pp. 1–32 in G.M. White and J. Kirkpatrick, eds, *Person, Self and Experience: Exploring Pacific Ethnopsychologies*, Berkeley: University of California Press.

Wilson, T.M. (1993) 'Frontiers go but boundaries remain: the Irish Border as a cultural divide', pp. 167–87 in T.M. Wilson and M. E. Smith, eds, *Cultural Change and the New Europe: Perspectives on the European Community*, Boulder: Westview Press.

Winch, P. (1958) *The Idea of a Social Science, and its Relation to Philosophy*, London: Routledge & Kegan Paul.

Wirth, L. (1938) 'Urbanism as a way of life', pp. 46–63 in A.K. Hatt and P. Reiss, eds, *Cities and Society*, New York: Free Press.

Wolfe, T. (1988) *The Bonfire of the Vanities*, London: Picador.

Zabeeh, F. (1968) *What is in a Name? An Enquiry into the Semantics and Pragmatics of Proper Names*, The Hague: Martinus Nijhoff.

Zonabend, F. (1980) 'Le nom de personne', *L'Homme*, 20 (4): 7–23.

Index